How the
Liberal Machine
Brainwashed
My Generation

OBAMA

Jason **Mattera**

ZOMBIES

OBAMA

ZOMBIES

THRESHOLD EDITIONS

NEW YORK   LONDON   TORONTO   SYDNEY

Threshold Editions
A Division of Simon & Schuster, Inc.
1230 Avenue of the Americas
New York, NY 10020

First Threshold Editions hardcover edition March 2010

THRESHOLD EDITIONS and colophon are trademarks of Simon & Schuster, Inc.

For information about special discounts for bulk purchases,
please contact Simon & Schuster Special Sales at 1-866-506-1949
or business@simonandschuster.com.

The Simon & Schuster Speakers Bureau can bring authors to your live event.
For more information or to book an event contact the Simon & Schuster Speakers
Bureau at 1-866-248-3049 or visit our website at www.simonspeakers.com.

Designed by Ruth Lee-Mui

Manufactured in the United States of America

10   9   8   7   6   5   4   3

ISBN 978-1-4391-7207-0
ISBN 978-1-4391-7209-4 (ebook)

To Charissa, Rachel, Justin, Becky, and Kristian:
Our future, our fight

Contents

Introduction

I seriously think I had an emotional seizure or
something. My whole body seized up. I couldn't breathe.
It's like I really mattered. . . . I picked the president!

—Sarah Phillips, student and Obama Zombie

What is an Obama Zombie?

Glad you asked.

Rewind to the night of the 2008 election. Obama's victory
wasn't just political; to many young people, it wrought salvation.
Supporting Barack during the election was one thing. But him
defeating John McCain?

Oh gracious God!

After Obama was pronounced the victor, throngs of students
at Maine's Bowdoin College huddled in a circle; some hands were
held, others were raised to the sky (from whence Dear Leader
descended) as they collectively wept, bowed their heads, and

sang . . . "Amazing Grace." We were the "wretches," once blind and lost, until B.H.O. opened our eyes with his outstretched rod touching the land. How sweet the sound indeed!

As one patchouli-smelling hippie on campus exhorted, "It's definitely the most spiritual experience I've had in a while."[1] Meeting Ozzy Osbourne in the flesh was her previous one.

Hyperemotional reactions were everywhere.

In what can only be described as an O-gasm, one Florida female student proclaimed, "It's probably the most excited I've ever been in my entire life. I seriously think I had an emotional seizure or something. My whole body seized up. I couldn't breathe. It's like I really mattered. . . . I picked the president! That was me! . . . I think I'm in love with America right now!"[2]

Outside the White House, legions of young people organized an impromptu rally through text messaging and word of mouth. By the time it concluded, they all needed new underwear.

One young lady, holding an Obama balloon, proclaimed that B.H.O. was going to bring "peace to everybody in the world."[3]

Cars honked. Partyers climbed streetlamps. There was dancing, whooping, and hollering. Even conga drums made it onto the scene. The commotion had the flavor of New Year's Eve. The alcohol and mindless speeches were on full display.

I'm drinking "change," one person yelled when prompted to disclose her choice adult beverage.

"We got the key now," a dude mawkishly shouted. "After-party in the Oval Office. Open up!"

The chants and musical odes were aplenty. Students from George Mason University (GMU) led the crowd to this ditty:

Barack Obama
Mighty Obama
Everywhere we go

People want to know
Who is our president
So we tell them.

Only to be interrupted by "Whose House? Our House! . . ."

Which was interrupted by a "Na Na Na Na, Hey Hey, Good-bye" tribute to George W. Bush.[4]

One of the GMU organizers even gave a shout-out to Obama's manhood, urging McCain supporters not to hate on the new president. My description of events is quite generous in its lucidity. Like those of most Obama Zombies, his statement was virtually incomprehensible. Judge for yourself: "Today, everybody represent Obama as a man. You know, don't disgrace Obama. Represent Obama as a man. And today, we're gonna sing, uplift, and bring Obama's presidency, because that's what we're gonna do, that's what we're here to do, man."

Deep, bro. Deep.

At the University of Pennsylvania, students who had packed into a gymnasium erupted into chants of "yes, we can" from the bleachers. Obama acolytes at Emerson College in Boston were equally apoplectic, with one female student proclaiming "Oh my God!" in the midst of covering her mouth in utter disbelief, like a prepubescent girl at a Jonas Brothers concert. At Ann Arbor, thousands of students ran, jumped, and high-fived through the streets of the University of Michigan.[5] Students at Virginia Commonwealth University took a different tack: they roared *and* set off an array of firecrackers.[6]

THAT, MY FRIENDS, is what Obama Zombies look like. They placed Barack on a pedestal reserved for no mere mortal. It led to the mental mummification of my generation and is why there are masses of Obama Zombies who desperately need awakening.

This book is a countercultural statement. It is out of step with the thoughts of many of my generation, and that is precisely why this book matters. This is a book for every freethinking, freedom-loving person who is fed up with the left's lobotomy of a generation. Ours must be a generation that stands athwart history yelling, "Hey, jackass! Get your government off my freedom!"

Some believe it's too late, that the legions of Obama Zombies are beyond awakening. I don't. I believe they can be revived. I'm an optimist. But I'm also a realist. It will take jolting the Obama Zombies of our world with facts, the kind of facts that sappy, hyperemotional liberalism loathes. Evidence, logic, thinking—those are liberalism's gravest threats.

There's nothing wrong with wanting to be inspired. But getting swept up in a marketing machine's manufactured emotion does not good citizenship make. Tons of young people, just like the ones described above, looked to B.H.O. for inspiration, for light, as though he was going to drop iPods from heaven and melt away student loans forever.

Obama promised the obligatory liberal smorgasbord of programs and free goodies that would help his loyal subjects overcome their "struggles." Obama would give us health care. Obama would pay for our schooling. Obama would stop glaciers from melting. Obama would guarantee us better jobs. Obama would end all wars, curb racism, and tackle terrorism. And, while he's at it, Obama said, he would send a government unicorn down from the sky to fly us up to the left's government-run world where people dance across streets of government-owned gold, eating FDA-approved candy canes while watching multiculturally appropriate edited re-runs of *Baywatch*—guilt-free. Just the usual liberal goodie bags of free gifts galore—and all paid for on the backs of those darned evil rich folks.

Young people, in their heart of hearts, actually believed that a scrawny street-agitator-turned-presidential-candidate could save mankind, renew our faith in American politics, and restore our faith in government. It was a message that hoodwinked my generation. A message of false inspiration in bureaucracy—not in individual freedom and initiative—that churned out a generation of Zombies. And it was a message that was a heat-seeking missile aimed at otherwise clear-thinking individuals who come from the most coddled, overprotected, information-drenched generation in American history. We are the "give me, give me, give me" generation. And Team Obama and his marketing mavens knew every button to push to program us, to set us up like an iTunes playlist.

TO THE TRUE Obama zealots, this book is an act of heresy. It seeks to shatter the media-created halo that radiates from Obama's anointed head. It is the response from the millions of my generation who are disgusted by what Obama and his minions have done to lobotomize our generation.

We're calling you out.

Yeah, you know who you are in academia.

You know who you are, the beta males at MTV who use the network to intravenously make liberalism cool and palatable.

You know who you are, you inane celebrities who helped popularize the meaningless yet catchy slogans of "hope" and "change" and "yes, we can."

Yes, we can? Yes, you did . . . become hapless tools used to remake America in ways that breed unemployment and multiple job losses, create further economic collapse, embrace weakness, cling to pacifism, and trample on every freedom we possess. Congrats, fools. This is our generation. It's a clarion call to all those who don't want to see our future flushed down Nancy Pelosi's and Barney Frank's toilets.

If you want to see just how creepy the Obama Zombie cult has become, go YouTube a video called the "Obama Military Youth Brigade March in Formation." Pledging fealty to any man is, well, scary. But this takes it to a whole new level. Around ten young men enter a room, bopping back and forth while chanting "Alpha, Omega . . . Alpha, Omega . . . Alpha, Omega." One after another, these clueless runts talk about how Obama inspires them to be the next this and the next that:

"Because of Obama, I aspire to be the next doctor."

"Because of Obama, I aspire to be the next lawyer."

"Because of Obama, I aspire to be the next chef" (says the fat kid, of course).

The pledges were all there: to be a fireman, engineer, mechanic, you name it. They then turn to face each other, chanting "Yes, we can!"

"Take core responsibilities of our own lives—yes, we can!"

"Have our own dreams—yes, we can!"

"Demand that more fathers spend more time with their children—yes, we can!"

The madness all ends with a shout of "Aooo!"—whatever the hell that means.

Seriously. Do you need Obama to inspire *fatherhood*? You need Obama to inspire career dreams? Really? And if Obama is a miserable failure as a president, which he's shaping up to be, will then your dreams be dashed? Will it then be okay to revert to being a deadbeat dad with no direction or ambition? Wouldn't it make more sense to invest your energy in, say, core values, not a man? Isn't that, after all, the American way?

• • •

AT AN EVENT in Manchester, New Hampshire, during the primary, Kimberley, a young volunteer, introduced B.H.O. to a crowd of young supporters. She captured the essence of the Obama Zombie: "Hope is an idea, it's a feeling, a belief, a revolution, a role, a possibility," she said before Obama took to the stage. Obama then delivered what *Newsweek* writer Andrew Romano called "pure millennial uplift."[7] Obama said:

> It's time for us to put aside the partisan food-fighting. If you know what you stand for, if you know what you believe in, if you know who you're fighting for, then you can afford to reach out to those who don't agree with you on everything. We can create the kind of working majority that we haven't seen in this country for a long, long time. If I've got the American people behind me, I fear no man. Nobody can stop us. We can do everything that we want to get done.

Now, back to reality. What the hell are you going to do about radical Islamic jihadists, sir? How many billions of dollars are you going to confiscate from me and my grandchildren to pay for your redistributionist schemes and political kickbacks to your ACORN and SEIU cronies? How many banks and car companies are you going to seize? How many police officers will you call "stupid," all while race-baiting? How many speeches will you deliver to the hostile regimes begging and pleading for forgiveness for America being . . . well, America?

"But how can you blame Generation Y?" you say. "After all, look at the slobbering lovefest they were subjected to by the most in-the-tank liberal media in presidential history." Fair enough. And, indeed, the media-driven marketing marvel that was the Obama campaign created Obama Zombies with lightning speed.

Take Luke Russert. On election night he was in Bloomington, Indiana, on the campus of Indiana University. This is what he told NBC's Brian Williams:

> I think what the significance of this evening means comes through in a text message that I received from a childhood friend of mine, is that it's our turn now. And he's referring to our generation, the millennial generation, who really invested their time and effort in Senator Obama, President-elect Obama, and *view him as this blank slate where all their hopes and dreams and aspirations will be put upon.* . . . For the first time in their political lives they feel like they have their own leader, somebody that understands them, feels their concerns and will fundamentally bring a difference to Washington, something that we've never seen in our lifetime. And I think just on the face of it, a lot of young folks never thought they'd see an African-American president. And these are the young people, these are the romantic people who are supposed to be optimistic. And it happened tonight. (Emphasis added.)[8]

Ah yes, the good ol' racist canard of voting for a man because of the color of his skin, not the content of his character. Only this time the color is black not white. Fixation on one's skin color is just wrong. It's antithetical to everything good in America. It is anything but postracial. Indeed, we won't truly be a postracial society until we vote against Barack Obama in 2012 because he is on course to be an abysmal failure as president, not because he happens to be biracial. That will be the moment when we have truly transcended race in America, as our liberal race-baiting friends like to say.

And yet . . . still we get these whimsical, postracial words of harmony and healing from two celebrity Obama supporters, rappers Young Jeezy and Jay-Z, at a D.C. election celebration:

> I know ya'll thanking a lot of people right now. . . . I want to thank two people. I want to thank the motherfucker overseas that threw two shoes at George Bush, and I want to thank the motherfuckers who helped them move they shit up out the White House. Get it moving, bitch! My president is motherfucking black!

Well now. Can't you feel the postracial unity in the air? Nothing to do with skin color here. Nope. Not in the least.

But the fact is that young people are the biggest suckers for the diversity hustle. During the primary, a student at Tennessee State University couldn't decide whom to vote for. Her diversity radar was going off the charts. She told an MTV reporter she couldn't decide between voting for Clinton or Obama: "It is a big issue with black women, whether we want to [vote for] a woman or an African-American. I would love to see a joint ticket."[9]

Here's an idea. How about vote for the one with the best ideas. Groundbreaking, I know. Let it be said, I don't care if your name is Juan Carlos, John Smith, or John Wong, I will vote for you if you have the right ideas. Diversity is, um, irrelevant. The best thing about multiculturalism is the food.

Hans Riemer, national youth director for Obama, and former operative for the—ahem!—"nonpartisan" Rock the Vote, confirmed just how postracial (snort) this election was: "This is the most diverse, multicultural generation ever; they embrace diversity, they think differences are cool. Young voters are turned off by anyone who is repulsed by differences."[10] In another interview, Riemer admitted that there's more fascination with B.H.O. because of his skin color, or as Reimer put it, "the chance to elect a black president."[11]

It is significant that a country where blacks were once slaves now has a black president, but rooting for and ogling over a candidate because of his skin color is one mighty backhand to the notion of a color-blind society—the true intent of the civil rights movement. Our support for or against a candidate should never be determined on the basis of race. Millions of truly postracial young people in this country didn't cry and weep like babies when Obama was elected. We mourned for our nation's future.

Here's some more puke-worthy racialist thinking from other Obama Zombies: "The youth have come out in droves like we've never seen before," said Kathryn Lavelle, a Rutgers University student, "and I think it's because it's an exciting election. It's the farthest an African-American has come, it's the farthest a woman has gone."[12]

Writing for the leftist toilet paper magazine the *American Prospect*, beta male extraordinaire Paul Waldman captures the diversity fascination with the left and Obama:

If Obama were to become president, the symbolic value of him taking the oath of office—a multi-racial man who was partly raised overseas in a Muslim country—would provide such an extraordinary contrast with his predecessor, the very embodiment of what many see as the worst of America in all his ignorance, arrogance, and parochialism, that it would instantly suck the life out of a good portion of the anti-Americanism that has presented such an obstacle in recent years.[13]

Obama's advisers, notably David Axelrod and David Plouffe, knew that the youth vote, steadily increasing since 2000, could play a major role in the '08 election. And they guessed right, creating the most coordinated, directed, interactive youth effort in modern history.

Team Obama set up "camps" around the country to train students to engage the youth vote on their campuses, equipping them with "the nuts and bolts of presidential campaigning."[14] So complete was the Obama campaign's obsession with lobotomizing the youth demographic that the cash-flushed Obama campaign even bought ads in video games, such as Guitar Hero and Madden NFL 09. As one campaign staffer bragged, "when you're buying commercials in video games, you truly are being well-funded."[15]

But the truly big money was spent on dominating college campuses with an unprecedented youth outreach effort. Team Obama's "youth consultants" soaked university campuses with radio and television advertising.[16] They had more than five thousand paid field organizers overall, in addition to the Obama boot camps that were organized around the country.[17]

Barack's mastery of new media and technology created an online presence that did far more than release campaign talking points; it was an interactive hub that identified and connected supporters with each other, encouraged community blogs, generated field material for door-to-door peer interaction, and stacked volunteers to man phone banks. Then there was the cutthroat community organizing and the Students for Obama chapters that sprouted up on every major campus nationwide (one thousand in all). And how about those youthful gestures—"brush the dirt off your shoulder" reference comes to mind—which included the fist bumps, the three-on-three basketball tournaments, the DJs, and the ubiquitous assumption that Obama was, well, one cool cat. After all, Dear Leader uses a BlackBerry, we were told! Stop the presses! All the components were assembled to churn out the Zombies.

And churn out the Zombies they did. When Obama appeared before Super Tuesday outside the MTV studio, eighteen-year-old Michael Madison confessed his bro-mance with B.H.O. "I am a straight man completely in love with Barack Obama," he said. "In 2004, I heard him give a speech at the Democratic National Convention. I fell in love and I've been in love ever since."[18]

A student from Garden City, New York, who was also outside the MTV studio said, "The way he makes you feel, it's like when you're going to pick up a girl for a date."[19]

Most of us would agree that a politician shouldn't make you feel like you're on a hot date.

But tell that to blogger Michael Whack, at the College of Charleston in South Carolina. On O's website, in the community blogs section, we find this bit of reportage of Michael's encounter with Obama's radiant aura during a rope line appearance. After seeing a gentleman shake hands with Obama, Michael experienced the following:

> As the guy drew back his hand I asked him, "You shook his hand didn't you?" Happily the guy said "Yes." I then said, "give me some of that" and the guy shook my hand with the same hand he had just clasped with Barack's. A woman friend of mine who was standing next to me saw me shake hands with the guy. I turned to her and

said "He [the guy] just shook hands with Barack," to which she responded . . . "Hey, give it up." We then shook hands. . . . This chain of hand shakes went on for about five or six more persons. . . . I felt some solidarity with this stranger, consummated by a handshake and signifying some unspoken agreement presumably about Barack Obama and his core message of UNITY![20]

Nauseated? If so, you're probably one of those conservative racists. Either that or you're just not stylish and down with the coolness, yo.

Mark Buhrmester, young Obama supporter, had an honest observation: "Having a hip candidate like him makes it difficult to support someone else. Barack Obama is in style, so if you don't support Barack Obama, it's like you're not in style."[21]

And there's the rub. For Obama Zombies, it's all about style over substance. It's all about feelings, not facts. Young people become liberals through osmosis today, whether it's on campus, through the media, or even with allegedly chic MTV programming. In this book we will analyze and demolish the liberal conveyor belt that spits out Obama Zombies, a machine that has robbed brains by the bushel. And what you see will make your jaw drop.

But make no mistake. We are on a collision course between government control and individual freedom, between the empowerment of people and the empowerment of massive and sprawling bureaucracies. This administration will shackle our generation to the whims of Washington if we don't get our act together and shake off the Obama hangover. "Youth is easily deceived, because it is quick to hope," said Aristotle.

And don't think your liberty is not at risk. But don't take my word for it. Hans Riemer—remember, he's B.H.O.'s youth director—

explained this redemption: "government is a powerful way to make this country a better place."[22] So, when B.H.O. says, "Change in America has always started with the young. They are not tied up with the world as it is, but rather, the world as it might be," pay careful attention through the means by which this "change" comes. Obama's "remaking" of America, as he dubbed it, comes through the power of Washington, the power of a few marshalling their desires on 300 million people.

And when more than 75 percent of college grads can't identify what purpose the First Amendment serves, and only slightly more than 50 percent can describe what a free market is, America is in real trouble.[23] Perhaps that's because college students are subjected to so much liberal pablum. In fact, so lopsided was the support among college professors and administrators for Obama that they donated $19 million to his campaign, more than *twelve times* the amount academia donated to McCain![24] Think about that for a moment. Professors supported Obama by more than a 12-to-1 ratio. That's how out of step with the rest of the country the radical professoriate has become. Aren't liberals always talking about diversity? Where is it? Especially when you consider that 46 percent of the people—46 percent!—voted for John McCain, and B.H.O. barely eked out a majority. Some diversity!

Nevertheless, the confluence of the Liberal Machine's Hollywood tactics, the mainstream media's collective wet kiss for Team Obama, and the radical professoriate's unending love affair with Barack all combined to create a massive throng of Obama Zombies. On Election Day, 68 percent of voters ages 18–29 cast their ballots for B.H.O., whereas only 32 percent backed McCain. There has never been a gap that wide in any previous presidential election.[25]

In Florida, 61 percent of the youth vote went for Obama, while the race was about even in every other age demographic.

In North Carolina, Obama won an eye-popping 74 percent of young people, while McCain accrued all voters over thirty.[26]

In Indiana, 63 percent of young voters chose B.H.O., even though McCain prevailed with everyone else.[27] But it wasn't enough. Heck, if only youth votes counted, McCain would have lost nearly every state.

Each election cycle there's much ado about the youth vote. Everyone tries to get it. There are an estimated 35 million voters ages 18–29. And of that, around 23 million voted. Conservatives cannot overlook the youth vote any longer. The 35 million "Millennials" must not be ignored. And in this regard, McCain was an awful candidate with an awful outreach to young people.

Besides, Gramps looked like death.

And you know what? We bought the Obama bulldoodle. Pure, unadulterated bulldoodle. During the campaign, Barack tried to shield us from his radicalism. Talking about it was "scare tactics" and typical Washington politics. But after just a year with B.H.O. in office, we know the truth: Quashing our freedoms is a daily sport for this bunch. And each freedom lost screws our generation for years to come.

It's time to slam educated elbows into the rib cages of the Obama Zombies.

The mindless followership must stop.

We helped make this mess.

We must clean it up.

Can we do it?

Yes, my brothers and sisters. Yes, we can!

OBAMA

ZOMBIES

1

The Media Muzzle and the Hope-a-Dope Mantra

Liberal Media? What Liberal Media? No Biased News Media Here!
(Pssst . . . Vote for Obama!)

During the 2008 campaign, I saw the most honest, fair, and intrepid reporting of the candidates, especially of then-senator Barack Hussein Obama. Hard-hitting questions, engaging profiles, skeptical eyes, distrust of the politician—I saw it all.

And then, I woke up.

In the real world, no "reporting" or "investigating" occurred. Instead, journalists became fawning teenage schoolgirls licking the heels of their teen idol. Indeed, the sexual undertones (overtones?) were hardly secret. We had legions of Nina Burleighs covering Obama, zombies masquerading as reporters. I call them Nina Burleighs because Nina Burleigh was the *Time* contributor who said she'd be happy to give Bill Clinton a blow job for "keeping abortion legal" and "the theocracy off our backs." Back then, journalists were even surprised by Burleigh's comments. Sure, the press corps is overwhelmingly liberal, but few were that open about it, let alone *sexual* in their commentary.

How times have changed. It's amazing the power a skinny dude with big ears and a deep voice can wield. During the primary, when on his campaign plane talking on his cell phone, Barack Obama caused a gaggle of female journalists to get funny feelings in their pants. And by funny, I don't mean ha-ha funny. While being filmed, in the background you hear these female journalists moaning and wetting themselves over B.H.O. "Agent, sit down," several members of the press shouted. Their view of Obama was blocked. "You're killing us" and "Move, please move," they snickered, all while clicking away at their cameras like adoring fans to photograph Obama spanning his left leg across a row of seats. Yes, Obama was stretching. That's it. CNN even put the video on their website with this caption, "Obama in jeans: Sen. Barack Obama surprises the press corps by wearing jeans."[1] Luckily, Nina Burleigh was at the tarmac when the plane landed to hand out knee-pads to each of the oohing and aahing "reporters." And these are the people we're expecting to give us balanced, fair, and straight-forward coverage? Yikes! While volumes upon volumes can be filled on the press corps's—dare I say erotic—love affair with B.H.O., the crowning moment of acknowledging the bias came out of the mouth of King Zombie himself!

During the star-studded White House Correspondents Dinner, packed with more than twenty-five hundred journalists, politicians, and celebrities, B.H.O. said this of the media: "Most of you covered me; all of you voted for me. Apologies to the Fox table."[2]

Well, you gotta give the man credit for that one; he's right. Hey, even a broken clock is right two times a day.

Speaking to the *New York Times*, longtime columnist Clarence Page inadvertently confirmed the gist of B.H.O.'s joke. "With this president, they [the media] just want to be in the same room," he gushed.[3]

Richard Belzer, the faux cop on *Law & Order: Special Victims Unit*, summed up the night and the Obama presidency this way: "The difference is palpable. It just seems more glamorous. Now it's rock-star, Kennedy elegance," to which he added smugly, "Nothing wrong with being cool."

Belzer and Page may have forgotten that they elected Barack Obama, not Will Smith, to lead the country. But hey, for liberals, it's all about what you *feel;* facts are stubborn realities. Conservative media critic Brent Bozell summed up the news media's infatuation by saying that their new motto should be: "B.H.O., you had us at hello."

The cheering, fawning, slobbering, and lip-puckering had its benefits: jobs. After the election of His Holiness, more than a dozen prominent members of the media turned in their zombie media credentials for zombie White House credentials. They went to work for Barack! Yes! From reporting his campaign, to getting a biweekly check from him. These supposedly unbiased members of the media actually cashed in! Prostitutes don't have sex for free, you know. And if you think *prostitute* is too strong of a word, let's recall that the *Washington Post* was offering inside access to Obama officials for as much as $250,000 until the ruse was uncovered and made public.[4]

But don't take my word for it. Meet a few of the prostitutes for yourself. The following reporters were rewarded with administration jobs.

- Warren Bass: *Washington Post* Outlook deputy editor, now adviser to Susan Rice, U.S. ambassador to the United Nations
- Daren Briscoe: *Newsweek* Washington correspondent,

now deputy associate director of public affairs for the Office of National Drug Control Policy

- Jay Carney: *Time* magazine Washington bureau chief, now the director of communications for Vice President Joe Biden
- Linda Douglass: ABC News Washington correspondent, who was a senior campaign spokesperson for the Obama campaign and is now the assistant secretary for public affairs at the Department of Health and Human Services
- Kate Albright-Hanna: CNN producer, transitioned to director of "new media" for the Obama campaign, and was involved in the Obama transition website
- Peter Gosselin: *Los Angeles Times* Washington correspondent, now speechwriter for Treasury Secretary Tim Geithner
- Sasha Johnson: CNN senior political producer, now press secretary at the Department of Transportation
- Beverley Lumpkin: Justice Department correspondent for ABC News, now press secretary at the Justice Department
- Roberta Baskin: a veteran of CBS News, ABC News, PBS, and ABC's Washington affiliate, now with the Office of the Inspector General at the Department of Health and Human Services
- Vijay Ravindran: chief technology officer for Catalist, a voter database provider which worked for the Obama campaign, now chief digital officer and senior vice president of the Washington Post Company. (Notice how this prostitute went in reverse—from the Obama campaign to the media. Can someone say "George

Stephanopoulos," the Bill Clinton hack who is now host of ABC's Sunday news show *This Week*?)

- Rick Weiss: *Washington Post* science reporter, now the communications director at the White House Office of Science and Technology
- Jill Zuckman: *Chicago Tribune* Washington correspondent, now the director of public affairs for the Department of Transportation[5]

Okay, so you might be thinking, "Who cares? They work for Obama. Big deal." Well, it is a big deal. I wish it weren't, but it is.

Let's take Daren Briscoe as the first example. He was a Washington correspondent for *Newsweek*, writing extensively about the 2008 campaign. He penned one article with his colleague, a huge Obama Zombie, Richard Wolffe, on how Obama transcends race and is able to bring black and white together. It repeated the postracial narrative that Obama injected into his public persona, the narrative that the media unscrupulously ran with. The July 16, 2007, article was titled "Across the Divide: How Barack Obama is Shaking Up Old Assumptions About What It Means to be Black and White in America."[6] The puff piece, masquerading as a legit report, gave credence to the lie that Barack "Typical White Person" Obama is a bridge to white Americans, that he is above and beyond the racial grievance-mongering that has defined demagogues like Jesse Jackson and Al Sharpton. Briscoe took his cue:

Many of Obama's supporters are enthralled by the content of his character—by his earnest desire to heal the nation's political divisions and to restore America's reputation in the world. Many also are excited by the color of his skin and the chance to turn the page on more than two centuries of painful racial history.[7]

The postracial meme certainly wasn't carried only by Briscoe and *Newsweek*. Obama staked his campaign on it. Other journalists followed suit in reporting it. NPR, for instance, said the "postracial era, as embodied by Obama, is the era where civil rights veterans of the past century are consigned to history and Americans begin to make race-free judgments on who should lead them."[8]

The next up to bat is Jill Zuckman. She used to be the Washington correspondent for the *Chicago Tribune*, that is, before she found her true love: working in the Obama administration.

On *MSNBC News Live* on July 8, 2008, host Tamron Hall discussed a TV ad by John McCain that emphasized his time as a POW, obviously noting McCain's love for his country. Hall asked Zuckman, still a "reporter," of course, how Obama could compete with such a powerful and moving personal biography. Her reply:

Well, look, Senator McCain's got this great story about what he survived and what he endured and his campaign wants to tell that story as much as possible because they think that that's something voters respect and it gives them a sense of what he's made of. But Senator Obama's got a great American success story, too, and it's just a different one and I think voters are equally impressed with what he's all about.[9]

Ah, yes, the story of a kid who was sired by Ph.D. parents, went to two Ivy league schools, and grossed millions in book deals is somehow comparable to the hellish brutality Senator McCain faced as a prisoner of war. Beam yourself back down to reality,

Zuckman. As a "reporter," Zuckman has referred to Obama as an "electrifying orator."[10] Shortly after McCain tapped Sarah Palin to be the vice presidential nominee, Zuckman wrote, "On the campaign trail this week for the first time without McCain, Palin's down-to-earth persona has generated wild enthusiasm and boosted McCain in the polls. But it remains to be seen whether swing voters will interpret that persona as showing a lack of sophistication and seasoning at a time when Wall Street is in crisis and the nation is at war."[11] Earn those leftist creds, Zuckman. Suggest that Palin is an inexperienced dolt. You go girl! Why not attach your résumé at the bottom of the article with a note that says, "Hey Plouffe, Axelrod, and Obama: If you liked this hit piece call me and we'll do lunch and discuss my salary requirements."

Jay Carney, formerly *Time*'s Washington bureau chief, now over in Joe Biden's office, was certainly no surprise. From the time that Obama announced his candidacy, *Time* ran seventeen Obama cover stories, all showing glowingly iconic images, cementing his cool factor. "How Much Does Experience Matter?" was one cover story, featuring Obama. Then-senator Obama's biggest knock against him was his age and his inexperience, especially when lined up against someone like John McCain. *Time*'s editors understood this shortcoming of Obama, and as a result, helped carry water on his behalf.

There's something egglike about the concept of experience as a qualification for the highest office. At first blush, the idea appears to be something you can get your hands around. Presidential experience means a familiarity with the levers and dials of government, knowing how to cajole the Congress, understanding when to rely on the Joint Chiefs of Staff and when to call on the National

Security Council—that sort of thing. But bear down even slightly, and the notion of experience is liable to crack and run all over.[12]

The *Time* correspondent then poses this question: "Was it Franklin Roosevelt's experience as governor of New York that gave him the power to inspire in some of the nation's darkest hours? Or was that gift a distillate of his dauntless battle with polio?"[13]

The core of it: Experience may or may not matter, but for Barack, it doesn't matter. He's Barack, after all.

Newsweek has had some of the most embarrassing, slobbery covers of Obama yet. That weekly definitely gets the Nina Burleigh award! After his victory in Iowa, *Newsweek* carried an iconic photo of Obama smiling with this quote from him: "Our time for change has come." In it, the editors called Obama an "icon of hope" who won't "kneecap" his foes. His campaign, *Newsweek* ogled, is "not about Red America or Blue America, but Obama's America."[14]

Other fawning cover stories on Obama included one with him stepping into what is presumably Air Force One with the caption "How to Fix the World." Another with him praying and the caption "What He Believes." But probably the most outrageous and the most prescient of how badly the media would be biased toward him during the presidential campaign was the December 20, 2004, *Newsweek* cover story with Obama: "Seeing Purple: A Rising Star Who Wants to Get Beyond Blue vs. Red." The entire premise was built off one speech, the speech Obama gave during the 2004 Democratic National Convention. Bear in mind that this speech was one giant heap of nothingness, offering little detail.

Astonishingly, many "reporters" were open about their bias. At an Obama rally, Lee Cowan, the NBC correspondent assigned to cover B.H.O. on the campaign trail, had this exchange with Brian Williams: "From a reporter's point of view, it's almost hard to remain objective because it's infectious, the energy, I think. It sort of goes against your core to say that as a reporter, but the crowds have gotten so much bigger, his energy has gotten stronger. He feeds off that."[15]

If that weren't unbelievable enough, Cowan doubled down on his bro-mance, confessing to the *New York Times* that it's "especially hard" for him and his colleagues "not to drink the Kool-Aid."

"It's so rapturous, everything around him. All these huge rallies," he added.[16]

Hey, at least this dude's honest about his love affair with Barack. I'll give him that much. As the 2008 election demonstrated, our fearless journalists' cup runneth over with "Kool-Aid." In a *Time* cover story (yes, another one) titled "Why Barack Obama Could Be the Next President," Joe Klein described Obama as "the political equivalent of a rainbow—a sudden preternatural event inspiring awe and ecstasy."[17] I'm sure being compared to a rainbow was even a first for Obama. Klein's exaltation really had no limits. In fact, B.H.O. would eliminate all discord in America, according to Klein.

> There aren't very many people—ebony, ivory or other—who have Obama's distinctive portfolio of talents. . . . He transcends the racial divide so effortlessly that it seems reasonable to expect that he can bridge all the other divisions—and answer all the impossible questions—plaguing American public life.[18]

The Pew Research Center's Project for Excellence in Journalism picked up on the bias. Before the Iowa caucus, Pew noted that Obama had gained nearly double the favorable coverage that Hillary Clinton had received, and nearly four times more favorable coverage than John McCain.[19] I wonder what tipped Pew off? Perhaps the comparison of Obama to a rainbow?

In a similar study, Pew found that in the time period from the Republican National Convention to the final presidential debate, John McCain was getting pilloried by the press: negative stories outweighing positive ones by a factor of more than 3 to 1.[20]

Politico's John Harris was asked on CNN whether he thought journalists were, in fact, rooting for Obama. Harris said yes, relaying this monumental gem from his days at the *Washington Post:* "a couple years ago, you would send a reporter out with Obama, and it was like they needed to go through detox when they came back—'Oh, he's so impressive, he's so charismatic,' and we're kind of like, 'Down, boy.' "

It turns out "reporters" at the *Washington Post* never did get those detox sessions. On Christmas Day of 2008, the paper ran a front-page story on Obama's workout routine that highlighted his "chiseled pectorals." I kid you not. Meet Eli Saslow:

> Between workouts during his Hawaii vacation this week, [Obama] was photographed looking like the paradigm of a new kind of presidential fitness, one geared less toward preventing heart attacks than winning swimsuit competitions. *The sun glinted off chiseled pectorals sculpted* during four weightlifting sessions each week, and a body toned by regular treadmill runs and basketball games.[21] (Emphasis added.)

For more than thirty years now, study after study has shown that, by an overwhelming majority, the journalists we rely on to give us the news straight vote for liberal candidates.[22] Even

MSNBC.com noted the newsroom is filled with a bunch of lefties. The website identified 143 "journalists" at prominent news outlets across the country who made political contributions during the previous two presidential campaign cycles. Of them, 125 "gave to Democrats" and other "liberal causes," while only "16 gave to Republicans."[23] Liberals are indeed covering liberals.

IN ADDITION TO devouring B.H.O.'s talking points like manna from heaven, the lapdogs in the press felt it was their duty to protect Obama's fanciful image. During the primaries, all the big three networks covered Obama marking the forty-second anniversary of the 1965 Bloody Sunday march for voting rights in Selma, Alabama. "There was something stirring across the country because of what happened in Selma, Alabama, because some folks are willing to march across a bridge. So they got together and Barack Obama, Jr. was born,"[24] Barack recounted. "This is the site of my conception. I am the fruits of your labor. I am the offspring of the movement. When people ask me if I've been to Selma before, I tell them I'm coming home."[25]

There's one problem with Obama's claim: It was total bunk. He was actually born *three years prior* to the march. No worries for him, though. The media cleaned up the mess. CBS's Gloria Borger acknowledged that Obama was born three years earlier but, "Even so, [Obama] says, he's still the product of Selma."[26] Oh come on, Gloria! Obama can't even tell the truth about his own birth, and all you can do is make excuses for him? ABC and NBC ignored the gaffe altogether.[27]

CHRIS MATTHEWS, WHO may be the mother of all zombies, is an anchor at the faux news network MSNBC. In an interview with the

New York Observer, Chris Matthews compared B.H.O. to . . . the New Testament!

"I've been following politics since I was about five," said Matthews. "I've never seen anything like this. This is bigger than Kennedy. [Obama] comes along, and he seems to have the answers. This is the New Testament. This is surprising."

It gets better (worse). Matthews even compared Obama to . . . Mozart!

> I really think there's a Salieri-Mozart thing going on here. . . . Salieri was the court composer who did everything right. He was impressive. Along comes Mozart. And everybody couldn't get the music out of their heads. Hillary is really good at doing what she is supposed to do. She's impressive. He's inspirational. That's the difference. One's the court composer. And one is the genius. There's something he does. I don't know what. Oprah said it. It's not that he's black. It's that he's brilliant.[28]

Matthews himself embodies the revolving door of the news media and liberal circles, having worked for Jimmy Carter and Democrat Speaker of the House Tip O'Neill.

Did I say that Matthews takes home the prize for the mother of all Zombies? Well, I may have spoken too soon. Martin Snapp of the *Contra Costa Times*, located near San Francisco, may give Matthews a run for his money. Snapp compared Obama to Moses, King David, and the Jedi warrior Luke Skywalker. And as if that weren't bad enough, Snapp writes that Obama's biggest draw among supporters is that "they love him because he's taught them to love themselves—specifically, that part of themselves that is responding to the better angels of their nature."[29]

Do you think I'm kidding about erotic coverage? One contributor to the *Huffington Post* postured that Hope and Change stimulated a new generation of lovemaking! Yes! As the writer exclaimed, "Barack Obama is inspiring us like a desert lover, a Washington Valentino . . . couples all over America are making love again and shouting 'yes we can' as they climax!"[30]

One young Obama supporter named Noah Norman, a twenty-five-year-old tech consultant, captured the liberal media's irrational exuberance for Obama when he candidly told the *Washington Post*, "Obama has this almost irrational following and I myself can't sometimes explain why I'm supporting him. He's all things to all men. At least that's how I put it."[31]

Did the fawning dry up once Obama got elected? Yeah right. I bring to you this gem, courtesy of *Politico:*

> During his first 100 days as president of the United States, Barack Obama revealed how different he is from all the white men who preceded him in the Oval Office, and the differences run deeper—in substance and style—than the color of his skin. Barack Hussein Obama is the nation's first hip president.[32]

And why is B.H.O. our first "hip" president? "See the body language, the expressions, the clothes. He's got attitude, rhythm, a sense of humor, contemporary tastes," blathered *Politico*.

The message was that if you were not down with Barack, it meant "you were not hip—you were square." Exactly the point. It's about image and not ideas. And if not being down with Obama's socialist power grab is "uncool," well then, I will settle for that label.

Obama is apparently so hip that some Zombies have coined the term *Baracking,* and even embrace each other by saying "What's up, my Obama?" Instead of "God bless you" or "Gesundheit" after a sneeze, the Zombie, er, hip, response is now "Barack you." No joke, people!

Got beef with your people? Well, "Barack's in the White House" now means "Show some respect."[33]

Deborah Tannen, professor of linguistics at Georgetown University, approves of the new Obama lingo. She told *Politico* it's "the most emblematic, positive thing that kids could say. It's connecting them to him, saying that there's something special in the connection between them."[34]

When I think of terms of endearment, "What's up, my Obama?" doesn't come to mind. It sounds cultlike and creepy.

In promoting Obama's "hipness," CNN may have had one of its more embarrassing segments to date. To mark his first hundred days in office, the network's T. J. Holmes and Kyra Phillips had an entire segment "assessing" Obama's "swagga."[35] Seriously! Kyra enters the segment with Jay-Z's "Swagga Like Us" hip-hop song in the background, chuckling that the "white" cameraman is "trying to swagga" with the camera. After that, she wants to make it clear to the CNN audience that "swagga" is different from "swagger" (it's "swagger" with "a lot bit more flava"). Kyra then goes on to introduce the "swagga guru," her fellow anchor T. J. Holmes, a black male who has just concluded a panel discussion with black men to celebrate their perception of Obama as another "brotha" who has "swagga."

Kyra has this unbelievable exchange with T.J. And remember, this segment is meant to fit into the meme of Obama's first hundred days in office.

Kyra: "So bottom line, every white president has had absolutely no swagga. Is that what you're saying? They're stuffy, uptight presidents." She laughs, as this is all a big game.

The resident black man, swagga guru T.J.: "Some would say that . . . and maybe it's not one of these things you're supposed to say, but you can go to Billy D. Williams to Shaft to whomever you want to talk about, there's just a bit of a swagga sometimes that people associate with black men." Swagga guru T.J.'s proof of Obama's swagga? "He sits courtside at basketball games; he goes out on the town; he goes out to nice dinners; he's not scared to be this young, hip guy." [36]

Kyra finishes off the segment by giving T.J. a fist bump. How "down" you are, Kyra. Holla!

But Obama's connection to reporters hits much closer to home. David Axelrod, B.H.O.'s chief political strategist, was himself a *Chicago Tribune* reporter before he segued into political consulting. His clients have ranged from the Clintons, to liberal U.S. senator Chris Dodd of Connecticut, to John "I may or may not be yo' baby daddy" Edwards, to Obama's current chief of staff, Rahm "Ballet Dancer" Emanuel (Rahmbo used to be a ballet dancer . . . Kid you not . . . Google it). David Plouffe, Obama's campaign manager, was also an embedded Democrat operative since his college days, having worked his way from Congressman Dick Gephardt's staff to Axelrod's Astroturf (artificial gassroots) operation, AKPD Message and Media. This gang knows politics, that's for sure. But they don't represent change. The mainstream media embarrassed themselves, prostituting their journalism and surrendering their professionalism to cozy up to the "cool campaign."

But those who saw Obama close-up in Chicago knew that he came from a thugocracy and was no reformer. *Chicago Tribune* columnist John Kass, a straight-shooting newspaper writer and an expert on Chicago's political machine, had this to say: "Why is Obama allowed to campaign as a reformer, virtually unchallenged by the media, though he's a product of Chicago politics and has never condemned the wholesale political corruption in his home town the way he condemns those darn Washington lobby-ists?"[37]

Kass pointed out that B.H.O. backed Mayor Richard Daley, Jr., and the thoroughly corrupt Chicago machine, never making "waves," so that he was in a position to move up the political lad-der. That ladder was mounted by Illinois state Senate president Emil Jones. Just so you're aware, the Associated Press described Jones as Obama's political "Godfather" and as an "old-school poli-tician" who "has relatives on the state payroll, steers state grants to favorite organizations and uses his clout to punish enemies and bury GOP legislation."[38]

B.H.O. was anything but a reformer, even though the media carried that narrative for him to high heaven. In fact, some of B.H.O.'s colleagues in Illinois were pissed that Obama was allowed to take credit for nearly every high-profile piece of "reform" legis-lation even though he would have very little to do with it. In Chi-cago, such action was called "bill jacking."[39] One colleague described "bill jacking" as carrying "the ball 99 yards all the way to the one-yard line, and then give it to the halfback who gets all the credit and the stats in the record book."[40] Obama was the halfback.

B.H.O., you may have figured out, was allowed to bill-jack be-cause he needed a record to run on for the United States Senate. Sounds like Obama learned under quite the reformers, eh?

And in regard to his running for president, how can we forget Obama promising to accept public financing of the campaign, then reneging on that promise because he said the financing system was broken. Make that before Obama's campaign realized they could rake in historic levels of financing, he was all about aggres-sively pursuing "an agreement with the Republican nominee to preserve a publicly financed general election." Not so much when he opted out.

The point is that Obama is not a man of integrity; he's a man of callousness and calculation; he and his advisers are ruthlessly savvy in getting what they want, and the mainstream media went right along like the prostitutes they are. Not only was and is Obama a doctrinaire liberal, but he's prone to mind-blowing lies and deception. The media gave Obama a pass. And they continue to do so.

At an online forum on health care, Obama said this: "There's something about August going into September where everyone in Washington gets all 'wee-weed' up." And he used *wee-weed up* the same way you might say you "tinkled" the bed as a toddler. While Obama instantly became the butt of jokes within the blogosphere, Katie Couric took a different approach: a defense of the phrase *wee-weed up*!

The aging CBS anchorwoman did a segment on "neology," which, as she defined it, is the invention of a word, or breathing new life into an old one. She then went on to give a history of presidents who've coined new terms, including Teddy Roosevelt's *lunatic fringe* and George W. Bush's *misunderestimate*. Barack Obama, she noted, introduced Americans to *wee-weed up*. Couric wondered if the phrase would make it into pop culture and the dictionary, as past presidents were "proud" neologists.[41] You know it: Couric gets the Nina Burleigh award as well!

Or what about Obama's increasing power grab on private capital? Americans are voicing frustration and alarm as he hits us with record deficits and national debt, car company takeovers, and liberal, big-government forays into health care, the economy, and the environment. Americans want to be left alone, with Uncle Sam out of their wallets. Conservatives have accurately pointed out that the Messiah's policies toward nationalization are socialist. Heck, his key influences were committed and outspoken socialists. But did you know that, according to MSNBC, when conservatives call Obama a socialist, what they're really doing is calling him the n-word? If you didn't know that, have no fear, because MSNBC's Carlos Watson is here! He can find a racial epithet in an empty room. Here's good ol' Carlos doing the tired ol' race-baiting two-step:

> Today I want to talk about a word that we're hearing more and more, and that's the word socialist. You hear it from a lot of conservatives these days, that's usually critiquing the President, or more broadly Democrats. And while that's certainly a legitimate critique, there certainly is an ideology that can and should be critiqued at certain times, it also sometimes is just a kind of a generic conservative bludgeoning tool. And that's all right, too, because you hear it on the Democratic side as well: rightwingnut, what have you. But what concerns me is when in some of those town hall meetings including the one that we saw in Missouri recently where there were jokes made about lynching, etc., you start to wonder whether in fact the word socialist is becoming a code word, whether or not socialist is becoming the new n-word for frankly for some angry upset birthers and others.[42]

Actually, Carlos, calling Obama the n-word would be like calling him . . . well, the n-word! Labeling someone a socialist, especially when all races and creeds are out protesting Obama's agenda, is obviously not racist. But MSNBC is in a league all its own. And the White House acknowledges that. One cabinet official actually stated publicly that "at the White House, as we always like to say, we love MSNBC." As one blogger put it, what kind of thrill would this give Chris Matthews?[43] I'd say a big one, of the wee-weed up variety.

It comes down to the members of the "mainstream," or as talk radio icon Rush Limbaugh calls them "drive-by" media, are nothing more than a bunch of beta male types slobbering over Obama and refraining from asking probing questions of his administration; they're more likely to ask about his adjustment to the White House than about any of the scandals and contradictions of his administration. These members of the media are the Screeches of *Saved by the Bell*, the Carlton Bankses of *Fresh Prince of Bel-Air*. They were the dorks who got picked on in high school but who now relish their roles of importance. And even though they still can't land the prom queen, they've substituted their affection for Barack Hussein Obama. When they watch *Napoleon Dynamite,* they see themselves.

The media, though, have outgrown the traditional outlets. Besides the big three networks, which are becoming more and more unimportant (thank goodness), there's talk radio, the blogosphere, and cable news. Yet there's also a part of the news media that has a huge effect on liberal coffers: Google. The Internet search engine giant is a household name, quickly morphing into everyone's favorite verb . . . Who did you *google* today? But it was also a high-stakes player in electing Obama. According to the Center for Responsive Politics, Google contributed more than $800,000 to Obama's presidential bid.[44] To be clear, Google as a company did not give to Obama, but employees and family members of employees "bundled" money together. In fact, Google was the fifth-largest industry campaign contributor to Obama, out of the twenty largest. Dwarfing Google was the University of California college system, Goldman Sachs (yes, the large bankers on Wall Street that Obama decried!), Harvard, and Microsoft, another tech-savvy giant. Google also gave more than $200,000 to the Democratic National Committee.[45]

In fact, Google affected the election with more than just cash. Its chief executive, Eric Schmidt, went out on Obama's campaign trail, stumping for the One just shortly before the election. It was a natural progression for Schmidt, since he was serving as an unpaid adviser to Obama. Besides technology (obviously), one of Schmidt's core stump issues for Obama was "clean energy." As you'll see later on in the book, *clean energy* is just another one of the left's euphemisms for seizing private capital and rationing energy. Schmidt, specifically, has proposed "cutting oil use for cars by 40 percent" within the next twenty years. He thinks that the transition away from oil would cost "trillions of dollars" but would save money in the long run, with an annual cost less than "the $700 billion offered to" Wall Street.[46]

"Clean" is the new "red." Schmidt was the perfect Zombie, paying lip service to the greatness of the free market but really pushing for more government expansion and more government control. After the election, Schmidt spoke at the left-wing New America Foundation and called for a fusion between socialism and capitalism. "The right answer is a balance between these," he said. "The objective is to win as a country."[47] The Google leader was one of Obama's "advisers" helping him to sell the "stimulus" package that turned out to be an absolute disaster. Schmidt oversees the Internet giant, but he's a run-of-the-mill liberal, believing, as does Obama, that we can spend our way into prosperity. "Businesses, by law, have to serve their shareholders," he explained at the conference. "They're not going to invest in R&D. . . . It takes government policy." He, like every other left-wing special interest group out there, came begging like a pauper for your money. Schmidt acknowledged he is also "a big fan" of alternative energy subsidies and "startups with funny names" financed by . . . Uncle Sam.[48]

Continuing his voyage into loony-liberal land, Schmidt advised Obama to pay bonuses to auto companies that go beyond the current CAFE fuel-efficiency standards—with your money, of course![49] Um, earth to Schmidt: Consumer demand and not Washington bureaucrats should determine the types of vehicles that are offered. This guy is straight-up Obama Zombie.

Like the media, Google had its own revolving door to the Obama administration. Andrew McLaughlin, Google's director of global public policy (otherwise known as the "head" lobbyist), and Katie Jacobs Stanton, Google's business development executive, were both tapped to work for Obama, McLaughlin as the deputy chief technology officer and Stanton the new director of citizen participation.

The website Gawker described Obama's incestuous relationship with the Silicon Valley behemoth this way:

> It's Google's presidency. We're just watching it. Six Google executives, including CEO Eric Schmidt and cofounder Larry Page, have donated $25,000 apiece to fund President Barack Obama's swearing-in party. Taken as a whole, the Googlers' cash is one of the largest corporate donations to Obama's inaugural committee.[50]

Now on to Google's cousin, Apple. Even though Apple and Google are competitors, that didn't stop them from teaming up to design Gmail and Google Maps for Apple's iPhone. As one tech website observed, "The iPhone drives a lot of traffic to Google, which dominates Internet search and advertising."[51] Google is the Internet titan, while Apple is the computer titan. And like Google, Apple is run by liberals. Steve Jobs is a big left-wing donor. His employees follow in his footsteps; Obama swept in six times more in campaign contributions from Apple workers than did McCain.[52] In fact, the average across the twenty largest Silicon Valley companies is five times in favor of Obama! So much about liberals being for the little guy, eh?

But the left-wing activism continues.

Both Google and Apple share a senior adviser of sorts: Al Gore. Gore is a member of the board of directors of Apple Inc. and is also a senior adviser to Google, a good indicator that Google and Apple are open to environmental alarmism and liberal policies in general. It should be no surprise that Schmidt is flacking for Obama when his own senior adviser is Al Gore.

Google and Apple are overflowing moneymakers. In 2008, Google generated $4.2 billion in net profits, while Apple posted a net quarterly profit of $1.14 billion at the end of the same year. Can someone say "capitalist cows"? And the big winner is, of course, liberals.

Bottom line: Google and Apple are liberal media titans. Ironically, both Apple and Google make good products, and unlike liberal policies, they actually create jobs. But they are liberals nonetheless and have aligned with a liberal president. Liberals before business, I guess. They are part of the Obama-biased media, the sleek, beta-male crowd that could never land girls in college but now have enough money to pay for all the high-priced journalist prostitutes they want.

YOUNG PEOPLE ARE consumers of information. They're not always up to speed on the activist nature of the media—old or new. They have better things to worry about, such as school and family. Unfortunately, that means they have a big red zombie target on their foreheads. During the 2008 election, *World News Tonight* anchor Charlie Gibson asked his colleague George Stephanopoulos, "How do you run against hope?"[53] With a compliant, fawning, and sycophantic press corps. That's how, Charlie.

2 Will You Be My (Facebook) Friend?

Digital Tactics for Luring and Creating Obama Zombies

Barack's much-popularized "Yes, we can" speech after the New Hampshire primary enshrined those three words in every good Zombie's dictionary. Yes, we can heal our nation! Yes, we can seize our future! Yes, we can prevail over cynicism and fear. Yes, we can unite . . . like Japan did after Hiroshima!

Huh? Remember that *Sesame Street* skit "One of these things is not like the other"? Spot the culprit? Good. That means you're already three brain waves ahead of will.i.am, the cofounder of the hip-hop group Black Eyed Peas. It was that genius who compared B.H.O.'s speech to the reconstruction of Japan after World War II. See for yourself: "Let's all come together like America is supposed to . . . like Japan did after Hiroshima . . . that was less than 65 years ago . . . and look at Japan now . . . they did it together . . . they did it . . . We can't? Are you serious? We can!!! Yes we can . . .

A United 'America' Democrats, Republicans and Independents together . . . We can do it 'Together.' "[1]

Here on planet earth, Japan didn't exactly "come together." After the United States military dropped an atomic bomb and following Japan's surrender, we ordered the Japanese rebuilding effort and wrote their constitution. Japan may have "come together," but it was through the will of the American military, not from happy talk and incense-burning hippies.

will.i.am may want to stick to singing "boom, boom, pow" and leave the analogies to folks who capitalize the first letter of their names. That aside, will.i.am was so moved by Barack's words that he and his tortured analogy produced a musical rendition to the "Yes, we can" speech. That production turned out to be the mother of all campaign videos in 2008, garnering more than 19 million views on YouTube. To put that in perspective, for all of John McCain's 330 videos, he only had 25 million views on YouTube.[2] One video by will.i.am nearly matched all views of the Arizona senator's videos combined, a feat attainable when you're able to assemble the likes of John Legend, Kareem Abdul-Jabbar, and Scarlett Johansson to star in your production.

will.i.am's Zombie credentials are unquestionable. "When you are truly inspired . . . magic happens . . . incredible things happen . . . love happens . . . (and with that combination) 'love, and inspiration' change happens . . . 'change for the better.' . . . Inspiration breeds change . . . 'Positive change.' "[3]

Still, his online video is emblematic of how the Internet has shaped and influenced how we elect presidents. In short, Obama became the YouTube president and has set the standard of how elections in the future will utilize the power of the Internet.

• • •

THE 2008 PRESIDENTIAL campaign was the first presidential race to pack the full punch of online mass media, and Obama, to his credit, took full advantage of it. B.H.O.'s team was way ahead of the curve when it came to harnessing the power of the Internet. It paid off. Obama's digital domination of John McCain was staggering and helped create the impression of an online army marching to victory. The numbers speak for themselves:[4]

- Facebook friends on Election Day: Obama, 2,397,253; McCain, 622,860
- Unique visitors to the campaign website for the week ending November 1: Obama, 4,851,069; McCain, 1,464,544
- Number of online videos mentioning the candidate uploaded across two hundred platforms: Obama, 104,454; McCain, 64,092
- Number of views of those videos: Obama, 889 million; McCain, 554 million
- Number of campaign-made videos posted to YouTube: Obama, 1,822; McCain, 330
- Total amount of time people spent watching each campaign's videos, right before the election: Obama, 14.6 million hours; McCain, 488,000 hours
- Number of Twitter followers: Obama, 125,639; McCain, 5,319
- Number of references to the campaign's voter contact operation on Google: Obama, 479,000; McCain, 325

The data are truly jaw-dropping. Old man McCain got destroyed in the online medium. As Internet gurus Andrew Rasiej and Micah L. Sifry stated, "When the history books are written, McCain's failure to invest similar resources in developing the widest possible online network will go down as a strategic error of the highest order."

And while the numbers above represent mostly official campaign statistics, there were hundreds of other videos posted to YouTube, or groups started on Facebook that pimped the celebrity candidate. will.i.am was one of the videos. The slutty Obama Girl was another.

You've probably seen Amber Lee Ettinger's melons and big booty plastered in your face. Actually, you and 16 million other Americans have. You know Amber as "Obama Girl." She dropped her half-naked self onto the scene in the summer of 2007, before the primaries kicked off, expressing her "crush on Obama." Instantly, a star was born.

The fact that Amber quickly became a hit—her 16 million-plus views on YouTube is more than double any one of Obama's videos—is hardly surprising. Sex sells. Well, let me clarify that: sex sells when you look like Amber Lee Ettinger, not when you look like Joy Behar.

Obama Girl morphed into stardom by lip-syncing a gushy song about the then–Illinois senator while prancing her "enhanced" body around for a site called Barely Political. In the famous "I got a crush on Obama" song, Amber advocates "universal health-care reform" and even has this ditty: "you tell the truth unlike the Right; you can love, but you can fight; you can Barack me tonight."[5]

OTHER ONLINE INFLUENCES included the allegedly nonpartisan "Declare Yourself" campaign, sponsored by—surprise, surprise— Norman Lear, a left-wing celebrity. Declare Yourself is anything but nonpartisan, but produced widely viewed and effective viral videos nonetheless. In two YouTube videos called "Hollywood Declares Themselves," a ragtag team of known actors satirically try to get young people to register to vote by telling them that they shouldn't vote. It is a star-studded cast: Leonardo DiCaprio, Ellen DeGeneres, Tom Cruise, Tobey Maguire, Shia LaBoeuf, Sarah Silverman, Will Smith, Harrison Ford, Snoop Dogg, Justin Timberlake, and even Borat!

Basically, Declare Yourself used Hollywood celebrities to get young people to vote and to the polls on Election Day. Lear maintains that his group is nonpartisan, despite his own liberal views.

Just how nonpartisan, you ask? Well, Declare Yourself's Jamie Foxx says, don't vote. "Who cares about global warming" and "the fact that our polar ice caps are melting," chimes in DiCaprio. "Who cares about the war on drugs," adds another. "I've never fought a war on drugs. I've never done shit on drugs, besides play Halo 2." Don't vote, don't vote, don't vote! "Who cares about Darfur? I don't even know where the fuck that is. That sounds like a T-shirt company to me," says Jonah Hill of *Superbad* and *Knocked Up*.[6] The satire is soon realized, with the celebrity entourage telling young people why they *should* be voting. "Don't vote unless you care about health care," one actor proclaims. "If you think that everybody deserves to be taken care of when they're sick," then maybe you should vote, says Forest Whitaker. "If you care about gun control," proclaims *Friends* star Courtney Cox, then you should vote. Dustin Hoffman brings up "gay rights" and "abortion rights." Minimum wage and the Iraq War are also issues on which young people are urged to cast ballots. If all these issues matter to you, the viral ad reads, then you should go vote.

Snoop Dogg, a onetime member of the Crips and a convicted felon, tells the YouTube audience to "vote because for the first time ever an African-American could end up in the White House." Nothing like a little pre-election race-baiting from a former gang member!

Sarah Silverman urges people to register to vote while "pooping" and asks viewers to send the Declare Yourself video to friends so that the message can spread "rampant like herpes." That lends a whole new meaning to the term *viral marketing*.

The Declare Yourself videos were catchy and well produced. But nonpartisan? Each one of the issues came from a decidedly left-wing stance that reflected the views of Declare Yourself creator Norman Lear. He is rabidly left-wing. He's also the founder of People for the American Way, an activist group started to resist the so-called influence of the "religious right." PBS host Bill Moyers, for instance, once asked him, "Did your heart leap with joy last week when the Federal Court in California said that the Pledge of Allegiance is unconstitutional because that phrase 'one nation, under God' violates the separation of church and state?" Lear replied: "I won't say that I was pleased; [but] I wasn't upset."[7] Lear is even one of those crazy lefties who support the cop-killer-turned-cause-célèbre Mumia Abu-Jamal.

During the election, Lear refused to endorse a candidate: "That isn't something that belongs in a 'Declare Yourself' conversation," he said. But the *New York Times* noted his choice was obvious: "prominently displayed in his office during an interview was a yarmulke decorated with a campaign sticker for Senator Obama."[8]

Lear, who is one of those old rich-dude creeps (at eighty-seven he has two teenage daughters), has access to any celebrity he wants. The impact is unquestionable. Declare Yourself boasts that it registered more than 2.2 million young people to vote, which is plausible considering that just two of their Hollywood YouTube videos nearly garnered a million hits. In total, they claim that more than "6 million people viewed their online videos and public service announcements," and that its "Only You Can Silence Yourself" print, video, and billboard campaign, which featured Jessica Alba, reached more than "100 million impressions" through publications including *People, Seventeen, Rolling Stone, Sports Illustrated*, and *US Weekly*. As if that weren't enough, Lear's group blasted text messages to more than 5 million people reminding them to vote. An impressive left-wing operation, to be sure.

The lesson is clear: the Internet is open to any group or individuals who want to make political statements, whether those statements are worshipful (will.i.am), salacious (Obama Girl), or ideological (Declare Yourself). ObamaMania didn't materialize in a vacuum.

STILL THINK THAT the Internet is not important? Food for thought: According to the Pew Research Center, 33 percent of Americans go online to get their political news. Skip along to young people between the ages of eighteen and twenty-nine and the number jumps to 49 percent. Nearly 50 percent of younger voters get their news from the Internet. Then there's the 25 percent of new voters who said they had joined a social networking group for a campaign.[9]

B.H.O.'s online legions were largely the work of Chris Hughes and Joe Rospars, two twenty-somethings who changed the game of online politicking. Even if the name Chris Hughes doesn't ring a bell, I'm sure you've heard of his creation: a little something called Facebook. Yep, that's right—the cocreator of Facebook, the most interactive, innovative, and popular community forum to date—

was part of B.H.O.'s online operation. As a McCain-Palin online adviser self-deprecatingly observed, "Memo to self: next time get the co-founder of Facebook on your team."[10]

Joe Rospars, cofounder of marketing firm Blue State Digital, oversaw the campaign's new media progress. Rospars is no stranger to the online world himself, having worked on Howard Dean's Web team before Dean imploded with his "I have a scream" speech.[11] After the infamous episode, Rospars and two other Deaniacs founded Blue State Digital, an Internet strategy firm designed to beef up online fund-raising, voter outreach, and social networking for liberal politicians and causes. These "Boston geeks," as one paper called them,[12] did online work for both Ted Kennedy and John Kerry before getting hired by the Obama campaign to create and run what turned out to be the ultimate Web-based political machine.

The online operation surrounded B.H.O.'s website, my.barack obama.com, or MyBO for short. MyBO was an interactive hub that identified and connected supporters with each other, planned events, encouraged community blogs, raised money, provided talking points and campaign logos, generated field material for door-to-door interaction, and stacked volunteers to man phone banks. MyBO was the one-stop-shop for the Obama campaign. It succeeded beyond expectations. As one report put it, "By the time the campaign was over, volunteers [on MyBO] had created more than 2 million profiles on the site, planned 200,000 offline events, formed 35,000 groups, posted 400,000 blogs, and raised $30 million on 70,000 personal fund-raising pages."[13] Whoa!

Rospars and Hughes were asked to build a movement, to build a community of Obama Zombies, and that's exactly what they did. Hughes said he brought Facebook's founding principles to the Obama campaign: "Keep it real, and keep it local." As the *New York Times* reported, "Hughes wanted Mr. Obama's social network to mirror the off-line world the same way that Facebook does—by fostering more meaningful connections by attending neighborhood meetings and calling on people who were part of their daily lives. The Internet served as the connective tissue."[14]

Two million profiles; 200,000 planned events; 70,000 personal fund-raising pledges. He certainly fostered "meaningful connections." One of those events was organized by Zombie Valli Frausto. After seeing B.H.O. on *Oprah,* Frausto said, "I've never been involved in a political campaign before, but it was like a call to action for me." She told the *Boston Globe* that "the way he [Obama] put his campaign together, with all these tools available to us, it allowed me to get involved."[15]

The *Globe* chronicled Zombie Frausto's interactivity through B.H.O.'s Web operation in the key state of Ohio, noting that through MyBO more than three hundred support groups were established. "When Frausto attended her first meeting of Obama supporters from around Ohio's capital city [before the primaries], about 40 people showed up. Today, groups she identifies with around Columbus have about 1,700 Obama backers." The army of online supporters organized multiple festivals, fairs, fund-raisers, phone banks, brainstorming sessions, and happy hour gatherings. "It was all done through my.barackobama.com," Frausto said. "We would not exist if not for that tool. It's phenomenal to me."

So how did MyBO assist with new votes? One feature offered was an "online calling-and-canvassing tool" referred to as Neighbor-to-Neighbor. It worked as follows. After logging on to MyBO, and through proper training (mostly viral), users were allowed to access a list of their neighbors who were undecided or who were categorized as "leaning Obama." According to tech industry leaders, MyBO was "highly integrated with data sets—geography, age, profession, languages, military service—to match volunteers with undecideds they might relate to."[16] All in all, volunteers used this specific instrument on MyBO to make nearly 8 million calls.[17]

Some states even held contests on who could make the most phone calls. In Ohio, for instance, the top ten call makers won a meeting with Dear Leader himself.[18] Can you think of a more fitting reward for the Zombies?

This level of "microtargeting" by Team Obama was the norm. Students who joined an Obama Facebook group were immediately contacted by the campaign. After studying the person's Facebook profile, "you have a common ground to talk to them about something," said Menno Goedman, an Obama volunteer. Once rapport was established, the new Facebook groupie was invited to an Obama event.[19] "It's one thing to get somebody to sign an online pledge saying, 'I'll vote for Obama.' But it's another to look them in the eye and get that same promise,"[20] Goedman added. On Election Day itself, more than 15 million people logged onto Facebook to follow what was happening and to encourage friends to vote.[21]

Such "peer pressure" to garner support for Barack was actually a centerpiece of the campaign's website. MyBO users saw an "activity index" that measured how hard they were working to get Obama elected.[22] B.H.O.'s team defined "activity" as "calls made to voter lists, events hosted, and funds raised." A ranking of between 1 and 10 was given. And the rankings were made public, on purpose, to other members of MyBO. As *BusinessWeek* remarked, "It could be uncomfortable to be exposed to friends and fellow supporters as having done little for a shared cause. It would be especially embarrassing if a member's friends learned they hadn't even bothered to vote."[23] Uncomfortable? Bad word choice, *BusinessWeek*! Refraining from campaigning for the Messiah would be nothing short of blasphemy!

• • •

TEAM OBAMA WAS always adroit on the Internet front. Not until the 2006 midterm elections did Facebook allow candidates to create profile pages. This came before the era of Facebook fan pages, which companies, celebrities, and laymen now use with increasing regularity. In 2006, Obama wanted a profile, even though he wasn't an official candidate. "I liked the Facebook idea,"[24] said Jim Brayton, who handled Obama's U.S. Senate online operations. Obama and his people immediately realized the potential. "We quickly wanted to be able to do more with it," he added.

It was actually B.H.O.'s online presence that gave him the advantage in states throughout the primary. Obama's campaign manager, David Plouffe, described the upper hand this way:

> When we turned to the community, they were there. We sent staff into Colorado and Missouri for caucuses, and the staff was already half-organized. We were there to support the people, but that simply would have not have been possible if we did not have a set of online tools that enabled us to do that. It wasn't just a tactic.[25]

To Plouffe, Chris Hughes made that happen. "Technology has always been used as a net to capture people in a campaign or cause, but not to organize. Chris saw what was possible before anyone else."[26]

Connecting people and sharing information in rapid speed: that was the name of the game. "People have always communicated, organized around campaigns," explained Hughes. "We just made it easier." And the resources flowed. "Our team just exploded in size," said Nikki Sutton, Obama's voter-contact manager. Of

MyBO's versatility, one official bragged: "Everywhere we went, we could plug in a zip code, and a list of really excited volunteers would pop up."

Without a robust online strategy, Plouffe admits his candidate's chances would've gone up in smoke: "Indiana? North Carolina? We wouldn't have won those states without the grassroots."[27] Plouffe also observed that they "were able to build a state-by-state organization during the primaries because of the Internet."[28]

When Obama defeated Hillary Clinton in the Virginia primary, local B.H.O. organizers credited the Internet team. "We couldn't have done this without the MyBO site," said Marcia Carlyn, a volunteer in Loudoun County. Even Obama staffers were stunned by what MyBO accomplished. According to Jeremy Bird, the Zombie director for Maryland, grassroots organizers in his state had used MyBO to set up "an office with seven computers, phone lines, a state structure, county chairs, and meetings every other Saturday."[29]

In the end, Obama's Internet team consisted of ninety people.[30] Yes, you read that right. Ninety peeps concentrating on the One's online message. And they were integrated into every portion of the campaign. They weren't shoved off to the side like some disposable "techie." In fact, Joe Rospars maintained that in order to build a powerhouse online animal it must be synergized with communications, finance, and grassroots organizing.[31] It just so happens that raising more than $700 million will produce that type of synergy.

Meanwhile, McCain was still fiddling with an abacus.

COLLEGE STUDENTS IN swing states were heavily targeted by Obama's digital minions. Through MyBO, students were asked to submit their home state and the state in which they attend school.

After gleaning that information, B.H.O.'s team would determine which state was most important for them to win and encourage students to register there. Overall, MyBO registered a million people, whereas around two thousand paid staffers and volunteers were needed to register the same number of people by going door-to-door.[32]

The online strategy was a massive success: The top Internet searches for Yahoo in 2008 included Britney Spears, WWE, and . . . Barack Obama.

Besides MyBO and Facebook outreach, Team Obama broke the backs of their opponents using YouTube and text messaging. Obama's YouTube channel was headed by Kate Albright-Hanna, an Emmy-winning CNN producer who was acquired by the campaign to flood YouTube and BarackTV, the video section of BarackObama .com, with as much content as possible. And flood she did. Remember that B.H.O. had more than eighteen hundred official videos . . . six times the number of official McCain videos! Obama's mug was everywhere during the campaign (and sadly, still is). His videographers filmed in all different angles, from "rallying his troops in his Chicago headquarters, scrimmaging with the University of North Carolina men's basketball team, mingling with the regulars at a barbershop in South Carolina, helping out with a phone bank in Colorado."[33] We saw Obama from every flattering, manipulated angle.

But not only did the campaign post the videos to YouTube and MyBO, it also "screened them at rallies and e-mailed them to voters who could not attend. Videos became part of the campaign's rapid responses and a presence on the personal pages of social network users."[34]

David Plouffe, in particular, was quite the YouTube aficionado. He'd routinely give updates to subscribers of their page on how the campaign was progressing. These videos included fund-raising pitches and viral get-out-the-vote strategy sessions. He also used it to respond directly to John McCain's attack ads. For instance, two weeks before the election, Plouffe posted a video on YouTube telling subscribers that "John McCain's campaign is 100 percent negative" and doesn't have any "positive ideas" to strengthen the country. As an example, Plouffe played some of the "vile" ads to show the viewers how "nasty" McCain was getting. Plouffe went on to play the clip of Sarah Palin accusing Obama of "palling around with terrorists." (That would be Bill Ayers, folks.) Plouffe reminded the online audience to continue to knock on doors, send emails, and donate money to fight the "unprecedented sleaze factory." Wrapping up the video, Plouffe called on all the Zombies to get "ferocious" for Obama.[35]

Plouffe had many of these videos. They were quick and to the point. And they added a personal touch, talking to the viewers as though they were all in this together. It was, as Joe Rospars said, lowering "the barriers to participating through technology, and to raise expectations about what we need from our supporters."[36]

YouTube was also used as a powerful defensive weapon. After B.H.O.'s Philadelphia speech on race, the campaign created a video featuring students at a high school in the Bronx, New York. The video shows black and Hispanic students watching Obama's speech and nodding in approval like the good Zombies they are. Once Obama's speech concluded, the students are seen discussing their own school's racial atmosphere. "I like . . . how [Obama] always says blacks, whites, Spanish, Asian," says a junior on camera. "He says all the races, so you can see that he's not focused on one group of people."[37] Another Zombie adds: "Just the fact that he wants to unify the country . . . everybody is agreeing because we're tired of dividing Republicans, Democrats, black, white, Asian. It's tiring."[38]

Of course the video was pure agitprop, attempting to position Obama as this racial harmonizer even though he sat in the pews of a church whose pastor was a racial divider. But the rapid response was effective and well produced, and like all of B.H.O.'s material, it offered us a candidate who never did exist.

The thirty-seven-minute speech on race itself at Independence Hall in Philadelphia was packaged as an online video and was viewed in its entirety by more than 6 million people—no commercial breaks and no color commentary. YouTube was one of the ways to bypass the mainstream media (even though they were in the tank for him anyway) and speak directly with supporters, with links to the campaign website and a "Contribute" button that enabled those watching the video to donate up to $1,000 using Google Checkout. McCain didn't offer this option.[39] At all.

OKAY, SO HAVING B.H.O.'s campaign manager make personal appeals to you on your YouTube account is a powerful appeal. But so is getting a text message from him, and one from Barack, the Messiah, himself.

Besides employing one of the founders of Facebook and an award-winning producer from CNN, B.H.O. added a savvy public relations entrepreneur who whipped up the idea for mobilizing voters through text messaging. Originally the campaign was skeptical, as such an idea had never been practiced on a large scale before. And plus, it does cost money to send and receive text messages. Would the payoff be worth it? Um, I'm gonna go with "yes."

At first the campaign started off small, just sending out dozens of texts here and there, asking supporters to tune in to a debate and reply back with thoughts on how B.H.O. did. But as the primaries and caucuses got closer, the text outreach started to yield results. When Oprah Winfrey addressed a rally of twenty-nine thousand people in South Carolina, campaign officials asked the crowd to text "SC" to a specific Obama number. Thousands of cell phone numbers just like that! The campaign also printed more than thirty thousand fliers with contact information of undecided voters and a call script with instructions on what to say over the phone.

The script read: "Hello,_____. This is [your name]. I am calling from Williams-Brice stadium where several thousand South Carolinians are gathered to see Presidential candidate Barack Obama and his supporter Oprah Winfrey."[40] According to the *Guinness Book of World Records,* this stunt turned out to be the largest phone bank ever.[41] B.H.O. eventually won South Carolina by a 28-point margin.

The campaign continued to collect a gold mine of cell numbers, and especially when they announced that if you texted your number to the campaign, Barack himself would notify you of his vice presidential pick first—via text messaging! The cell numbers poured in.

Once the campaign had your cell number, they were going to use it: asking for financial support, encouraging you to vote, encouraging your friends to vote. It was a personal appeal directly to you. "To me, texting is the most personal form of communication," said Scott Goodstein, the Obama official who hatched the scheme. "Your phone is with you almost all the time. You're texting with your girlfriend. You're texting with your friends. Now you're texting with Barack."[42]

The real text-messaging coup occurred at the Democratic National Convention. While the seventy-five thousand supporters were shuffling into Invesco Field in Denver, the Obama team turned them into campaign volunteers. Obama's Colorado director,

Ray Rivera, asked the crowd to pull out their cell phones and send a text message to a designated number. "We're going to do some work," he said. Of this strategy, the Associated Press noted that "the speech itself may or may not become a seminal moment in the campaign" but instead "a shrewd and groundbreaking calculation to expand Obama's vote base."[43]

If you're thinking it, you're correct: that was seventy-five thousand new numbers—direct contacts—added in one night. Do you even need to ask if McCain's people added text-messaging features to their outreach? Please, don't.

In addition to the text messages, Obama's campaign arranged 130 telephone stations throughout Invesco and asked attendees to take turns making "scripted" calls to unregistered eligible voters. Young people were the specific target. Through microtargeting techniques, B.H.O.'s legions identified 170,000 people between the ages of eighteen and twenty-four in Missouri who were eligible, but unregistered to vote.[44] Guess who got a call from Invesco Field?

Text messaging zipped at lightning speed also helped manufacture crowds. Before Obama hit up a rally in Colorado, his online crew sent a text to his supporters in the area saying "Rally with Barack in Denver this Sunday!" along with an address and a reminder that it was "Free & open to public." More than one hundred thousand people descended from all over Colorado to attend this gathering in a key battleground state that His Holiness eventually won.[45] Voilà: how to create an Obama Zombie, text-messaging-style. All in all, Team Obama collected a million cell numbers through their text-messaging outreach.

And what would be a discussion about new media without mentioning the O-phone? Yes, Obama even had his own *ringtone*! Before the election, Rospars and company unveiled an application for the iPhone that, like any good Zombie material, was advertised as a "comprehensive connection to the heart of Barack Obama."[46] The application even featured portions of Obama's speeches "mashed up" into ringtones. Sadly, campaign officials declined to include sermons from the radical reverend Jeremiah Wright and book readings from the terrorist Bill Ayers mixing to the beats of the Black Eyed Peas.

In addition to fluffy Obama speeches, the application served as a mini MyBO, enabling volunteers to organize their phone directory so that those individuals located in contested states appeared first.[47] The *New York Times* observed that "Obama will have not just a political base, but a database, millions of names of supporters who can be engaged almost instantly."[48]

SO WHAT DOES the McCain camp do to hop into the Internet game? Pork Invaders, people. A doofy little video game called "Pork Invaders." The goal of the game was to shoot down pigs while dodging their flying projectiles. Once victory was claimed over the vermin, numbers appeared before the viewer detailing Obama's massive requests for "earmarks," a congressional provision that wastes funds on specific projects in the home state of senators and congressmen, usually to curry favor with donors and lobbying organizations.

That was the McCain campaign's Internet outreach. Freaking "Pork Invaders." Don't count on me to defend it; it didn't look like Halo, that's for sure. More like Pacman, circa 1980s.

Obama hires Facebook dude and Emmy winners, unveils an iPhone application, compiles 13 million email addresses that sent more than 7,000 messages,[49] and organizes the largest phone bank in the history of mankind. And we conservatives get Pork Invaders. I'm gonna take a wild guess and say that it's hardly a surprise that nearly 25 percent of all young people had personal contact with someone from the Obama campaign, and why 28 percent of young voters in battleground states—far greater than in any other age bracket—said they had attended an Obama campaign event.[50]

THE IRONY IS that the conservative message is in direct alignment with young people's craving for individual choice and services, all of which new media fuel and foster. That's something big government can never provide. The Web empowers individuals in ways unimagined a generation ago. Online participation is the ultimate endorsement of limited government. We choose; we decide; we are not regulated, coerced, engineered, or taxed. The world is a mouse click away.

The very existence of things like Facebook and YouTube is a testament to the power of what a free people can do, and also gives conservatives relatable talking points when confronting the Zombie. Government bureaucrats never told Chris Hughes, or his roommate at Harvard, to create Facebook. The same goes for the innumerable number of social networking sites today, including the amazing cell phone technology we have—a multiple array of BlackBerrys to pick from and an iPhone with more than twenty-five thousand applications. These are the fruits of ingenuity, innovation, and the profit motive. Ever wonder why the aforementioned industries thrive while highly regulated programs such as health care, Social Security, and housing are all jacked up? Ever notice that when a free market isn't suffocated, prices plunge and choices spike? Free markets have made available to everyone—rich and poor alike—gadgets that we could never dream of living without: air conditioners, microwaves, stoves, refrigerators, washing machines, clothes dryers, and computers of all shapes and sizes.

We couldn't fathom a society without such luxuries. Thank you, capitalism.

But Obama's Congress continues its descent into bigger government and less freedom, offering legislative bills topping a thousand pages, all with new schemes for regulation and redistribution of wealth to the cronies of their choice. In fact, Obama is on track to have more "czars" than Ben & Jerry's has flavors!

My generation is easily deceived into believing the left's grandiose promises. Our idealism and relative comfort clouds our judgment. We tend to be healthy, without mortgages, not yet parents, carefree relative to past generations of Americans. So when some politician, especially a cultic one like Obama, promises universal health care, an end to poverty, or to heal our nation and fix the economy, we place undue trust in the power of government, because we've never experienced its inefficiencies and pathologies. It's time to wake up! It's time to spend more time thinking, and less time following!

3

The Dave Matthews Electoral Magnet—
And Other Ways to Manufacture a Crowd

*Why Whacked-Out Celebrities Matter Far More Than You Think,
and How They Create Electoral "Laboratories" for Obama Zombies*

What would make you be a good mother or father, sister or brother, or even a caring neighbor? Human decency? Your values? Or the election of a president?

For the Tinsel Town know-nothings who inhabit Hollywood, electing B.H.O. was nothing short of a rediscovery of the basic adult responsibility.

Following the election, Demi Moore and her *Punked* husband, Ashton Kutcher, produced a video pledging their support to Dear Leader. With them were an all-star cast of Hollywood heavyweights, including Cameron Diaz, Dakota Fanning, Jaime Pressly, Ashlee Simpson, Nicole Richie, Tobey Maguire, Diddy, Alyssa Milano, Marisa Tomei, Courtney Cox, and David Arquette. The hyperbolic lovefest reached operatic heights.

I pledge to end hunger in America, went one line. In the history of the planet, hunger has never been eliminated. But somehow, when cometh Barack, the seas will part, the mountains will crumble, the skies will open, and poverty will henceforth be abolished.

Sweet, bro!

And that's just one line. Kutcher—whom I will grant some slack because he is, after all, married to Demi Moore—defended his video as a clarion call to Hollywood to stand up and help B.H.O. solve the world's ills.

"There's an assumption that this one man is going to take on his new job full-time and somehow wave a magic wand of change, and I don't believe that to be true," Ashton told Reuters. "I think that we have to be the leaders, and that's not celebrities—I think that we as citizens have to be leaders of the movement that we want to create."[1]

> *I pledge to smile more, to laugh more, to love more . . .*
> *I pledge to be a great mother; to be a great father . . .*
> *To be the voice for those who have no voice . . .*
> *I pledge to consider myself an American, not an African-*
>   *American . . .*

This last line is delivered by then–New York Giants linebacker Michael Strahan. Here's a dude who raked in millions on the gridiron who will, now and *only* now, pledge to refer to himself as an American—because Obama got elected?! Earth to brother Strahan: You freaking won a Super Bowl under the tenure of President Bush. Were you not an American then?

The pledging to the most mind-numbing of basic duties of citizenship rolled on:

To always represent my country with pride, dignity, and honesty . . .
I pledge allegiance to the funk, to the united funk of funkadelica . . .

This last enlightening insight comes from Anthony Kiedis of the Red Hot Chili Peppers. Not gonna lie to you—I have no clue what this means. Then again, it's doubtful he did, either. So take heed, kiddies: drugs will make you pledge allegiance to funk.

I pledge to never give anyone the finger when I'm driving again . . .
I pledge to bring awareness to mental disease, to advance stem-cell
*   research . . .*
I pledge to show more love to strangers . . . [especially strangers who
*   hate America and loathe her existence]*
I pledge to be a better mentor to my younger sisters . . .
For the environment, I pledge to flush only after a deuce, never a
*   single . . . [Liberals have a strange fascination with doo-doo.]*
I pledge . . .
To work to make good the two-hundred-year-old promise to end
*   slavery . . .*
To free one million people from slavery in the next five years . . .
I pledge . . .
I pledge to never stop learning and growing each and every day . . .

And the finale, people:

What's your pledge?
I pledge to be a servant to our president and all mankind.

There you have it, folks. Prior to January 21, 2009, if you happened to have been a delinquent parent, experienced road rage, were ashamed of America, flushed the toilet for "number ones," were a hyphenated American, a pouter, and a supporter of the slave trade, well, no longer! Hollywood and Obama pledged to implant a moral compass in you.

You might be wondering, okay, who gives a donkey's rear about what some pampered actor has to say? And normally, you would be right. Demi Moore may strip with Oscar-winning elegance on camera, but she's in no position to be giving out life advice. But when it comes to my generation, Hollywood matters. Team Obama knew this. And thus they unleashed Tinsel Town like never before, deploying celebrity SWAT teams to battleground states, hosting swank mega–fund-raisers, organizing free concerts (perfect lure bait for aspiring Obama Zombies), cold-calling voters, emailing, and machine-gunning text messages with dizzying regularity and lightning speed.

Celebs were gaga over B.H.O.! And it wasn't surprising they'd help elect the most superficial and egomaniacal candidate we've ever seen. As Tina Daunt of the *Los Angeles Times* put it, "If Obama loses, there won't be a shrink in Beverly Hills with an hour to spare."[2]

Kelly Hu of *X-Men* and *Terminator: Salvation* declared that B.H.O. "speaks to Asian-Americans because he'd lived amongst us in Asia and in Hawaii." And what if he never was from Hawaii? Well, no matter because "he would still be the most inspiring candidate I've ever seen," added Hu.[3]

On Obama's victory, Oprah had this orgasmic reaction: "I'm vibrating." Oprah continued, declaring that the election "has been the greatest experience of my lifetime. I haven't seen a sense of unity like this since 9/11. Now, we're all brought together in the name of hope."[4]

And the always classy and tactful Madonna had this to contribute: "I'm so fucking happy right now."[5]

Sherri Shepherd of *The View* broke down in tears over Obama's victory, recalling that she looked at her baby and said mawkishly, "You don't have to have limitations."[6]

Singer John Mellencamp remarked that while he's written countless songs about racial harmony, even he couldn't believe that "a man of color could be president of the United States." He added, "I am so proud of America."[7] Nothing like believing that your fellow Americans are all racists, Johnny boy.

Actress Scarlett Johansson said the "overwhelming hope that Obama inspires is infectious."[8]

Hate to break the news to you, but there wasn't a landslide for hope. The election was much closer than you wished. B.H.O. won 53 percent of the vote. On the other hand, 58 million Americans gave your guy the middle finger, and there wasn't any Hollywood star around to pledge them out of it.

Hollywood had a stake in the election. In true self-absorbed lefty style, a victory for Obama would be a self-congratulating victory for the Hollywood elite. And thus the tactics were, in many ways, a confirmation of star power writ large.

For example, musician Dave Matthews sent out an email to a million of his fans to endorse Obama. *Rolling Stone* asked the musician why he was so passionate about Obama over candidates of the past. And in Matthews, not surprisingly, we have a guy who thinks lack of experience is actually a qualification to be president:

> The biggest argument that people can lay against him is his lack of qualifications, which is such an empty argument. The most important qualification a candidate can possess is being able to inspire people to want to do things for the country. The great presidential speeches by people like Kennedy or Lincoln—what made them great

were their words, and the fact that they moved mountains with their words. We don't remember JFK's qualifications. We don't remember his connections or his experience in the political arena. What we remember are the qualities that made him stand apart from all that. That's why people are being inspired by Obama. He makes me feel like it is possible to change the world.[9]

Somehow, comparing Abraham Lincoln, the first Republican president, ender of slavery, and preserver of our union, to Barack Obama seems—oh, I don't know—*insane*. In fact, the only thing the thug from Chicago and the president from Illinois have in common is that without Lincoln, Dave Matthews could have *owned* Obama.

But Matthews, strangely, went on to defend Obama's inexperience as a plus. He mocked the other candidates for insisting that "you need to have experience in order to be able to move forward."

"What a bunch of crap," said the South African–born singer. "I don't want someone who's experienced in the present-day arena of politics—it's hopelessly failed this country. Both sides of the aisle, without question, have dismally let the American people down. We need a person with fresh ideas and an incredible eloquence that really cuts to the core of so many issues with just a real frankness."[10]

Actually, neither Matthews nor any of his ilk can point to a fresh, new idea from Obama. It's warmed-over liberalism, plain and simple. It's more big government and a retread on redistribution of wealth or, as Obama put it famously to Joe the Plumber, "spreading the wealth around." Nothing new in any of this, but to Obama Zombies who have little knowledge of American history (after all, leftists have gutted it as a requirement in America's top colleges and universities), failed liberal policies may seem fresh and new, especially when advocated by their favorite singer or movie star. Ergo the following action hero Obama allusion from Dave Matthews:

> I really think Obama could move mountains, not because he's some kind of spectacular superhuman, but because he moves people in a real way. . . . When I look at Obama, I feel like, "Wow, here's this man who's going to try to break down some walls and try and revive the Constitution after the three-decade-long beating it has taken. Maybe we can finally resuscitate that poor old dusty piece of paper that's been kicked into the corner for a long time."[11]

But perhaps one of Team Obama's best and most effective uses of rockers like Dave Matthews came in the form of a little something I like to call the "Dave Matthews Electoral Magnet" tactic. During the Democrat primary, Obama's team deployed a smart if cynical campaign tactic that is a perfect representation of all that is wrong with the Zombification of my generation. At an Indiana University pro-Hillary rally, Bill Clinton was delivering one of his trademark finger-wagging lectures in support of his wife when Team Obama's Bloomington-based office leapt into warp-speed Zombification mode. As Clinton was speaking, B.H.O.'s minions began handing out free Dave Matthews tickets. You can imagine the viral marketing effect, with college kids burning up their texting keyboards and mad dialing on their iPhones to tell their soon-to-be-Zombified friends that, "Dude, Obama is hooking us up with free Dave Matthews tickets. Leave the Slick Willy speech and come get the free tickets, bro!"

Now you might think that such blatant, crass pandering would hold no sway on young, enlightened minds. But you would be wrong.

"I was leaning toward Obama," said Jason Schechtman, nineteen, of Deerfield, Illinois, a student at IU, "but this sealed the deal for sure." "The Obama campaign announced this right as [Bill Clinton] was about to speak, and it brought everyone from over there to over here."[12]

Behold! The Obama Zombie conversion right before your very eyes!

It's really that depressing and basic. The "feel good," "be cool," "here's free stuff" so-called "dorm storming" tactics that managed to woo historic numbers of young people to vote for Obama by a 2-to-1 margin produced the kind of ephemeral electoral spike it was intended to. A year later, the excitement has vanished. Reality has set in. As the Associated Press's Martha Irvine reported, since the election the Obama "fervor has died down—noticeably." What's more, in a classic case of buyer's remorse, some Zombies show small but encouraging signs of beginning to awaken from their slavish slumber. For example, the AP also conducted a poll that showed only half of 18- to 29-year-olds approve of the way Obama has handled health care, and only 38 percent say they support the health-care plans under consideration by the Democrat Congress.[13]

Still, despite these encouraging tremors of life within the Obama Zombie masses, the fact remains that an entire generation, nodding to the beat of the latest YouTube Zombie clip, helped elect the most unprepared, untested, far-left radical in U.S. history. That chief Obama henchmen David Axelrod and David Plouffe understand the power of celebrity branding and the winning tactics such as the deployment of Dave Matthews Electoral Magnets is certain. As advertising guru Chuck Brymer, president and CEO of DDB Worldwide, which is one of the largest and most influential advertising agencies in the world, noted, the 2008 presidential election "was the election heard round the world. Plouffe's blend of digital and traditional media was spot on and the key driver behind the successful brand story and record campaign fundraising." [14]

ANOTHER IMPORTANT ROLE the Obama campaign gave Hollywood involved stoking the flames of Palin Derangement Syndrome.

Samantha Ronson, Lindsay Lohan's onetime lover, said that her fans should vote for Obama because if Palin is elected "my green card probably won't get renewed!!!" [15]

Lohan rhetorically asked, "Is our country so divided that the Republicans [sic] best hope is a narrow minded, media-obsessed homophobe?" [16] Lohan also pulled Palin's female card from her: "Women have come a long way in the fight to have the choice over what we do with our bodies. . . . And its [sic] frightening to see that a woman in 2008 would negate all of that." [17]

Matt Damon said that it would be a "really scary thing" if Palin became president because McCain didn't survive his first term. A "really bad Disney movie," as he put it. "The hockey mom, you know, 'oh, I'm just a hockey mom' . . . and she's facing down President Putin. . . . It's totally absurd . . . it's a really terrifying possibility. . . ." [18]

Pamela Anderson told Palin to "suck it." [19]

Pink said, "This woman hates women," and added, "If I were writing a letter to Sarah Palin it would be a lot of *whys* and *hows*. Who are you? Do you know? Why do you hate animals? Please point out Iraq on a map. . . ." [20]

Pink, Palin does love animals—the way most Americans do: killed, fried, and ready to eat.

"Palin, what's that?" erupted Russell Simmons at MTV's VMA awards. "He [McCain] went all the way to the right and got the most conservative person who knows nothing about the struggle of most Americans and made her the vice presidential nominee. That's amazing. Any skirt will do."[21]

Nothing like a sexist lecture on the plight of the common man from a rap mogul who spends his time in million-dollar mansions and zipping around the planet in his private jet.

Diddy, on one of his YouTube videos, had this message to John McCain: "You are bugging the fuck out. I don't even understand what planet you're on right now . . . Alaska? Come on man. I don't know if there are even any black people in Alaska. . . ."

Not only did the alleged lack of black people in Alaska "bug" Diddy out, but he was also concerned that "there's not even no crackheads in Alaska." Ah yes, the gold standard in the picking of a vice president. Does your state have any crackheads? No? Well then, clearly you aren't qualified. Crackheads by the dozen in your state? Straight to the front of the line for leader of the free world!

Diddy summed up his Obama Zombie logic with this stirring message: "I'm calling all youth. All Colors. All youth voters. November 4th we have to protect our future, and John McCain is bugging the fuck out, okay? . . . You need to get versed on black policies and youth policies."[22]

AXELROD AND PLOUFFE'S ability to manufacture crowds led by Hollywood's brightest lights was only the beginning, though. It was the transition from concert to get-out-the-vote strategy that delivered Change We Could Believe In. Enter the Boss, Bruce Springsteen. In the leadup to the election, Springsteen volunteered his time to star at Obama rallies in key battleground states. In Pennsylvania, Springsteen drew tens of thousands at the Benjamin Franklin Parkway. After heaping angelic levels of praise on Obama, the New Jersey rocker called President Bush a "disaster" and claimed that too many people have "lost faith" in the American dream.

"I've spent 35 years writing about America and its people and the meaning of the American promise—a promise handed down right here in this city. Our everyday citizens . . . have justifiably lost faith in its meaning."[23]

Springsteen's free concert at Ohio State University drew more than ten thousand young people, fresh subjects for Obama-style lobotomies. The Boss said Obama would lead an "American reclamation project" to revive the country's global image. "Despite the terrible erosion to our standing in the world," said the international-relations expert Springsteen, "we remain for many people a house of dreams. And 1000 George Bushes and 1000 Dick Cheneys will never be able to tear that house down." With its usual savvy for well-timed and seamlessly coordinated get-out-the-vote tactics, Springsteen's appearance was designed to capitalize on a loophole that allowed Ohio residents to register and vote on the same day.[24]

The Boss performed a free concert at Eastern Michigan University and even a fund-raiser in Manhattan with the Piano Man, Billy Joel. The ritzy event offered another chance at some good ol' Palin bashing. In front of twenty-five hundred people, Springsteen told the gathering, "Billy and I have rehearsed a little, but I hope you consider this more like the vice presidential debate. You have to sort of Palin-ize your expectations. We seem like we know a lot, but we don't, really." The crowd laughed on cue.[25]

The NBA superstar LeBron James and famed rapper Jay-Z also

got in on the action, hosting free concerts in Ohio called "Last Chance for Change." Before Jay-Z began spitting out lyrics, the twenty thousand fans packed inside Quicken Loans Arena in Cleveland were shown a thirty-minute Obama informercial on the JumboTron.

Once the rally kicked off, Jay-Z had this to say of B.H.O.: "Rosa Parks sat so Martin Luther King could walk, and Martin walked so Obama could run. Obama is running so we all can fly, so let's fly."[26] LeBron, meanwhile, spent his time bobbing and bouncing on stage, possibly in the hopes of scoping out another baby momma for him.

To be sure, Obama pays lip service to rap music being misogynistic and offensive, but in reality he is all too happy to use individuals for vote getting and fund-raising who've been rapping about the thug life and sexing multiple "bitches" and "hos."

"So what?" you may ask. "Are young voters really influenced by this kind of celebrity endorsement silliness?"

Yes, say mass communication scholars. One study conducted by two Washington State University professors found that "celebrity endorsed campaigns successfully lowered complacency and helped young people believe in their own impact on the political system." Furthermore, the researchers found that, after being subjected to celebrity endorsements, "young people got involved at higher levels and became increasingly aware of societal issues."[27]

Natalie Wood, assistant director of the Center for Consumer Research, agrees: "Politicians are like businesses—name recognition goes a long way, and celebrities can help make that happen. Obama is a classic example of that because most people had never heard of him before."[28]

One person who made sure that Barack Obama became a household name was Oprah Winfrey. By Team Obama's own estimation, Oprah's emergence on the campaign trail led to record-setting rallies and at least ten thousand new volunteers.

An economist at Northwestern University, Craig Garthwaite, and one from the University of Maryland, Timothy Moore, confirmed the impact of Oprah's endorsement. MSNBC.com reported, "After analyzing sales of Oprah's Book Club selections and subscriptions to Winfrey's magazine *O*, the pair estimated she captured about 1 million additional votes for Obama in the primary election." [29]

Liberals' overwhelming domination of the entertainment industry has given the left a massive advantage in leveraging outreach to the youth demographic. The emotional connection between young people and their music makes the left's use of pop culture as an electoral tool an especially potent electoral brew.

"Musicians in particular have this deep connection with their audience on an emotional level that really gets to the identity of the individuals," says Andy Bernstein, the executive director of HeadCount, a voter registration organization created in 2004 by a group of artists, music industry professionals, and fans. "Young people really define themselves with the music that they listen to. When someone like Dave Matthews steps to the microphone and urges people to vote, you can't even measure the impact. Fans are very, very engaged and they're not just feeding off of the musicians, but they're communicating with each other." [30]

HeadCount poses as nonpartisan, but Bernstein acknowledges that the group was birthed during the '04 campaign to defeat President George W. Bush. "I was a reporter at the time," he says. "I was on the phone with somebody, and the conversation turned to politics. I was so riled up, I was like, 'I've got to do something, what am I going to do?' And, like a minute later, I said, 'You know what? If I can do something to get fans of the bands I listen to to vote, that's what I can do.' "[31]

This "nonpartisan" organization had the weight of Dave Matthews Band, Pearl Jam, Jack Johnson, Nine Inch Nails, Wilco, Phish, John Mayer, and numerous others behind them. The organization then set up voting registration tables at a thousand concerts across the country, registering tens of thousands of Obama Zombies-in-training. And surprise, surprise, they're all libs. The Medill News Service analyzed the campaign contributions of the musicians affiliated with HeadCount and found that most of them gave to Democrat candidates in the 2008 presidential race.[32] In fact, HeadCount is so nonpartisan that Andy Bernstein found a way to encourage people to vote for Obama: "It's okay to say 'Jerry Garcia' " when informing registrants who is preferable to vote for. "That's allowed. As long as you don't say what party Jerry Garcia will be running on."

Translation: vote for B.H.O., bro, and pass the joint.

HeadCount wasn't the only "nonpartisan group" with a readily apparent point of view. The Hip Hop Caucus's "Respect My Vote" campaign pimped out rapper T.I. to get young people, mostly in the hip-hop community, to register to vote. The group targeted Baltimore, Philadelphia, Richmond, Atlanta, Cincinnati, Raleigh/ Durham, Houston, Dallas, St. Louis, Indianapolis, Columbus, Detroit, Cleveland, and Charlotte. The founder, "Reverend" Lennox Yearwood, Jr., wears a traditional collarless reverend shirt with a hat backward. He enrolled T.I. "to work towards the elimination of poverty, the highest quality public education and the elimination of racism, racial profiling and police brutality."[33]

T.I., who pled guilty to weapons charges in 2008, was all too happy to campaign for Obama under the nonpartisan banner.

"This was the first election I voted in myself," said T.I. "I guess it was Barack who influenced me. Politics just didn't move me. I didn't feel like it made a difference one way or the other. I looked at politicians and just thought, either way we're fucked. They don't really care about us anyway. Now, I look at Obama's government and I feel like someone's in there who has our best interests at heart."[34]

Hip-Hop Team Vote, another "nonpartisan" group, targeted Philadelphia youth, registering more than one hundred thousand voters.[35] Participants included our buddy T.I., Russell Simmons, and Flo-Rida. T.I. described himself as "a felon two or three times over" and Flo-Rida is the Romeo rapper who sings sweet odes about . . . blow jobs.

Flo-Rida told the youth, "Here's the chance to make your children's children's world a better place." Yes, voting can make change. Also, refraining from singing about blow jobs may lessen the coarsening of the culture.

WITH SUCH STAR power, the left will always have a sizable advantage over conservatives. When artists like Jay-Z or the Boss perform for free at Obama rallies, they are donating far more than they are able to do financially under federal campaign restrictions. Individuals are allowed to donate $2,300. That's it. But Obama would far rather have Springsteen, who made $70 million in concerts and album sales within the past year, donate his time than a measly $2,300. Now, while there should be *no* restrictions on the amount of money an individual can donate to a campaign (free speech doesn't have limits), it's fundamentally unfair to cap one's giving yet allow huge donations in the form of rallies (read: infomercials) that are worth millions and where cell phone numbers and emails are gathered to mobilize a youth marketing militia.

The greatest irony in all this is that so much of the success Hollywood entertainers achieve is the result of one of the core tenets of conservatism: namely, that able-bodied human beings are responsible for their own human flourishing. The life stories of so many entertainers exude all the best qualities that a strong conservative work ethic can bring. Their success was not wrought through the chamber of a government bureaucrat; it was individual initiative, individual drive, and individual responsibility.

Sean "Puffy" Combs is a prime example. As a boy, Combs was born in the public housing projects of Harlem, New York, and was only a child when his father was tragically murdered. He attended Howard University in Washington, D.C., while interning at Uptown Records in New York City. His love for music led him to shuttle back and forth between the two cities, even with a full load of school work. He did drop out of college, but at age nineteen became the youngest executive ever at Uptown Records. Today, for better or worse (for worse), Combs is a household name. He has established a record label, a clothing line, and a cologne; has created his own television show; and has produced and promoted some of the biggest names in hip-hop. He made *Fortune's* list of the "40 Richest People Under 40" and has a net worth exceeding $300 million.

Diddy loved music, loved promotion, loved the spotlight, and worked his derrière off to achieve his dreams. Uncle Sam didn't orchestrate it. He did. Not Washington.

When Obama talks about "individual responsibility and mutual responsibility," it's the mutual responsibility part he uses to justify the redistribution of wealth that he openly favored during the campaign and is carrying out by targeting the most productive members of society. In Barack's world, all money is the government's, no matter how much time, money, and effort you put into earning it. Wrap that ideology inside the left's usual class warfare rhetoric and—voilà!—you can turn otherwise hardworking, individualistic achievers like Diddy into head-bobbing Obama Zombies who will mindlessly campaign for a man who preaches a message antithetical to the very virtues that helped them achieve their success.

It's an effective if cynical trick. And, unfortunately, it's a trick that has produced many Obama Zombies.

The Peacenik Phantom

*How Peace and Love and Obama Granola Goodness Threaten Your
Life—And Why That Warmongering U.S. Military Is Your Best Friend*

Whom would you rather have protecting your family and nation?
Rambo? Or Bambi?

That was your choice in 2008. And, thanks to Obama Zombies,
America elected Bambi. The only difference is that the original
Bambi had far more foreign policy experience, what with all that
negotiating with the squirrels and birds of the forest and whatnot.
Plus, Bambi never hobnobbed with anti-American radicals or apol-
ogized for American power.

John McCain was a woefully weak spokesperson for the conservative cause. Still, on military matters, the man was unmatched.
And listen up, all you Obama Zombies: Your civil liberties don't
mean squat if you're dead! Got it? That's why presidents are commanders in chief before all else. We elect presidents to do the most

important thing a government can do: keep us from being murdered by hostile regimes.

McCain's military credentials are beyond compare in politics. A brief biography goes like this: McCain graduated from the U.S. Naval Academy, following in the deep military footsteps of his family. His father and grandfather were both four-star admirals. McCain became a prisoner of war in Vietnam after he was shot down while on a mission in Hanoi. As a POW, McCain was brutally tortured, day after day. The North Vietnamese eventually realized how important Mac's father was in the military. As a show of respect, they offered him early release, but he refused the special treatment. Get that: the Vietnamese offered to release him, but McCain rebuffed the offer, choosing to let the next compatriot in line go first. In the end, McCain's war wounds left him with life-long disabilities, such as not being able to lift his arms above his shoulders or type on a computer. By any standard, the man is an American hero.

After getting elected to the U.S. Senate in 1986, he served as a member of the Senate Armed Services Committee, keeping him deeply enmeshed in and informed on all military and intelligence operations affecting the United States of America.

Here are Barack Obama's military experience and credentials:_____.

Yet with all of McCain's experience and all of Obama's lack thereof, young people distrusted the former when it came to foreign policy.

A poll conducted in the fall of 2008 by Harvard's Institute of Politics found that 44 percent of young people ages 18–24 still trusted Obama over McCain on the issue of Iraq (28 percent trusted McCain).[1] More shockingly, 40 percent trusted Obama more on the broad category of "Foreign Policy" (27 percent sided with Mac).[2] A whopping 51 percent thought Obama would "improve the U.S. image abroad," while only 17 percent believed that of McCain.[3] Young people were evenly split over who would better protect them from terrorism.[4]

Who could forget the drama over Bill Ayers, the unrepentant bomb-thrower-turned-university "educator"? The relationship he had with Obama—political activity, foundations, and directing education projects together—rightfully called into question where Obama's allegiances lay. After all, Ayers's terrorist activity was not a relic of a rejected past but rather of a past he proudly bragged about on numerous occasions. I'm not looking to relitigate the relationship, especially since McCain stupidly took the "high" ground and tiptoed around the issue. But Obama Zombies need to understand how Ayers and his radicalism felt right at home in academia.

When Ayers became a problem for Obama, due to the dutiful coverage the relationship received on talk radio and the Fox News Channel, Ayers's colleagues constructed a website dedicated to his defense, SupportBillAyers.org. The main page of the website read as follows:

> It seems that the character assassination and slander of Bill Ayers and other people who have known Obama is not about to let up. While an important concern is the dishonesty of this campaign and the slanderous McCarthyism they are using to attack Obama, we also feel an obligation to support our friend and colleague Bill Ayers. Many, many educators have reached out, asking what they could do, seeking a way to weigh in against fear and intimidation. Many of us have been talking and we agree that this one gesture, a joint statement signed by hundreds of

hard-working educators, would be a great first step. Such a statement may be distributed through press releases or ads in the future.[5]

The website also pledged to combat the characterizations of Ayers as an "unrepentant terrorist" and "lunatic leftist." To them, he was just working "passionately in the civil rights and antiwar movements of the 1960s, as did hundreds of thousands of Americans. His participation in political activity 40 years ago is history."

Ayers was no MLK, peacefully marching through the streets of Selma, raising awareness of injustice. Rather, Ayers was judge, jury, and executioner—and he relishes that to this day. In his 2001 book, *Fugitive Days*, Ayers gloats how he "participated in the bombings of New York City Police Headquarters in 1970, of the Capitol building in 1971, and the Pentagon in 1972."[6] This is what he had to say about the Pentagon bombing: "Everything was absolutely ideal . . . The sky was blue. The birds were singing. And the bastards were finally going to get what was coming to them."[7]

It gets worse. On September 11, 2001, the day of the terrorist attacks, Ayers told the *New York Times* that he doesn't regret setting off bombs and laments that he didn't do enough.[8]

With that in mind, do you want to take a wild guess on how many "academics" pledged solidarity at SupportBillAyers.org? More than four thousand! And many of these professors "teach" at prominent institutions, including Columbia University, New York University, the University of Chicago, Rutgers University, and George Mason University, among hundreds of others.

Bill Schubert, a professor of education at the University of Illinois–Chicago, signed the letter to stand by his colleague. "I certainly support him in the sense that I think he's an outstanding faculty member and a good colleague," Schubert said. "I'm very disheartened by any discrediting kind of material in the news."[9]

Discrediting? Only in academia are you not disqualified from a posh tenured position on a campus if you lament not having eviscerated more people and property with dynamite. Rather, it's grounds for a promotion.

The disturbing thing is that intellectual thugs like Ayers are precisely the types of dirtbags that Obama hung around with in college. In *Dreams from My Father*, Obama recounts that he consciously connected with all the radical students to "avoid being mistaken for a sellout." Obama hung with the "Marxist professors," "structural feminists," and the "punk-rock performance poets" who got exercised about "neocolonialism," "Eurocentrism," and "patriarchy,"[10] which are all leftist buzzwords for overthrowing America as a world power.

And in a recently discovered op-ed that Obama penned at Columbia for a student magazine, he took aim at our country's culture of "militarism" and advocated nuclear disarmament. The title of the piece said it all: "Breaking the War Mentality."[11] As the *New York Times* put it, Obama "agitated for the elimination of global arsenals holding tens of thousands of deadly warheads" and railed against what he called "the relentless, often silent spread of militarism in the country" amid "the growing threat of war." In the article, Obama profiled two peacenik groups, Arms Race Alternatives and Students Against Militarism, which helped lead efforts to incorporate "peace, disarmament, and world order" into Columbia's curriculum to shift America from its "dead-end track."

Fast-forward to today. Now president, Obama is seeking to establish global coalitions that start the path to a "nuclear-free world." Obama has also cut back on developing missile-defense systems home and abroad that can protect America from rogue regimes; he wants America to decrease its weapons stockpile and wants to play patty-cake with Iran and North Korea to beg them, pretty please with sugar on top, to halt their nuclear ambitions.

At a forum sponsored by MTV and MySpace during the campaign, Obama explained to the young audience how he'd handle Iran:

> I'm going to tell them, "Should you develop a nuclear weapon, it's going to set off an arms race in the Middle East. You have to stop funding terrorist activities." But I'm also going to offer them some carrots and say to them, "But you know what? If you stand down on the nuclear issue, then potentially you could be admitted to the World Trade Organization. You can potentially have a greater economic benefit. Ultimately, at some point, we may be able to set up normalized diplomatic relations." [12]

Obama added that having these types of conversations would send a signal to Iran and the rest of the world that America is "listening" and not just "telling them what to do." [13]

Such rhetoric sounds nice, but it's why Obama had egg all over his face when it was revealed just eight months into his presidency that Iran had built an undisclosed, second nuclear facility. Obama's gullibility borders on willful negligence. It's one thing to be stupid, it's another thing to turn a blind eye to facts and overwhelming evidence.

The mullahs in Iran have made it clear that they seek the destruction of America. They don't want diplomatic relations; they want worldwide domination. Such hatred for us is driven by their interpretation of Islam. "Death to America" chants are common enough to be almost like a greeting for many of them. In fact, what type of meaningful diplomatic overtures can Obama legitimately expect from Iranian rulers who don't blink an eye when it comes to brutalizing their own people? We saw exactly that when the "supreme leader" of Iran ordered his Basij force to club, shoot, and ax to death young people protesting Iran's staged and fraudulent election.

North Korea is similar. Kim Jong Il has made it crystal clear that he seeks the West's annihilation, and he stymies every attempt by the United Nations to curb his weapons programs. Obama prefers to "negotiate." Meanwhile, back in the real world, we take our enemies at their words and view their actions as a middle finger to sane diplomacy. As military analyst Frank J. Gaffney commented, "If the implications were not so serious, the discrepancy between Mr. Obama's plans and real-world conditions would be hilarious. There is only one country on earth that Team Obama can absolutely, positively denuclearize: Ours." [14]

It's as if Obama wants to say to North Korea and Iran, "Now, fellas, I know you say you want to destroy Western civilization, but I think you're just misunderstood. I know you really don't mean what you say." Um, B.H.O., when Mahmoud Ahmadinejad declares that the Holocaust was "a false pretext to create Israel" [15] and that attacking them is a "national and religious duty," or that a world without America is "attainable," what type of negotiations could you possibly bring to the table without brute force and fierce sanctions? Especially when Ahmadinejad says that Iran has its own "war preparation plan" for "the destruction of Anglo-Saxon civilization." [16]

Obama seems not to care. After all, he fancies himself the "apologizer in chief." Such moral equivocating is insane and morally loathsome. Worse, it's downright dangerous. But why should this surprise us? If Obama Zombies would have taken their earbuds out of their ears long enough to actually research and listen to this man, they would have known just how radical he truly is.

• • •

EIGHT DAYS AFTER 9/11, Obama wrote an op-ed for Chicago's *Hyde Park Herald* in which he argued that Americans needed to have compassion for those who had just slaughtered our brethren:

> The essence of this tragedy, it seems to me, derives from a fundamental absence of empathy on the part of the attackers: an inability to imagine, or connect with, the humanity and suffering of others. Such a failure of empathy, such numbness to the pain of a child or the desperation of a parent, is not innate; nor, history tells us, is it unique to a particular culture, religion, or ethnicity. It may find expression in a particular brand of violence, and may be channeled by particular demagogues or fanatics. Most often, though, it grows out of a climate of poverty and ignorance, helplessness and despair.[17]

Obama kept with the same meme when addressing the MTV/MySpace presidential forum, specifically tailored toward youth. In it, he was asked this question via an interactive instant message: "The current administration has significantly affected global opinion about the United States. How do you hope to change the global opinion of our nation, and what are the most important American principles that you feel should be emphasized if you get a chance to represent the United States globally?"[18] The *Washington Post* reporter who conveyed the instant message followed up with this: "What's the face that we need to put out for the world?"

Obama's answer: "Mine."

That was fitting with the line the campaign fed us that only someone with a "multicultural" background can bring peace and harmony to the world, which coincided with hilarious rhetoric that he'd heal the planet and bring everyone to suddenly like America.

But Obama continued in the forum, addressing how he would handle our "plummeted" standing in the world:

> A couple of things I would do very specifically. I would double foreign aid because I want to send a message that we are concerned about other people, we're not always just talking about our agenda. We want to build schools around the world to teach math and science instead of hatred in America.

Reality check: The Muslim fanatics that have waged and are waging war against us did not do so because of poverty. Dropping rice and beans from the skies along with Hooked on Phonics lesson plans won't curb terrorism. As columnist Mark Steyn has pointed out,

> There's plenty of evidence out there that the most extreme "extremists" are those who've been most exposed to the west—and western education: from Osama bin Laden (summer school at Oxford, punting on the Thames) and Mohammed Atta (Hamburg University urban planning student) to the London School of Economics graduate responsible for the beheading of Daniel Pearl. The idea that handing out college scholarships to young Saudi males and getting them hooked on Starbucks and car-chase movies will make this stuff go away is ridiculous—and unworthy of a serious presidential candidate.[19]

During the MTV/MySpace forum, Obama gave us a taste of liberals' curious logic. He told the kiddos that we must quash "the genocide in Darfur" because "it's the right thing to do." But then in the next breath, he declared that "we've got to end this war in Iraq" by "focusing on diplomacy." Let's see if I got this one right: Intervene in some remote African country that has no national security relevance at all, but abandon Iraq, where the U.S. military is killing al-Qaeda operatives and other terrorist cells by the thousands (19,000 terrorists killed and more than 25,000 detained, just so you know[20]).

It's easy to be a liberal. It's easy to say you'll pull out of war and restore diplomacy and make everything better. Never mind that America finally went into Iraq after a decade of "diplomatic" sanctions from the United Nations. Obama paints a world that doesn't exist. Moreover, being a superpower, a world leader, means that other countries may not like you, that other countries may not support your actions. But that's American leadership: we lead and do not follow. Quite frankly, it's a good sign when terrorist states don't like what you're up to. That means you're doing something right.

One reason Barack and his ilk push to disarm America is that they view this country through the prism of the Vietnam War. They view America as constantly walking in sin, in need of redemption. On several occasions, B.H.O. has sought to apologize to foreign audiences for the actions of the nation that made him the most powerful man on the planet. By the Heritage Foundation's Nile Gardiner's count, Obama begged for forgiveness to "nearly 3 billion people across Europe, the Muslim world, and the Americas."[21]

Where do you think Obama delivered this whopper? "In America, there's a failure to appreciate Europe's leading role in the world. Instead of celebrating your dynamic union and seeking to partner with you to meet common challenges, there have been times where America has shown arrogance and been dismissive, even derisive."[22] In Strasbourg, France, last April. Yes, yes: Obama apologized to the French for haughtiness! *The French!*

Obama's apologies to the Muslim world, a common favorite of his, are even more menacing considering the fact that the terrorist threats we face today are coming from radical Islamists—not Buddhists, Christians, Jews, Sikhs, atheists, but radical Muslims.

In an interview with Al Arabiya, Obama said, "My job to the Muslim world is to communicate that the Americans are not your enemy. We sometimes make mistakes. We have not been perfect. But if you look at the track record, as you say, America was not born as a colonial power, and that the same respect and partnership that America had with the Muslim world as recently as 20 or 30 years ago, there's no reason why we can't restore that."[23]

Or how about our illustrious leader standing in the Turkish parliament apologizing for slavery and torture:

> Every challenge that we face is more easily met if we tend to our own democratic foundation. This work is never over. That's why, in the United States, we recently ordered the prison at Guantanamo Bay closed. That's why we prohibited—without exception or equivocation—the use of torture. . . . The United States is still working through some of our own darker periods in our history. Facing the Washington Monument that I spoke of is a memorial of Abraham Lincoln, the man who freed those who were enslaved even after Washington led our Revolution. Our country still struggles with the legacies of slavery and segregation, the past treatment of Native Americans.[24]

Obama even seems hell-bent on exalting Islam at the expense of facts and evidence. As Alex Alexiev, an adjunct fellow at the Hudson Institute, pointed out, it's amazing how wrong Obama is on the history of Islam, especially since he has an unlimited resource of researchers, fact checkers, and experts on call all the time. Regarding Obama's Cairo address, Alexiev observes,

> Obama touted Islamic contributions to music (an art form prohibited among the devout) and printing (regarded by the mullahs as the devil's invention, and not available to Muslims until three centuries after Gutenberg), and his preposterous promotion of Saudi King Abdullah, ruler of the most religiously intolerant country on earth, as a champion of "interfaith dialogue."
>
> More telling still are Obama's historically inaccurate portrayals of Muslims as being at "the forefront of innovation and education," and his blaming colonialism and the Cold War for their falling behind. In fact, Muslims have not been at the forefront of anything since *ijtihad* (reason) was declared un-Islamic ten centuries ago and replaced by blind obedience to reactionary sharia dogma, which, in turn, ushered in a cultural and intellectual stagnation that is yet to be overcome.[25]

As commander in chief, Obama has a duty to present America in the best possible light, not to bring up every misgiving of the past. Our human rights record is unmatched worldwide, but Obama's vision of a flawed America blinds him from realizing this. He does not believe that America is special and unique in its virtues. At the G-20 conference in Europe, a reporter asked Obama if he subscribed to the idea of American exceptionalism. He replied,

"I believe in American exceptionalism, just as I suspect that the Brits believe in British exceptionalism, and the Greeks believe in Greek exceptionalism."[26] In other words, No, nothing exceptional, America is like any other country. Big deal. Shoulder shrug.

During the Summit of the Americas, Obama sat idly and even took notes while Nicaraguan president Daniel Ortega ripped the United States as a terrorist and imperialist nation. When asked about Ortega's diatribe, Obama said, "It was 50 minutes long. That's what I thought."[27] At another point he jokingly said, "I'm very grateful that President Ortega did not blame me for things that happened when I was 3 months old."[28]

Way to defend your country, champ.

The left rejects American exceptionalism because they want to put big bad America in its place by disarming us to give other countries around the world leverage to counterbalance our power. But don't take my word for it. Leading leftist "intellectual"—and I use that word sparingly for the left—Deepak Chopra wrote an article for the *Huffington Post* called "Can We Stop Being a Superpower, Please?" In it, Chopra shows the left's true intentions for America.

"It's been roughly 20 years since the fall of the Soviet Union," he grieves, "which means that the U.S. has experienced two decades of being the world's sole superpower. The experience hasn't been positive." His beef? The "enormous waste of resources involved in being a superpower," for starters. "Has the Stealth bomber justified its staggering cost? Has the nuclear submarine, Polaris missile, Titan missile, not to mention Star Wars? Most of these weapons haven't seen the slightest use. Billions of dollars have been spent on a defense system that is protecting us from a foe who long ago neutralized its threat."[29]

Forget the fact that having a strong military arsenal is for defensive and preventive measures. After all, it's not like we have crazy regimes around the world who seek our death and destruction. Nah.

Folks, as the saying goes, when you fail to prepare, you prepare to fail. We live in dangerous times. Peace is an anomaly. But Chopra, like his fellow lefties, naïvely believes that "peace is achieved by being peaceful, no matter what the military-industrial complex claims to the contrary." [30]

Sadly, young people are prime consumers of Obama's and the left's moral equivocating. The concepts of "right" and "wrong" are a blur to them. Political correctness—the fear of offending liberal orthodoxy—already handcuffs us from speaking our mind on basic Christian principles, including marriage and sexuality—à la the blond bombshell, Miss California. But the PC stranglehold also has deleterious effects on our understanding of how real the terrorist threat is.

In two national surveys conducted by Barna Research Group, young people were asked if they believe that there are "moral absolutes that are unchanging or whether moral truth is relative to the circumstances." Seventy-five percent of those ages 18–35 answered the latter. [31] This notion of "if it feels good do it" no doubt gut-checks us from saying that Rachel Maddow looks like a dude, but that's far less serious than moral relativism allowing us to define Islamic terrorism, the spade of which Obama will not call as such. Instead, liberals demur each time conservatives mention the constant specter of terrorism.

During George W. Bush's last State of the Union address, for instance, the College Democrats over at Brigham Young University decided to mock the president by taking a shot of alcohol every time he used the words *terror, enemy*, and *evil*. [32]

Grandmaster liberal bloviator Keith Olbermann typified the

idea that conservatives hype terrorism when he said this on the air at the 2008 Republican National Convention:

> ... 9/11 has become a brand name. A Republican campaign slogan. Propaganda of the lowest form. 9/11 has become 9/11 with a trademark logo. "9/11 TM" has sustained a president who long ago should have been dismissed, or impeached. It has kept him and his gang of financial and constitutional crooks in office without—literally—any visible means of support. "9/11 TM" has made possible the greatest sleight-of-hand in our nation's history.[33]

Similarly, on student reactions to 9/11, Professor Patricia Somers of the University of Texas found that students she interviewed worried that retaliation for the terrorist attacks would result in the death of more innocent Americans. Moreover, her subjects feared that members of the American Muslim community would be wrongly targeted. One student complained that "patriotism blinds people to what's really going on." Others said the "cheering for America as if it were a football team" sickened them.[34] The patriotic mood of the country at the time, according to Somers's respondents, was "hypocritical and false," while others were alarmed that Americans got caught up in the moment of "waving a flag." Instead, in the words of a *USA Today* story on Somers's work, the post-9/11 campus environment settled for "blood drives, community service, and group hugging."[35]

According to liberal authors Morley Winograd and Michael D. Hais, young people are more inclined to "group unity" than to unilateral action. That influence, they argue, was cemented into the hearts of millions of Millennials from their childhood days of watching *Barney*! "They all solved their problems by the end of the half hour, and they all accept one another,"[36] the duo concluded. That's right, folks. We're the Barney Generation. And only to liberal ears would that be cause for celebration. Good grief. I'd hope to think that the big purple dinosaur is not why younger Americans are more blinded about Islamic terrorism. The terror organization Hamas, by the way, has its own cartoonish character. But "love" and "unity" are not themes of the show. Nope: It's a Bugs Bunny look-alike who declares, "I will eat the Jews!"[37] Not a joke.

But of course American college students have been bamboozled. Just look at the classes and textbooks we're subjected to. Peace studies, offered on hundreds of campuses, is one big political think tank for leftist foreign policy. For example, a widely used text in such courses is a book called *Peace and Conflict Studies*, written by Professor David Barash of the University of Washington and Professor Charles Webel of the University of California–Berkeley. The preface reads, "The field [of peace studies] differs from most other human sciences in that it is value-oriented, and unabashedly so. Accordingly we wish to be up front about our own values, which are frankly anti-war, anti-violence, anti-nuclear, anti-authoritarian, anti-establishment, pro-environment, pro-human rights, pro-social justice, pro-peace and politically progressive."[38]

Liberal bias in academia? What liberal bias in academia?

As Islamic radicals are determined to perpetrate more terrorist attacks against America, the authors of *Peace and Conflict Studies* analyze the events of September 11, 2001, through the prism of moral relativism. First off, say the authors, "Any actual or threatened attack against civilian noncombatants may be considered an act of 'terrorism.' In this sense, terrorism is as old as human history."[39]

Befogged in such moral equivocation, Professors Barash and Webel conclude that the American Revolutionary War was actually launched by terrorists, not patriots: terrorism is "a contemporary variant of what has been described as guerrilla warfare, dating back at least to the anti-colonialist and anti-imperialist struggles for national liberation conducted in North America and Western Europe during the late 18th and early 19th centuries against the British and French empires."

The professors acknowledge that placing *terrorist* in quotation marks "may be jarring for some readers who consider the designation self-evident." But, as they argue, "one person's 'terrorist' is another's 'freedom fighter.'"

Translation: The murderous bastards who took the lives of three thousand Americans on 9/11 died for the cause of liberty.

Peace and Conflict Studies offers further reflection:

After the attacks on the World Trade Center in New York City and the Pentagon in Washington, D.C., many Americans evidently agreed with pronouncements by many senior politicians that the United States was "at war" with "terrorism." Yet, to many disemboweled people in other regions, "Americans are the worst terrorist in the world." ... Following the attacks, President George W. Bush announced that the United States would "make no distinction between terrorists and the countries that harbor them." For many frustrated, impoverished, infuriated people—who view the United States as a terrorist country—attacks on American civilians were justified in precisely this way: making no distinction between a "terrorist state" and the citizens who aid and abet the state.[40]

Second translation: Here's hoping the authors of *Peace and Conflict Studies* get captured by al-Qaeda so they can see just how *similar* the Islamists are to our troops.

DESPITE JOHN McCAIN'S military credentials, the liberal machine had no shame in falsely painting him as a warmonger. Sadly, it's gotten to the point in America that those who are honest about the serious threats to national security are slimed as just wanting to stir up conflict. Here on planet earth, Islamic terrorism cannot be wished away.

During the campaign, Barack's military adviser, retired general Wesley Clark, bad-mouthed John McCain's war record, noting that "I don't think riding in a fighter plane and getting shot down is a qualification to be president," and falsely adding that McCain hadn't held any executive responsibility.[41]

But the McCain trashing didn't stop there. Senators Jay Rockefeller and Tom Harkin got in on the action. In an interview with a West Virginia paper, Rockefeller all but accused McCain of cold-blooded murder: "McCain was a fighter pilot, who dropped laser-guided missiles from 35,000 feet. He was long gone when they hit. What happened when they [the missiles] get to the ground? He doesn't know. You have to care about the lives of people. McCain never gets into those issues." In reality, McCain's plane was shot down because of military orders to fly combat missions at lower altitudes to *avoid* collateral damage.[42]

Senator Harkin of Iowa actually argued that the military tradition of McCain's family was "dangerous" for the country. He told reporters, "Everything is looked at from [McCain's] life experiences, from always having been in the military, and I think that can be pretty dangerous. It's one thing to have been drafted and served, but another thing when you come from generations of military people and that's just how you're steeped, how you've learned, how you've grown up."[43]

Liberal talk radio host Ed Schultz, a wannabe Rush Limbaugh on the left, was even more direct, calling John McCain a "warmonger" at a fund-raiser for Barack Obama. On CNN, Schultz continued to be inflammatory, repeating the feckless charge. "John, fit the description [warmonger]. There's no question about that. . . . He's saber rattling with Iran. He wants to throw the Russians out of the G-8. And yesterday, on your network, he said he wants to increase the military. Now I ask Americans this morning, what kind of message does it send to the world when we're occupying Iraq and we've got a candidate calling for more of a military buildup. This is outrageous. The man is a warmonger."[44]

John McCain understood that there are deadly terrorists and he would do everything possible to deter them.

The narrative that McCain was an out-of-control, bellicose warmonger was so prevalent that even the liberal *Washington Post* called out the left, claiming their charge a "caricature" and stating that "McCain is no warmonger."[45]

It's no wonder liberals make up a small percentage of the armed services. And boy, is it pathetic. According to a *Military Times* poll, the largest ideological bloc in the active-duty military are those who describe themselves as conservative: 46 percent![46] Now the embarrassing part for liberals: only 8 percent call themselves liberal. That's dismal. Among the National Guard and Army Reserve, the number of conservatives climbs to 54 percent, while liberals continue at 8 percent.[47]

Better leave the fighting to conservatives.

In any event, why would Obama encourage young people to sign up for the military, an institution he's been taught to believe is evil and oppressive?

The false leftist view of America as an evil dictatorship has gotten to such a hysterical level that two goofballs writing for the left-wing website CampusProgress.org were actually debating whether supporting the home team in soccer reinforces American "hegemony." Asheesh Siddique argued that our "dominance of international soccer [would] only reinforce detrimental anti-American sentiments from the world, since our pursuit of global political hegemony has done precisely" that.[48]

The madness continued: "By reaching out and supporting great soccer teams even if they aren't our own, especially given our team's general badness, we demonstrate that we favor cooperative co-existence over chauvinistic and backlash-inducing dominance. That could have positive repercussions for international diplomacy and our standing in the eyes of other countries."

CampusProgress.org is heavily funded by the liberal sugar daddy George Soros. Where does he find such "winners" like Asheesh?

With such a barrage against the military coming from the left, it's no mystery why 53 percent of young people polled distrust the U.S. military to do the right thing.[49] A majority! But when their elders are polled on whom they trust more, the military always receives a percentage of support north of 80. In fact, priests and judges are usually the only categories considered more trustworthy than the military. But young Obama Zombies?

It's disgusting that every time you hear a liberal define or say they are for "freedom," they don't take a stand against tyrannies around the world, even if only for moral support. They don't even talk about freedom when it comes to protecting America from Islamic nutjobs. That's "arrogant" and "unilateral," they tell us. Freedom, to them, is the freedom to kill third-term babies in the womb.

The fact is that young people benefit by American power. They benefit from America's strong military and constitutional form of government, even if liberals despise both. The closest most young people come to a foreign country is either a study-abroad program in a safe place, on a safe campus, or in meeting foreigners who have work visas in the United States or are studying here. The disconnect of terrorism for young people is typified with silly Facebook groups such as "No, I don't care if I die at 12 a.m., I refuse to pass on your chain letter," which has nearly a million members, or other groups such as "Hey, Facebook, breastfeeding is not obscene!" which has similar large numbers. Young people in Iran don't bother with such stupidity. After all, when you're getting hacked to death with an ax, shot at from rooftops by government officials, and clubbed mercilessly for peacefully protesting in the streets, well, Facebook and Twitter are utilized, but it's for spreading the word about your government's atrocities, not about who you butt-smacked the night before. Similarly, we see legendary man-on-the-street interviews where young people can easily identify Jordan Sparks, Derek Jeter, or Britney Spears, yet have no clue who the secretary of state, vice president, or similar important official is. Ironically, such ignorance is a testament to our military greatness. We're able to enjoy clueless lives precisely because we don't have to worry that some government death squad might round us up. Unfortunately, though, this complacency breeds lazy logic, the hallmark of the Obama Zombie.

It's easy for Obama to say he will usher in a new form of diplomacy; it's easy for him to say he will talk to Iran and North Korea. It's easy to promise peace. Liberalism is easy. It requires no thought, just feel-good messages. What's hard is to acknowledge the ubiquity of evil—and that the military might be needed to defend against it.

5 Global-Warming Ghouls

Why We Long for No Flush Toilets, Yearn to Adopt Glaciers,
and Desire Camels Over Cars

John F. Kennedy dreamed of putting a man on the moon.

Ronald Reagan dreamed of a world without the Berlin Wall.

Barack Obama and his minions dream of . . . a world built with straw homes?

You think I'm kidding? I wish I were. But I'm not.

Alas, I present to you *The Live Earth Global Warming Survival Handbook*, which is the official companion guide to the Live Earth concerts. The concerts were a prime magnet for Obama Zombies if ever there was one: they attracted mostly teens and young adults wanting to sneak a peek at their favorite celebrity icon. But, as is emblematic with this generation, while the Zombies were smitten with Hollywood fanfare and hype, they overlooked the radicalism professed by Live Earth organizers. On page 142 of the guide, that's where we first meet the idea of starting your own *zoo* to save the planet from intergalactic collapse. The guide is a perfect example of all that is wrong (and insane) about liberalism, wherein logic and reason are jettisoned in favor of emotional paroxysms parading as serious policy.

How else do you explain a movement that urges college kids to create their own zoos? Indeed, in a rare moment of clear thinking, the guide acknowledges that it will, in fact, be difficult for you to stock your personal zoo with every animal on the planet, even "with a dedicated team of roving naturalists" at your disposal.[1] The species the guide implores us to stash include polar bears, penguins, tigers, and pandas. "Tigers?" you say. "Liberals want us to have pet *tigers*?" Yep, argues David de Rothschild, the book's author.

In July 2007, Al Gore assembled the largest rock concert ever, stretching seven continents, filling stadiums, and reaching hundreds of millions more on television. He called it Live Earth. The goal was to bring awareness to the idea that man, in all his finiteness, is responsible for scorching the planet. Live Earth showcased popular entertainers including Madonna, Kanye West, the Red Hot Chili Peppers, Bon Jovi, Leonardo DiCaprio, Cameron Diaz, Raven-Symoné, Sting, and many others to echo the liberal line on all things environmental. Barack Obama said that Live Earth would go down as one of "the most significant days of action in the campaign against global climate change,"[2] and a major plank of his presidential campaign was a pledge to curb the release of carbon dioxide in the atmosphere. One online paper even noted that "Obama is the only presidential candidate to launch the 'Live Earth' concert on his official website," and that the symbol for Live Earth resembles Obama's official campaign logo.[3] Oddly, the pre-event advertising made little mention that concertgoers would be urged to start their own zoos or shovel tiger dung.

But here again, the world of the Obama Zombie is not one of logic and reason. No, instead Obama Zombies march to the beat of emotion. The herdlike youth cult that helped propel the Messiah to the White House was more akin to a Madison Avenue ad blitz than a serious policy debate. If not, please explain the Live Earth guide's advice that one additional way to save the planet would be for you to take a trip to Costa Rica so you could add to your animal kingdom zoo. Besides sanctimonious liberals, who has the time and money to hop a plane to South America to haul back Costa Rican frogs?[4]

Never mind the carbon footprint you'd leave behind as you hopscotched across the globe. But once you've traversed the earth and assembled your animal habitat, be warned, says Rothschild: "It's not an easy venture—a menagerie of this scale will require you to spend countless hours shoveling dung—but it is a rewarding one."

But it gets even worse. In all, *The Live Earth Global Warming Survival Handbook* lists "77 Essential Skills to Stop Climate Change—or Live Through It." If shoveling animal excrement isn't your thing, perhaps you and your band of merry Obama Zombies might enjoy trading in your cars for camels. Yes, "Your dog, cat, parrot, or even boa constrictor might seem like an ideal companion for today's world. But in the not-too-distant future, the camel may become the perfect pet for the environmental challenges of the 21st century."[5]

The wackiness has just begun. The eco-manifesto tells us that camels require easy maintenance (just the darn poop shoveling again), are a good source of protein, can be *milked* (yes, you read that correctly), and have long life spans. But don't let camel-racing your neighbor take up all your free time, dear Obama Zombies. You've also got some adopting to do. And I don't mean adopting the starving Ethiopian kid for thirty dollars a month.

No, liberals have something better for us. It's time to adopt . . . a glacier!

It's no joke. The twenty-sixth essential tool for combating global warming is to support financially a sheet of ice. From the Obama Zombie eco-bible: "Cherish your adopted ice floe by posting its picture in a prominent place and by checking on it each year."[6] Come on, people! Do your part! There's nothing like a random trip to Antarctica to become friends with . . . ice.

When tax season arrives, and while you're not romanticizing glaciers, or cleaning up tiger crap, or milking your camel, how about you audit your garbage! The Live Earth official handbook explains that "one of the best ways to understand your environmental balance sheet is with a little personal Dumpster diving."[7]

If diving into Dumpsters doesn't get you hot and bothered, fear not. Obama Zombies have even more ways for you to get involved. Like, say, building a house made out of straw. As the book notes, "Ditch the steel and glass, forget the neo-60s geodesic dome, and get past the Cinderella castle you once drew in your notebook. Instead, think simple. Think organic. Think straw."[8]

If the ferocious tornadoes and hurricanes that Barack Obama tells us are on our way due to global warming actually do land, well, no worries. Your straw house may not withstand the impact a steel-framed home would have, but, hey, you would've halved your CO_2 emissions. Just take shelter under your camel or the massive pile of crap amassing in the backyard. It's following a liberal's fragile heart, not safety, that counts.

The Live Earth Global Warming Survival Handbook has tons more other gems in the name of combating climate change: building a bat house outside your (straw) house,[9] giving worms a home in *your* home,[10] and partnering up on bubble baths ("scrub-a-dub with an organically grown loofah or sensual cotton sponge").[11] I wish this were all a joke. But it's real. It's how the left imagines running your life, and they are doing so on the fallacious premise of global warming.

What's so alarming is how many members of my generation have bought into the eco-hoax. It's not hard to understand why. We can't escape the propaganda. It attacks us from all sides: academia, MTV, Hollywood, musicians, the media. We don't stand a chance against the Obama-worshipping army that seeks to manipulate and control our lives.

That's why I'm here. I don't dig straw homes, camels, animal crap. I want to befriend people, not glaciers. I'm not looking to waste my time auditing the Dumpster outside my apartment. And most of all, I'm not idly standing by as the left bamboozles young Americans into believing that they are saving the planet when what the leftists really seek to do is erode the personal freedoms and liberties our founding fathers fought and died for.

Regardless of what Al Gore tells you, Antarctica is not melting, but has actually cooled over the past fifty years and ice on the continent has even expanded to record levels.[12] The polar bears are safe, increasing in numbers in some parts.[13] And if you change your lightbulb and build a straw home, you will have done nothing to "save the planet."

Liberals are duping you to satisfy their own big-government schemes.

What the minds of Obama Zombies fail to grasp is that regulating CO_2 emissions is a regulation of what you do: our choice of transportation, the temperature of our homes, the length of our showers, our choice of food (cows release more CO_2 emissions than other animals while belching, we're told), the Internet, washing machines, dryers, the fact that we drive instead of walk our children to school, buying food that's not locally grown, and the countless electronic appliances that make life more enjoyable.

You probably never thought your iPod would be under assault, but an article in the *Seattle Times* ran with this headline: "Charge Your iPod, Kill a Polar Bear?" File this away under "you can't make this stuff up." According to the article, the Paris-based International Energy Agency estimates that new electronic gadgets "will triple their energy consumption" by 2030. Gadgets include MP3 players, mobile phones, and flat-screen TVs. Paul Waide, a senior policy analyst with the IEA, lamented that the electronics industry is "the fastest growing area and it's the area with the least amount of policies in place."[14]

Huh? No "policies in place" for plasma TVs?

Authoritarian alert! Authoritarian alert!

In fact, Waide's casual reference to policing consumer electronics is mild compared to what one eco-princess columnist for Britain's *Guardian* proposes: rationing the personal carbon use of each citizen.[15] Once your carbon card runs out, you've got to buy credits from someone who has used less than "his or her quota."

Folks, this is scary. A major newspaper in Britain, the birthplace of the Magna Carta—the father to our Declaration of Independence and U.S. Constitution—is promoting the idea of the federal government devising how much energy you're allowed to use in your daily lives. For that is what a carbon footprint is: energy usage.

Young fools like Jessy Tolkan of the Energy Action Coalition can mindlessly testify before Congress and demand that the nation's carbon dioxide emissions be cut by 20 percent by 2015 and by 80 percent by 2050.[16] But when Tolkan flew in six thousand "experts" from around the country to lobby Congress, she unintentionally demonstrated how much Americans rely on CO_2 in our daily lives. When asked if such large-scale mobilization was worth it, considering the carbon footprint the people were leaving, she had a confession to make: "This is an issue we struggled with. Does it make sense to encourage travel from all across the country? In the end we feel that what is going to happen over the next four days was worth it."

And there you have liberal sanctimony at work. It's okay for them to fly around the country to engage in activities that *they* believe in, but they are the first to condemn *your* own buying choices and lifestyle habits. Now, there's an "inconvenient truth."

But who can blame them? They are merely following in the carbon footprints of their leader. On Earth Day, President Obama burned through 9,100 gallons of fuel when he parachuted into Iowa to give a speech on energy conservation.

SO HOW, THEN, has the left pulled this off? How have they managed to pull the organically grown wool over the eyes of the youth vote? The first primary tactic involves the left's total domination of American college campuses.

Meet Claire Roby, a college student in 2007. Claire wanted to make a statement with her Christmas gifts. So on Christmas morning, Claire gave "handmade clocks made from discarded CDs and scavenged electronic components," all of which were wrapped in newspaper. Why? She got dropped as a kid? No. According to a *New York Times* profile, Ms. Roby gave the gift of garbage to do her part to save the planet.[17] To her, Christmas was no longer the venue to give sacrificially of yourself, finding out what those closest to you actually want for the blessed occasion. No, instead it's an opportunity for political grandstanding. Christmas cards, you see, are evil because they waste paper. Christmas lights? Evil. They waste electricity. And as for those capitalist creations called presents? Well, what's the point of giving someone a gift they actually want when you can instead give the gift of propaganda?

"We'll see how much we can avoid a dinner table argument this year," Roby told the *Times*. Roby, eco-warrior princess, is not alone. At the time the article was written, Roby was an environmental studies major at American University. Bingo.

Unsuspecting students enter college expecting to be intellectually challenged. Instead, professors and administrators subject students to a blizzard of liberal global-warming talking points. What most students are never told, of course, is that the idea that man is warming the planet is relatively new. In the 1970s, the eco-drones were telling us that man was *cooling* the planet. In fact, the concern then was that the world might soon be imperiled by— are you ready for this?—an Ice Age! *Time*'s 1974 cover story "Another Ice Age?" and *Newsweek*'s 1975 story "The Cooling World" are now cult classics. But in a fashion similar to today's hysteria, these news outlets had falsely deduced that man's actions had triggered worldwide cooling patterns.

Time and *Newsweek* were not alone. Popular books in the '70s included *The Cooling* and *The Weather Conspiracy—The Coming of the New Ice Age*. What a difference a few decades make.

Obama Zombies now consider global warming all the rage. Their position, and the position of B.H.O., is that man's industrialization, fueled by the release of carbon dioxide into the atmosphere, will result in a polar meltdown if action is not taken immediately.

But many of those who study atmospheric conditions believe the exact opposite: that the mild, barely noticeable warming the temperature has seen over the last hundred years is the result of normal planetary motions and natural climate changes. They understand that warming and cooling are largely a function of—drum roll, please—the sun![18] Yes, the sun, that massive fiery ball in the sky that enables life on our planet. A bombshell, I know. But if you're losing sleep over such mild warming in the last century, don't. We've now entered a cooling period, one that has brought temperatures down to where they were in 1930.[19]

But rather than present students with both sides of the argument, our "academic" institutions have instead pursued the path of liberal propaganda. In an effort to gobble up as many federal research dollars as possible, once-freethinking and intellectually independent science departments have instead towed the Obama Zombie line while lining up at the federal trough to receive Al Gore–sized portions of taxpayer largesse. The goal: use academicians as megaphones to blast the liberal message far and wide with the hope that graduates will soon constitute a green voting bloc that will forever change the electoral map. Hence the brainwashed likes of a Claire Roby. Poor woman . . . by the time she graduated, her mind was so scrambled she was giving garbage to loved ones for Christmas.

Think I'm overstating academia's role? This headline from the *Chronicle of Higher Education* says it all. "Saving the Planet, by Degrees."[20] The reporter, Piper Fogg, detailed how courses premised on environmentalism have been injected into curricula. So what are students learning in these "saving the planet" courses? If the University of Minnesota–Twin Cities is any indicator, nothing useful. Students there maintain a "trash journal" to catalog "every scrap of paper used or banana peel chucked." One wonders how much carbon they emit punching their sinful deeds into a computer that emits carbon. Let's pray that professors don't actually make these students print out their work on—gasp!—*paper* when submitting class essays!

The indoctrination runs so deep that, in a moment of candor, the *Boston Globe* led off a story this way: "When historians look back on this decade and at what had college campuses most fired up, it won't be the war, or the economy, Obama-mania, or even Britney's babies. It will be a color."[21] As the *Globe* noted, there "is no Green Book of eco-friendly schools, but sustainability is already a campus buzzword." Ah yes, *sustainability*. That's the word academics use to push their green agenda these days. The *Globe* defines *sustainability* as "leav[ing] enough resources so our children can live as well as we do now."

The *Chronicle of Higher Education* defines a "sustainable university" as one "that promotes the concept of meeting present needs without compromising the ability of future generations to meet their own needs." Getting past the academic gobbledygook, college administrators are using the buzzword *sustainability* to promote the left's environmentalism. Specifically, explained the *Chronicle*, they're vowing to "curb carbon emissions," "buy green energy," "reduce waste," "serve organic food," "purchase hybrid cars," "appoint sustainability directors," "build green dormitories," and "plant native shrubbery."[22]

Other schools, including Skidmore College in upstate New York, are "fighting" global warming by imploring students to "Do It in the Dark."[23] How romantic. Nothing like saving the planet, one sex act at a time. Classy.

"Trayless Tuesdays" are another Obama Zombie favorite. Many institutions, including Cornell University, Skidmore, and the Rochester Institute of Technology, have banished or limited the use of trays in dining halls, all under the banner of "sustainability." The fewer trays, the less water used to wash the trays. The less water used, the less energy consumption. However, "trayless Tuesdays" have unintended consequences, as the *New York Times* points out: they clog up cafeteria lines and elongate dining hours, since students need to keep leaving their table to get more food than their two hands can carry without a tray.[24] And let's pray that all that walking back and forth doesn't make them increase their breathing, because then they might emit more carbon dioxide into the air.

But again, logic isn't the realm of the Obama Zombie. No, *emotions* and *feeling good* are all that matters.

Undoubtedly, liberal politicians like Obama have colleges to thank for young people's overwhelming support of climate change measures. Academia is whipping out an army of Captain Planets and Eco-Princesses who will stay beholden to liberal candidates if the brainwashing is not undone. It is a tall task. Many professors and administrators see it as their professional duty to preach Gore-based hysteria. For instance, Michael M. Crow, president of Arizona State University, has pledged to make his campus "climate neutral" and believes that his campus needs "to speak with a unified voice and to speak with action" on global warming.[25]

At Carnegie Mellon University, administrators openly admitted that the goal behind the construction of the "New House" dorm was to teach students about climate change. How? By being notified when their classmates drop a deuce.

To "pique students' interest in the environment," campus kiosks were outfitted with monitors that register every flick of a light switch or flush of a toilet.[26] That way you can chastise your fellow classmates for going to the dumper and crapping all over the environment.

These "sustainability measures" would be harmless if they weren't so financially costly. Indeed, the only thing that stinks worse than waterless toilets is the cost to install them—costs that further drive up the already astronomical price of higher education.

Leith Sharp, director in 2007 of Harvard University's Green

Campus Initiative, noted that Harvard employs twenty full-time staffers and forty part-time students to sustain its "sustainability" programs, and that's still not enough, according to her. "It's unbelievable how much work [sustainability] is going to be, and people are utterly blind to that fact."[27]

Get that? Harvard employs sixty people to combat global warming on campus, and it's still not enough. Cash-flushed Harvard may have that kind of dough to squander, but other schools who sign onto buying green energy and offsetting carbon don't enjoy fat-cat endowments.

In 2008, Middlebury College opened an $11 million biomass plant that burned wood chips "to help heat and cool campus buildings and produce electricity."[28] The high-priced plant was claimed to "reduce the college's consumption of fuel oil by 50 percent" and to "cut the college's greenhouse gas emissions." Tucked away in the eco-warriors' notepad is this bit of fine print: Middlebury needs "20,000 tons of wood chips to replace one million gallons of fuel oil each year."[29] The creation of twenty thousand tons of wood leaves one humongous carbon footprint. Extra trees need to be chopped down, reducing the plant life, which consumes carbon from the atmosphere, and the logging itself may raise greenhouse gases.[30]

Emory University in Georgia has a whole different approach: it sends an energy bill to each individual school. According to Ciannat M. Howett, Emory's director of sustainability initiatives, different departments "have a huge incentive to get everyone in the school to reduce usage because then those dollars can go to their core mission, rather than energy."[31] That's it: sacrifice the "core mission" of education on the altar of sustainability.

At the University of Florida, academic departments were charged three thousand dollars per parking pass in an effort to minimize car emissions on campus. Alan T. Dorsey, the chair of the physics department, attacked the policy because he had to dip into research funds in order to cover the new fees. "This cost comes at a bad time," he said.[32] Ed Poppel was one of the administrators responsible for the parking rate increase, "to get people out of their cars and onto bikes or two legs." Yet he was still driving to work. "I give myself the excuse that in my position I have to be very flexible. It's difficult to tell people to change behaviors if I'm unwilling to change mine."[33]

Can you say "eco-hypocrite"?

When you don't have the money for waterless toilets, sport a cactus. Pitzer College in Southern California doesn't have the money to provide organic food or construct fancy green buildings. Instead, they decided to replace their lawn with cacti. Large chunks of Pitzer's campus lawn were ripped up and replaced with prickly desert plants.[34] Sorry, Obama Zombies, there will be no more studying on the lawn. And if you do decide to study on the lawn, you dare not bring your iPod!

Yet, overall, in their efforts to "green" campuses, American colleges and universities combined to buy close to "1.1 billion kilowatt hours of green electricity," which is enough to power eighty-seven thousand homes for an entire year, according to the *Chronicle of Higher Education*.[35] Ironically, every time "green" power is purchased, colleges are merely paying higher prices for energy, because they have no way of knowing whether the energy they buy is actually alternative. This again underscores just how goofy all this hyperemotional eco-claptrap truly is, and why only an Obama Zombie would not take the time to actually research and think.

Here's how it works: When a wind turbine produces renewable energy, it sends electrons into the electricity grid, where green energy blends with nongreen energy. Thus, colleges that buy energy produced at a wind farm don't actually purchase the electrons that came from that wind farm. Instead, as the *Chronicle* clarified, "they buy standard electricity and then pay a *premium* for wind renewable energy credits, providing an incentive for utilities to build more green power facilities."[36] (Emphasis added.) New York University, for instance, bragged that it bought 118 million kilowatt hours of green energy, but in reality, the school received "credits" for wind power while the campus was being serviced by a standard electricity grid.[37]

The Obama Zombies have been swindled by those evil energy companies that have the audacity to provide humans with life-sustaining energy yet again.

Much of this would be funny if it didn't directly affect parents' and students' wallets. Green energy isn't cheap. In fact, it's considerably more expensive than traditional energy sources, including coal, oil, nuclear power, and natural gas. There's a reason why wind and solar "account for less than 1 percent of total net electricity generation" in the United States. A single percent![38]

There's more. In 2007, the U.S. Energy Information Administration (EIA) calculated the total dollar amount the government spent to produce energy. These supposed alternative sources of energy received around $16.6 billion, which came in the form of direct government subsidies and loans as well as tax breaks.[39] Because these "alternative" methods aren't viable on their own, we the taxpayers are forced to foot the high bill. The EIA found that solar energy receives $24.34 per megawatt hour from Uncle Sam, while wind gets $23.37 and "clean coal" rakes in $29.81. By contrast, as the *Wall Street Journal* observes, normal coal receives 44 cents, natural gas 25 cents, hydroelectric 67 cents, and nuclear power $1.59. In other words, wind is subsidized fifteen times more than nuclear power, even though nuclear power fuels 20 percent of this country's electricity production and wind less than 1 percent.[40]

Nevertheless, the only way a college can be completely carbon neutral, as many college presidents have promised, is to buy so-called carbon offsets. This of course is the scheme that pays other people to lower their carbon emissions or to plant trees to make up for your carbon production. There's nothing like out-sourcing your eco-sins for cash.

Everything we do is driven by energy production, but it's qua-drupled on a university level, as colleges involve housing, feeding, teaching, and entertaining tens of thousands of students. It's ir-responsible for schools to jack up already expensive tuition rates and ever-growing "student activity fees" (as many are doing) to absolve administrators and radical professors of their liberal eco-guilt. That said, there are a few fiscally responsible college presi-dents who refuse to go along with the charade. The president of Pomona College, David W. Oxtoby, has stated that before he goes blowing students' tuition on buying carbon credits he would first have to become convinced that doing so would be "really mean-ingful, and not just a way for the rich to make their consciences feel better."[41]

Alas, a pinprick of sanity.

ANOTHER MAJOR ECO-BLUDGEON involves the left's lock on youth-targeted media.

Consider the following. When Drew told Cameron that she took a crap in the forest, Cameron burned with envy. "I am so jealous right now," said Cameron. "I am going to the woods tomorrow." Drew laughed and boasted: "It was awesome." I was "hunched over like an animal" when I "took a poo in the woods."[42]

There you have it, folks, two of the most famed celebrities—Drew Barrymore and Cameron Diaz—euphoric about the idea of taking a dump in the forest. And this is precisely the primitive world they envision for you, too.

Barrymore and Diaz's animalistic adventures were part of the MTV 2005 series *Trippin'*, which the *New York Times* described as Diaz's unscripted "travelogue with a save-the-planet goal." Diaz produced the episodes (ten in all) and brought her celebrity friends along for the ecological ride: Jimmy Fallon, Justin Timberlake, Eva Mendes, and Jessica Alba. The show's goal was to target young audiences: "elementary schools taught about the cycle of life, the fragility of the fauna and the importance of recycling, but that when children turned into adolescents they tended to lose these interests."

Thus, the need for *Trippin'*.

The *Times* correctly observed that since "young viewers' appetite for scientific knowledge is limited, Ms. Diaz is betting that their interest in celebrities will draw them to the show and help them [find] a world beyond the exurbs and X-Boxes." The paper, however, dismissed Diaz's extremism as just fun and games: "she dwells on excrement, both for laughs and for edification."[43]

But we're not letting Diaz off the hook that easily. While visiting Nepal, she referred to village walls covered in cow dung as "beautiful" and "inspiring." Then she took to praising "pounding mud" with sticks as "the coolest thing."

In Chile, Barrymore told the MTV audience that spending time in a primitive village sans electricity was uplifting. "I aspire to be like them more." Barrymore, by the way, at the time of *Trippin'*, reportedly grossed $15 million a flick.

During the Bhutan episode, Diaz remarked that she loved how the "country's wealth was not based on dollar amount but on gross national happiness." Regarding the countryside still being relegated to undeveloped forest, she proclaimed, "That is so awesome.

I like Bhutan." On you Americans—you greedy Americans—Diaz, who reportedly makes $20 million a movie, said this: "It's kinda gotten out of hand how much convenience we think we need."[44]

And just when you thought it couldn't get worse, it does. It turns out that local officials actually had plans to bring some parts of Chile closer to, um, the twentieth century, never mind the twenty-first. There were proposals to turn significant portions of the forest into a highway and also build an aluminum smelter. But it turns out our Hollywood eco-princesses weren't too keen on these projects, because of their alleged harmful impacts on the environment. Diaz rhapsodized: "Each of us can make a difference. If everyone recycled the aluminum cans they used, there would be no need for new smelters. So stop being a fucking pig and re-cycle your aluminum cans," she chortled.

Now, if you're wondering how these celebrities found their way around the jungles of South America, you're a very astute reader. While Diaz and her team were celebrating the lifestyle of a caveman, *Trippin'* shows them flying on multiple carbon-spewing airplanes and chartering pollution-puffing helicopters and even gas-guzzling boats to reach their site locations. The cringe-inducing irony was made complete when the series also showed the celebri-ties being "chauffeured to the airport in a full-size Chevy SUV," notwithstanding multiple public service announcements aired on *Trippin'* trashing the use of those same big, bad SUVs.

Ah, the hypocritical life of the eco-celebrity: raking in mil-lions of dollars per film, being chauffeured around in private jets and SUVs, vacationing in the jungle, all while praising primitive life in parts of the world that can't provide basic infrastructure and sanitation for their own people. Forget hypocritical. It's de-praved, perverse, and downright cruel. But it's a perfect if small example of how Hollywood continues its radical, hypocritical environmentalism onslaught against those of us who consume but a tiny fraction of the energy that celebrity mansions and car collections suck up.

Kind of like Live Earth. Remember that? As we discussed, it was the biggest, most detailed and intricate concert, stretching seven continents, filling stadiums with thousands, and reaching millions more on television to raise awareness about global warming.

Again, celebrities who have the biggest carbon footprints of us all—with their mansions, private jets, spending sprees, vacation homes, movie productions, and concert tours—are telling ordinary folks like you and me that we need to cut down on our own carbon footprint. As those world-renowned climatologists the Red Hot Chili Peppers explained, "The climate change situation is the No. 1 problem facing humanity."

In a rare moment of journalistic integrity, even the *New York Times* was suspicious. "If less is more," the *Times* wondered, "then why is biggest better?" According to the *Times*, "this seven-continent, multimedia eco-extravaganza was colored by the very complacency it vowed to combat: No matter how dire the problem, the solution can be small and painless." [45]

The *Times* pointed out how the emcee at Giants Stadium, musician David Holmes, was "discussing alternative eco-products while balancing an Apple computer on his lap." Um, David, how on God's green earth do you think your laptop was produced? Wasn't through wind power, brother . . . and it definitely wasn't at the hands of a barefoot Chilean boy rubbing sticks together in his hut.

NBC, which is in the tank with the green agenda, televised the Live Earth concerts. And, as expected, their "reporter," *Today*'s Ann Curry, asked softball questions, such as the one to Trudie Styler: "Why do you care so much?" Hey, Ann, a better question, maybe to Kanye West and Ludacris, might have been: "Your lyrics gratuitously praise big cars, fat wallets, extravagant homes, bitches and hos, excessive partying, and big guns, and you tour the globe on concerts. Why do you think you're in a position to lecture the rest of us about cutting back?" If only Ann Curry were a real reporter. Then we might get an answer.

"So much star power assembled in so many places," notes the *Times*, "to assure fans that all they need do to save the planet is change a light bulb, choose paper over plastic or, as Cameron Diaz recommended, turn off the shower while shaving their legs."[46]

The *New York Times* wasn't the only news outlet to point to the extravagant hypocrisy of Live Earth. The London-based *Daily Mail* estimated that the total footprint of Live Earth was 31,500 tons of carbon emissions, given all the energy consumed while traveling to the concerts and powering the productions. The paper's investigation revealed that "far from saving the planet, the extravaganza generated a massive fuel bill, acres of garbage, thousands of tons of carbon emissions, and a mileage total equal to the movement of an army."[47] Add to that the estimated television audience and the carbon footprint exceeds 74,500 tons! In case you're curious (which you should be), the average Briton's carbon footprint is around 11 tons . . . *per year*. An interesting way for left-wingers to address a planet that is on the precipice of environmental Armageddon—to blow past a year's worth of carbon footprints, by 6,777 times. Makes sense, no? Come to think of it, adulterers should try this kind of lefty logic when pledging renewed fidelity to their wives: Cheat more—not once, not twice, but 6,777 times further!

If celebrities truly bought into all the climate meltdown talk that they spew, they would stop filming movies immediately. Their lifestyles and vocations produce more than triple the carbon footprint of the average household. Madonna can forgo simulating sex onstage and Cameron Diaz can crap in the forest without the cameras rolling. Diaz, prone to gross confessions, described to Jay Leno the type of life she pictures for the rest of us: "I do follow the 'If it's yellow leave it mellow, if it's brown, flush it down.' I believe in that 100 percent."[48] So, if you ever happen to be invited to one of Diaz's cocktail parties, don't be surprised that her bathroom reeks of urine.

THE FINAL TOOL used to lobotomize aspiring Obama Zombies involves the "scientific" shell game promulgated by the left against America's youth.

If a lie is repeated often enough, it's thought to be true. And nowhere is this more true than in the false notion that a "consensus" of scientists is that man is responsible for warming the planet. It's not true. But Obama Zombies don't want a real debate. They want an Al Gore slide show that leaves folks feeling all warm and fuzzy about saving polar bears.

U.S. senator Jim Inhofe of Oklahoma has himself assembled a growing list of more than 650 top scientists from around the globe who have challenged the global-alarming hysteria proffered by the liberal machine.[49] Consensus? What consensus? Slowly, even the reliably liberal media are noticing. *Politico* conceded that a "growing accumulation" of atmospheric data could signal that the "science behind global warming may still be too shaky to warrant cap-and-trade legislation,"[50] and the *New York Times*'s environmental reporter Andrew Revkin acknowledged that "climate science is not a numbers game (there are heaps of signed statements by folks with advanced degrees on all sides of this issue)."[51]

Interestingly, the *Times*, which editorializes with the belief that man is in fact warming the plant, still felt compelled to call out Al Gore and Barack Obama for sensationalizing the threat of global warming. On February 25, 2009, the paper ran a story with the headline "In Debate on Climate Change, Exaggeration Is a Common Pitfall." As they pointed out, Gore was forced to remove a slide from his presentation that correlated global warming to a sharp spike in "fires, floods and other calamities around the world," after the research group Gore quoted said he had misrepresented the data. The *Times* explained that "while climate scientists foresee more intense droughts and storms, there is still uncertainty, and significant disagreement, over whether recent patterns can be attributed to global warming."[52]

When the *New York Times* is scolding you as an eco-exaggerator, you *know* you have problems.

So let's get to the basics. Is carbon dioxide a pollutant that is causing the earth's temperature to rise?

I'm gonna go with no.

Here's why: Try this experiment. Breathe in the air that you exhale. Now, let me know if you faint, feel nauseous, or as if you're about to die. After all, we human beings *exhale* carbon dioxide, for crying out loud! Perhaps Barack Obama forgot, but carbon dioxide is essential for life. Plants and crops depend on it. Some farmers even deliberately generate increased levels of CO_2 to bulk up food production.[53] More "pollution," anyone?

In any event, there's no need to become apoplectic over CO_2. Geologist Dudley J. Hughes published a paper for the Heartland Institute pointing out that rising carbon dioxide levels are nothing to worry about, since it comprises less than 1 percent of the atmosphere. Nitrogen and oxygen, by contrast, cover about 99 percent. Hughes gives us a workable analogy to understand how absurd it is to say that CO_2 has any meaningful effect in our vast atmosphere. "For simplicity, let us picture a football stadium with about 10,000 people in the stands. Assume each person represents a small volume of one type of gas. . . . Carbon dioxide is represented as only about 4 parts in 10,000, the smallest volume of any major atmospheric gas."[54]

Basically, our world doesn't have a thermostat that liberals can toy with. Our climate is always changing, from the Medieval Warming Period to the Little Ice Age, which followed that. There is no such thing as a global mean temperature. Besides, the infinitesimal "warming" that certain parts of the world are experiencing—over the past hundred-plus years—is nothing to write home to Mom about and is a far cry from saying kids in Jamaica are going to burst into flames one of these days.

But the Jamaican kid can relax. In fact, let's buy him a sweater, because we may be experiencing global cooling now. In 2008, outlets that track global temperatures worldwide released data showing that the earth faced cooling cycles large enough to negate the warming documented over the past hundred years.[55] Baghdad, for instance, experienced snowfall for the very first time.

Which is it, Obama Zombies? Warming or cooling? I've got to know! You see, folks, meteorologist Obama can't predict the weather tomorrow, but he can predict a global climate catastrophe? Even Al Gore's most ardent believers have come to realize this fact, which is why now they prefer the term *climate change* to *global warming*. It's more vague that way.

Not only is 1934 the hottest year on record, but five of the ten warmest years transpired before World War II—well before we started pumping globs of CO_2 into the atmosphere.[56] So what was causing global warming in 1934?

Interestingly, environmentalists can't even make up their minds on whether to abandon fossil fuels for the much-hyped biofuels. One activist group is urging the British government to halt rules that require a percentage of transportation energy to consist of "green" fuels. According to Friends of the Earth, cutting down forests to plant and harvest crops for biodiesel purposes has the unintended consequence of generating an extra 1.3 million tons of CO_2.[57] Similarly, one study by professors at the University of California–Davis found that it could be more eco-friendly to drive an SUV than to take a train. Oil, gas, and coal, for instance, are used to produce electricity to power and build trains as well as the building of transportation infrastructure. When all is said and done, sticking with your SUV may actually be better for the environment.[58] Recycling may absolve you of inner guilt, but the process of cleaning and cataloging materials requires using an abundance of—gasp—energy.[59] Funny how that works, eh? And let's not forget about those second rounds of trucks that bulldoze through neighborhoods like tanks to pick up our color-coded recycling bins. The emission that comes out of those bad boys is no joke.

Move past the idea that mild warming in the earth's temperature is catastrophic (especially while we're cooling down now) and go find whatever mode of transportation you want. Recycle if it makes you feel better. Adopt a glacier. Befriend sheets of ice. Plaster your walls with cow dung. Choose to buy doofy-looking hybrids. It's called freedom. But please spare the rest of us the self-important chest thumping about how you're saving the environment. And above all, don't tread on our God-given freedoms. You do have the right to be duped by the "scientific" shell game, but you also have the right to think for yourself and not act like a Zombie.

IN THE END, I actually agree with Obama on one key point: global warming will affect my generation. But what we need protection from is not the warming (now cooling), but rather an authoritarian cult of blind followers who will attempt to remake our lives for the worse. Liberals like to speak of leaving their kids a better planet than what was given to them. If Obama Zombies don't wake up from their slumber, we will be paying for B.H.O.'s climate schemes, not only in higher taxes but also in less output as a nation; in lighter, less safe vehicles; in less innovation; and most importantly, in a loss of freedom.

Republicans, in many ways, have only themselves to blame for the plight we face. John McCain was a worthless candidate, in particular on the subject of climate change. His efforts to reach out to young voters amounted to little more than an embrace of the cockamamie eco-hype while cobbling together his own stack of government-run solutions.

Sorry, Barack. We want to keep our homes at whatever temperatures we choose. We want to drive whatever we decide. We want to eat whatever we damn well please. And we reject you and your liberal machine's attempt to create a perennial voting bloc of young people scared out of their minds that they are ruining the planet.

Health-Care Hypnosis

How to Destroy the Greatest Health-Care System the World Has Ever Known

You've heard it before: there are 46 million people in America without health insurance.

It's an outrage!

It's immoral!

It's unjust!

It's an abomination!

It's . . . a freaking lie!

Let's do the thing Obama Zombies hate the most: look at the actual facts.

The 46 million figure they spew forth with brainless obeisance is, in fact, a complete hoax, even by Obama's own admission. But that oft-cited figure is just one of the many reasons the liberal machine was so successful in conning so many members of my generation to swallow Obama's prescription for socialized medicine.

Let's break down the numbers using the Congressional Budget Office statistics:

- Nine million of the uninsured are *not* citizens of the United States.[1]
- Twelve million are already eligible for government assistance but for some reason have been too busy to sign up for free goodies.[2]
- Seventeen million of the uninsured have household incomes above $50,000.[3]

Pause and think about that last number for a minute. Seventeen million individuals who are being touted as the "uninsured" make more than $50,000.

How's that mythical 46 million number looking about now? Let's recap: We started off with 46 million, then we subtracted 9 million foreign nationals and illegals. Then we deducted the 12 million who are already eligible for some type of government assistance but haven't claimed it. From there we subtracted the 17 million who are banking more than $50,000, but choose not to purchase insurance because it's their God-given right to do whatever they darn well please with their money.

Where'd that 46 million figure vanish? In reality, the figure drops to around 5 percent—out of a population of 300 million people—who actually *may* slip through the cracks. And our health care is the envy of the world.

Still, affordability is a serious and important concern, and it's a concern that conservatives care about far more than liberals. So what is the conservative solution for rising health-care costs? Free markets and *real* competition.

The problem is that a free market where consumers and providers freely partake of each other's services does not exist. Governments work hand in glove with providers, such as chiropractors and drug-abuse counselors, to arrange a package of services (read: mandates) that we are forced to buy—it's corporatism at its ugliest. Every special industry lobbies for its crack at the mandate. It's money in their pocket, after all.

Obama is just like any leftist politician—he gives lip service to taking on special interests but in reality supports policies that are a lobbyist's dream, because they allow the special interests to get subsidized by the government. Obama officials have met privately with health-care executives and drug companies, a brazen violation of his campaign promise to have all negotiations of bills broadcast on C-SPAN for all to see. Of course the mainstream media haven't grilled Obama on this campaign promise. It took a blogger to uncover the truth.[4] But why broadcast for all to see a policy debate that only involves the takeover of a $2 trillion health-care system? That's peanuts to a liberal! I mean, it is only your money. Why should the White House negotiate in public when it can do so in secret, cutting deals with lobbyists[5] and pharmaceutical companies[6] behind the scenes?

Hope and change, people!

When it comes to mandates, it boils down to this: If you want to visit a chiropractor, great. Pay for it out of pocket!

But let's laser in on the kind of government intervention that stifles care and drives up cost. Take my own home state of New York. It is one of three states that have both "community rating" and "guaranteed issue." In a nutshell, *community rating* obliges insurance companies to charge everyone the same rate regardless of their age or health status. Young people get screwed by this formula: We're stuck paying higher prices to help subsidize the premiums of older Americans. *Guaranteed issue* means that insurers must "cover anyone at any time," usually at the same rate.

It's no surprise, then, that the states that pile on mandate after mandate and impose community ratings, thereby giving everyone nearly uniform premiums, are the states that have the highest annual insurance premiums. In New York, for instance, insurance is "roughly two to three times higher than the national average," and neighboring New Jersey has premiums for individuals bucking $5,000.[7] The result is that young New Yorkers pay through the nose.

It is government intrusion into health care that is screwing everything up in the first place. Rather than let people choose what they want covered, some government bureaucrat from on high lays down the law of the land. Such diktats are wholly at odds with a free society.

Now, to be fair, Barack Obama does have a point about "insurance security." If you lose your job, chances are you will lose your medical insurance. For most of the country, and for most young people, insurance is directly tied to employment. It's one of those benefits we're offered for employment, but it's also a government-created system that has turned out to be woefully inadequate for the twenty-first century. Young people are more fluid in the job market. We hop around. We're not like our parents or their parents, who worked at one company building up seniority and benefits over the course of their careers.

Employer-based health care started during World War II when the government imposed strict wage and price controls on American businesses. The result, among other things, was a shortage of people in the workforce. Entrepreneurs did what entrepreneurs do best: they devised a plan to attract skilled workers despite the government's onerous regulations. That plan was to pay for a worker's and his family's medical care. It was a hit. Repressed salaries were made up with "fringe" benefits. Congress eventually passed legislation that allowed those benefits to be tax-exempt, a response to IRS rules requiring that medical coverage be counted as salary and therefore subject to taxation.[8]

The implications are broad. Most individuals now rely on their employers for their health insurance. The trouble is that a system like ours punishes people who don't have employer-based health care and must therefore instead buy insurance privately. The reason this is problematic is that government-sanctioned mandates have driven up the costs of privately purchased insurance. And unlike large companies that buy insurance packages in bulk quantities (thus resulting in cheaper costs), small business owners can't band together with others to buy lower-premium insurance. Worse, those without employer-based health care must use after-tax income to purchase insurance, whereas employer-based coverage gets a huge tax break. It's inequitable.

THE LIBERAL MACHINE'S ability to churn out Obama Zombies on the health-care issue boils down to this: Unfortunately, young people are more susceptible to liberal bloviating about free health care and massive overhauls because younger Americans are the least likely to use health care. That means some left-winger comes along and talks about "shared sacrifices" and drops the 46-million-uninsured myth on a young person's unwitting head and, presto, you've got yourself a freshly minted Obama Zombie. The problem is that waving a magic wand won't produce free health care for everyone.

It's more complicated than that. The very instrument that created the mess in the first place (government) is the very instrument that liberals advocate can solve the mess (more government). Let's see: The government introduced the inefficient concept of employer-based health care, state governments imposed huge burdens with mandates, yet somehow we should trust the government even more?

In any case, the federal government is the reason for exploding costs and the ban on a free exchange of services from people to providers. Did you know that the federal government set up strictures that prevent people from purchasing insurance across state lines, another inhibitor to competition? Insurance companies must fashion health-care policies to the guidelines of each state. Competition does not exist on a national level. Instead we get a hodge-podge of fragmented markets and the large price differences that accompany them. This drives up the health-care insurance prices considerably, especially, as the Heartland Institute points out,[9] if you live in a state that must cover things like acupuncture and marriage counseling (about one-fourth of states), social workers and contraceptives (more than twenty-five states), and hairpieces and hearing aids (seven states).

Competition, as Obama likes to say, will drive down cost. But we need real competition and real deregulation that will rid costly mandates. Some insurance companies, for instance, steer up to 80 percent of the health-care market and pour money into whatever politicians' hands will protect their monopoly and not allow access across state lines. And while competition is hampered by so much regulation, so much bureaucracy, and so many mandates, liberals in Congress such as Barney Frank (and even Senator Obama while running for president) think they can undo the problems caused by a limited monopoly by converting it into an overall monopoly.

Columnist Ann Coulter said it best: "It's the famous liberal two-step: First screw something up, then claim that it's screwed up because there's not enough government oversight (it's the free market run wild!), and then step in and really screw it up in the name of 'reform.' "[10]

For too many young Americans, the clarion call for "reform" translates into thinking that health care is some magical right that somebody else must pay for and shouldn't be treated as any other commodity, such as food, electricity, or cars, for that matter. During the election, Obama called health care a right, not a privilege, adding that Americans have a "moral commitment" to provide health care to every American. It's a great feel-good sound bite. But such an entitlement mentality is a dramatic departure from the Declaration of Independence's guarantee to protect our life, liberty, and pursuit of happiness. The federal government accomplishes this, as our Constitution outlines, with less than twenty enumerated roles.

An MTV reporter in Delaware did a report on young people and health insurance called "The Young, Hot, and Uninsured." One individual interviewed, Gabriel Humphreys, a twenty-eight-year-old techie, grumbled that he didn't have health insurance, especially so he could go to the hospital after a snowboarding accident. "I actually hurt myself like eight weeks ago," Humphreys said. "I tore my rotator cuff while snowboarding and, you know, I couldn't go to the doctor. I could, but, you know, I didn't want to pay that out of pocket because it would've been horrible."

Zombie Gabriel said that he favors a "nationalized" health system, where everyone is covered, and he bemoaned the fact that we can fight wars but don't have the government insure people. Obama's generalities are an easy target for young people who are told they're in need of insurance, with catastrophe knocking on their doorstep.

Hey, dude, if you don't have health care, and you don't want to pay for it, then don't go snowboarding! If you still believe in personal responsibility, any personal responsibility, raise your hand. Why should you, I, or anyone have to fund this brother's snowboarding accidents?

During the campaign, story after story told us how young voters wanted health-care "reform." One Rutgers University student, Joe Shure, told an NBC reporter that "health care is a huge concern. And the fact that the U.S. is an industrialized country without universal health care is an embarrassment, I think."[11]

Obama certainly embodies this mentality. His rhetorical tactics are always the same: hook young people with big-government schemes by calling it the "empathy deficit," which is our inability "to put ourselves in someone else's shoes," as he told the students at Northwestern:

> We live in a culture that discourages empathy. A culture that too often tells us our principal goal in life is to be rich, thin, young, famous, safe, and entertained. A culture where those in power too often encourage these selfish impulses. . . . I hope you choose to broaden, and not contract, your ambit of concern. Not because you have an obligation to those who are less fortunate, although you do have that obligation. Not because you have a debt to all of those who helped you get to where you are, although you do have that debt.
>
> It's because you have an obligation to yourself. Because our individual salvation depends on collective salvation. And because it's only when you hitch your wagon to something larger than yourself that you will realize your true potential—and become full-grown.[12]

Nice do-gooder rhetoric, but my goodness, collective *salvation*? Obama's razzle-dazzle logic-free sound bites induced their intended Zombie effect: "I have listened to him and I liked what I've heard so far," said Julie Rattendi, a first-time voter. "I'm just looking for someone to believe in."[13]

Yet now that Obama is the leader of the free world, what's interesting is that young people have been visibly absent in supporting the government plan for health care. It's caught the eye of the media. Where are the Obama supporters, or the "Obamaniacs"? Where are those troubled, unconfident students who put all their faith in Obama during the campaign? They sang songs about him; prayed to him; rapped to him; made love to him; marched to him; fainted to him; obsessed over him; and now, well . . . they're absent.

The drop-off goes right to the cult of personality, and the fact that young people buy into the utopian bulldoodle that Obama serves on a platter but are generally healthy, so there's no urgency or need to engage in the debate. Plus, the campaign is over. They can wait another four years to grovel, faint, and copulate at the Messiah's feet. Leftists and youth vote poseurs of Rock the Vote such as Heather Smith dismiss the disinterest as a backlash from the partisan rancor seen at health-care town halls. So to step up interest, Heather gets blogger Perez Hilton and other celebrities together to try to get young people motivated to back Obama's policy.

But the reason none of this seems to be working is that it all smacks of further limits on individual freedom and choice. Heck, liberals are already calling on Obama to regulate the food Americans eat, just as New York City banned trans fats. One liberal, Michael Pollan, wrote in a *New York Times* op-ed that the Obama administration must declare a war on the "American way of eating"; Dear Leader must work with the food industry to "take a good hard look at the elephant in the room [fat people] and galvanize a movement to slim it [us] down."[14]

Jim Geraghty of *National Review Online* summed up the Obama pie-in-the-sky health-care philosophy quite nicely:

> We're expected to believe a Democrat-controlled Congress, with deep divisions in its ranks, will put together a bill that will keep everything the same for those who have health insurance through their jobs, Medicare, Medicaid, or the VA; mandate coverage of pre-existing conditions; ban caps on coverage; mandate coverage of routine check-ups and preventive care, like mammograms and colonos-copies; offer health insurance to 30 million uninsured; provide tax credits for small businesses; painlessly man-date coverage for the young healthy uninsured; provide hardship waivers; provide choice and competition; keep insurance companies honest; avoid taxpayer subsidies for public option plans; keep out illegal immigrants; not pay for abortions; and not deny care to the elderly because of cost-benefit analyses, all while not adding one dime to our deficits—either now or in the future.[15]

Let's punt all our personal responsibility and just lay it at the feet of Dear Leader. The government can't even make a profit delivering mail, yet they want to dictate a health-care policy for 300 million Americans?! Say what? That makes as much sense as letting Michael Vick take care of your dog while you're out of town.

You, as an individual, and you, as the head of a household, have the single biggest incentive to provide medical coverage. Keep in mind that "rights" never impose financial obligations on other people. But to claim that somebody has the right to health care means that somebody else must pay for it. My right to free speech doesn't guarantee me that you will pay for a microphone; my right to religion doesn't guarantee that you'll provide me with a collection plate, Bible, and hymnals. In reality, Zombies have as much of a "right" to health care as they do to taxpayer-funded trips to KFC to feast on a bucket of wings and biscuits. Food is a much more basic necessity than health care, yet we do not have food-based insurance, or even food-based savings accounts. The late, great economist Milton Friedman had this axiom: Nobody spends somebody else's money as wisely or as frugally as he spends his own. Only in Disney movies does redistribution of wealth work.

We should be allowed to choose our level of insurance, like we do car premiums: to provide risk pools for consumers that cover them against catastrophic and unanticipated costs! I definitely don't expect or want to get into a car accident, but I'm covered for that level of possibility. My insurance, however, doesn't pay for my oil change, my gas, my car washes, etc. I pay for that out of my pocket, and as a result, I search for the best deals. It is truly a free market in action. The closest thing we have to a free market in health care is in the world of cosmetic surgery. There are no heavy government regulations or subsidies. People pay out of pocket, competition flourishes, and consumers are satisfied. As Ed Morrissey of Hot Air explains,

> If anyone wants to see how a medical-care market could work rationally, all they need to do is see how plastic surgery and Lasik markets work. Because the consumer has to deal with the actual cost of service, these providers are not overwhelmed. Because the providers get actual market compensation for their goods and services, there is no shortage of providers. And because of both of these facts, competition between providers keeps costs

reasonable and rational. Health-care reform should learn from that example and move closer to that kind of market, rather than towards more scarcity, less choice, and less freedom.[16]

But the liberal lives in his own world, where your wallet is his piggy bank. And the power of their emotion is, well, powerful, but also infantilizing. Take Erica Williams of the George Soros-bankrolled group Campus Progress. She appointed herself to represent "youth" issues. In a column for the *Huffington Post* in support of Obama's health-care scheme, she impressively manages to showcase her ignorance. After admitting that she doesn't like to "haggle over the nuances" of health care, Erica writes:

> I could tell them that health care reform is my fight because my partner, 25 years old, is an entrepreneur, consultant, and all around brilliant guy who cares more about professional fulfillment than financial gain and has thus been without insurance for 3 years. I've cried myself to sleep many a night over his lack of coverage, terrified that at any moment, an illness or accident could push us into financial ruin in the beginning stages of our life together.
>
> I could tell them that health care reform is my fight because 60% of my friends (yes, I did the math . . .) have lost their jobs in the past 6 months and don't go to the doctor. . . .
>
> I could say that a young friend of mine is afraid to get a test that would tell whether or not he has a congenital heart disease because he is worried that he will forevermore have a pre-existing condition.
>
> I could also tell you that in addition to being young,

I'm a woman of color and that for my demographic in particular, health care is a life or death issue.

And all of those reasons would be true. But for my generation, health care reform is more than a personal story or experience: it is a moral and humanitarian mandate.[17]

Well, well. Her "partner" doesn't purchase health care, because he would rather invest his money elsewhere. Fine. That's freedom. Not a problem. If a person would rather spend his money on a BlackBerry and expensive dinners than insurance, cool. Go for it. But he made his choice. Furthermore, Erica claims that her generation has made health care a "moral and humanitarian mandate." Just one problem: she can't point to any such mandate in any of our founding charters. If she would truly represent the interest of young people, she would discuss the massive redistribution of wealth that flows from young to old.

Our system today, pushed by liberals in government, supports a scheme where grandparents steal from the pockets of their grandchildren. Current entitlements are so out of control that it is inconceivable that people like Erica Williams would try to foist yet another costly entitlement—socialized health care—on an entire generation. In 2008, the U.S. comptroller general estimated that the total burden in present value of our entitlement programs— the three largest being Social Security, Medicare, and Medicaid—is about $53 trillion! With a *t*! The comptroller, David Walker, said, "I know it is hard to make sense of what 'trillions' means. One way to think about it is this: Imagine we decided to put aside and invest today enough to cover these promises tomorrow. It would take approximately $455,000 per American household—or $175,000 for every man, woman, and child in the United States."[18]

As Walker notes, the federal government has been so inefficient with Medicare and Medicaid, completely government-run to begin with, that the two programs "threaten to consume an untenable share of the budget and economy in the coming decades. The federal government has essentially written a 'blank check' for these programs." [19]

Hey, Erica, how about we find a moral and humanitarian mandate to get the government's grubby hands off our wallets! If poseurs like Erica really cared about young people they would demand *in*action from a government that has already proven itself to be unworthy with our money. A better option would be to let individuals take control of their medical future. Remember the Friedman axiom: Nobody spends somebody else's money as wisely or as frugally as he spends his own.

In reality, we have been handed a broken health-care policy, not by greed, not by selfish "profit-mongers" (I'm sure Erica works for free, eh?), but by selfish government bureaucrats who think they can devise a health-care scheme for 300 million Americans.

The moral outrage is that young Americans are not paying for their own retirement, their own health care, but for that of others. Obama likes to talk about capping premiums that people will pay and subsidizing costs (with your money). But why doesn't he cap taxes? Why won't he cap regulation? People know best how to spend their own money.

Shawn Tully, editor at large at *Fortune* magazine, identified freedoms lost under ObamaCare. Keep in mind that there's little freedom to begin with. Still, the Democrat plan doubles down on stupid.

> The bills in both houses require that Americans purchase
> insurance through "qualified" plans offered by health-

care "exchanges" that would be set up in each state. The rub is that the plans can't really compete based on what they offer. The reason: The federal government will impose a minimum list of benefits that each plan is required to offer.[20]

The Department of Health and Human Services will be able to define what types of coverage are offered in these "exchanges," including the mandates that are driving up state insurance markets, as we touched on. Connecticut, for instance, forces providers to cover hair transplants, hearing aids, and breast reconstruction. Now, I know people like Erica don't like to get into the "nuance" of the debate and just like to speak in "general" terms, but why on God's green earth should young people have to cover any of that? Moreover, how does federalizing such superfluous mandates ensure that prices will go down? The thing is, liberals don't care about cost. All their pet programs—all of them—are dead broke. Yet they spend away. In a free system we would get to choose our coverage. But in Obama's system a health commissioner would. Seriously.

The Heritage Foundation points this out about ObamaCare:

The Health Choices Commissioner will decide what services health insurance must cover, and under what conditions. These choice ("standards") will apply to both employer-sponsored insurance and insurance purchased through the Health Insurance Exchange, which will be operated by the Health Choices Administration. There will be no other legal way to buy health insurance. There will, however, be a "Qualified Health Benefits Plan Ombudsman" to provide you with "assistance" in "choosing a qualified health benefits plan in which to enroll"—from among the plan or plans the Commissioner has already chosen, of course.[21]

I thought we fought a revolution to rid ourselves from kings.

In any event, ObamaCare also adopts "community ratings," which, as you may remember, means that patients pay the same rate regardless of age or health status. This no doubt drastically harms young people, as our level of care is much less than older folks. In fact, insurance companies will be forbidden from charging older people more than twice what they charge young people. Normally, the ratio is 5 to 1, but now it's 2 to 1. It's a significant transfer of wealth from the young to old.

As Tully points out, "So if a 20-year-old who costs just $800 a year to insure is forced to pay $2,500, a 62-year-old who costs $7,500 would pay no more than $5,000."

If car insurance companies had to charge everyone the same regardless of driving history, what would happen? Would your car insurance decrease or increase? In fact, this brings up a necessary point that is missed in this whole debate: Why don't you watch your own health care? You see, there is a big difference between health care and medical care. Health-care management is up to individuals. It's all the essentials we learn as a kid: eating right, exercise, watch those trans fats, lots of greens, lots of fruits, get good rest, don't be stressed, etc. That's health care, and it is entirely your personal responsibility.

If you have medical complications because of your diet, which consists of eating Wendy's every night of the week, then why should taxpayers have to pay for your bad choices? Is that harsh? Hell no! What's harsh is bankrupting a generation and not talking honestly about incentives and personal responsibility.

Hey, kids, forgo the latest Jordans, forgo the flat-screen TV, forgo the vacations, forgo the nights eating out, forgo the bling-bling, forgo the $120 cell phone plan. You don't need all the gizmos and gadgets. Grow up and rely on yourself for a change. Now, that's change we can believe in! If people are paying the costs themselves, they are their best prevention method. That's the real preventive cure. When the government controls costs, it will also allocate care. It's basic economics.

Any piece of legislation that forces—yes, forces—young people to purchase insurance that bureaucrats deem acceptable will be a disaster. And if young people decide not to opt in, they will be taxed. Taxed for not buying into a government-devised health-care scheme! To put this in perspective, our founding fathers went ape on a single, minuscule tax on tea. It's true that young people are accurately called the "young invincibles" because, barring some catastrophic accident or illness, we rarely get sick. Even the liberal Kaiser Family Foundation, in a survey of young people, acknowledges that 95 percent of all young people report that they are in good or excellent health. Yes, 95 percent. Why would we want to install community-rating standards or extra mandates that would drive up the cost for virtually every young person in order to subsidize older folks? When John Fund of the *Wall Street Journal* pointed this out in an op-ed, that Obama's disastrous health-care plans mean "lower prices for older (and wealthier) folks, but high prices for the young," Rock the Vote—stalwart defenders of liberalism, not the youth—responded thus:

> Mr. Fund believes young people will face higher costs if reform passes and cites as evidence proposals that would limit insurance companies to a 2-to-1 ratio on age-based health care premiums—that is, insurance companies

would only be able to charge older people double what they charge younger people for the same coverage. While the 2-to-1 ratio is designed to keep costs down for older people, Mr. Fund believes that will come at the expense of young people.

He ignores two critical facts. First, under proposals currently being considered in Congress, coverage would be made more affordable because premiums for young people would be based on their income levels. Second, premium increases would be addressed by the government in the form of credits. As such, young people's costs will remain low because of income-based premiums and subsidies to make up cost differences—not because insurance companies have free rein to discriminate against older people.[22]

Shall we remember how this group flacking for Obama posits itself as nonpartisan? Regardless, Rock the Vote is run by idiots, and here's why. Notice that they don't rebut Fund's correct point that premiums would increase on the new mandated ratio, but they instead defend the new and costly mandates by saying that the government will step in and provide "credits," which are basically welfare payments, to people who can't afford coverage. Again, it's the liberal two-step in action! The government's mandates, by Rock the Vote's own admission, would drive up the cost of coverage. But that's fine, because good ol' Uncle Sam will step in to subsidize the medical bill (with your tax dollars).

Health-care costs are high because of government intervention, yet the liberal machine advocates more government policies that will increase the price of admission.

The fact is that 70 percent of young people have insurance, and out of that 30 percent who do not have insurance, 94 percent report being in good and excellent health, compared to the 95 percent of all young adults—uninsured and insured—who claim that same health status.[23] Yes, Zombies, the drop-off is only 1 percent. There is no crisis. There is no emergency. Yet, as we've seen, the political left wants costly mandates that drive up the price for families and young people.

Obama and his liberal cohorts like to bemoan the fact that the United States is the only industrialized nation that doesn't ensure health care for every single citizen. They view this as a detriment. It's a great fluffy, substance-free talking point. But it misses the entire scope of what America is. The very core of our being is that we trust people over politicians. It's on that principle that America has been the center of opportunity. It is a testament to our Constitution and our self-reliance that the government has not (yet) taken over our health-care system. It's to be celebrated and admired.

The Economic Igor

The Five Economic Lies Liberals Tell and Sell to Obama Zombies in Training

In the left's magical land, the laws of supply and demand don't exist. They think that they can just wave a wand and give everyone more money without any consequences. It doesn't work like that. Liberals portray themselves as helping the little guy, helping families, but in reality, liberals help the little guy all right ... they help him stay little!

The liberal machine tells at least five economic whoppers to hoodwink Obama Zombies in training. So let's start with one of the biggies: the Virtues of the Minimum Wage.

Liberal support for having and raising the minimum wage is ubiquitous. As of July 2009, the minimum wage—varying in each state—is federally at $7.25. During the campaign trail, Obama promised to raise the minimum wage even further, to $9.50 an hour, which means that in the last five years, the minimum wage would have skyrocketed 85 percent.[1] That's all a cause of celebration for the left. They view it as helping "working families" and the "poor." For the late senator Ted Kennedy, it was one of his trademark issues. He famously erupted at conservatives in the Senate for trying to block increases to the minimum wage; Kennedy accused them of tampering with the economic prosperity of others.

And as *Politico* noted, the minimum-wage issue is specifically messaged toward younger people: "Through events on the Hill, visits to college campuses and regional conference calls to college newspaper editors, majority leaders in Congress are working to convince this potentially powerful voting bloc that they're delivering on a youth agenda."[2] Liberals on Capitol Hill emphasize the increase in the minimum wage as part of their youth outreach, *Politico* added, because it "disproportionately affects young workers." It is a message that Obama continues during his failed presidency. At a Labor Day speech in Cincinnati, he praised much of the "labor movement" for, among other things, the minimum wage, which makes our "economy the envy of the world."[3]

The Zombie is especially susceptible to the minimum-wage talk. It's all emotion and no substance. The Zombie thinks to himself, *If we only raise the minimum wage higher for workers who are trying to feed their family of six, then we can increase their standard of living. This family will now have bread to feed themselves!*

First off, most people on the minimum wage are young, usually teenagers. The families of four or six are statistically the exception. But what these do-gooders fail to grasp is that artificially raising wages comes at a cost to the worker, and that cost, especially during hard economic times, is getting fired. Raising the minimum wage hurts low-income workers, forfeits jobs, and negatively impacts the American economy. Minimum-wage jobs are entry points in the job market. Even though they try, liberals can't escape basic economics: There's an inverse relationship between price and demand, which means that the more expensive it is to employ workers, the fewer of them there will be. You may say, "But Jason, the minimum wage will add hundreds more dollars a month to a worker's salary, which translates into thousands more per year. It's fairness, Jason! Why are you against fairness?!"

Here's my response: If the minimum wage at $7.25 is such a great thing, why stop there? If it increases standards of living and disposable income, and if there are no negative economic effects, how about we raise it to $15? Why not mandate that every person make at least $50 an hour! That's $8,000 a month, which comes out to nearly $100,000 a year! We'd all be rich people!

Let's consider some facts. Only a small number of people out of a massive workforce earn the minimum wage—around 3 percent of wage earners, or about 2 million people, according to the U.S. Bureau of Labor Statistics. And the majority of those people are teenagers and young adults, working part-time and in school. In fact, most individuals earning minimum wage have a household income of around $50,000.[4] Not too shabby. But regardless, raising the minimum wage, especially in down economic times, is a huge tax on business that is ultimately paid in the form of lost jobs and higher prices.

Nestor Stewart, owner of Stewart Pharmacy in McMinnville, Tennessee, said that the increase in the minimum wage was "cat-astrophic."[5] He explained that "higher wages" prevent him and other small-business owners from expanding their operation. "I've got to eliminate and be more conservative about these part-time employees," he said. "I have to. I have to have something left in the bottom line. It's just creating a terrible problem." As ABC News noted, Stewart will have to raise his pharmacy's prices to cover the new salary costs. No worries, Zombie! It's the liberal intention that counts. Disregard the results: Stewart's cutting down business hours, slashing employee work hours, and his inability now to hire students returning to college—it's the *thought* that counts, people!

But this is not an isolated incident. According to economics professor David Neumark, "the bulk of the evidence—from scores of studies, using data mainly from the U.S. but also from many other countries—clearly shows that minimum wages reduce employment of young, low-skilled people. The best estimates from studies since the early 1990s suggest that the 11% minimum wage increase . . . will lead to the loss of an additional 300,000 jobs among teens and young adults. This is on top of the continuing job losses the recession is likely to throw our way."[6]

Sorry, Zombies, but your Messiah is kicking young people's economic rear ends. Minimum-wage increases mandate unemployment. How's that for fairness? But don't listen to me. A report in the *Journal of Economic Perspectives* noted that 71 percent of economists at America's top universities—many of which are liberal havens—agree that "a minimum wage increases unemployment among the young and unskilled."[7]

Currently, the teen unemployment rate tops 25 percent, and the unemployment rate for black teens is above 50 percent.[8] For young adults, that rate is closing in on 20 percent, more than double the national unemployment rate.[9]

Rather than reduce poverty, liberal policy is reducing opportunity for finding a job. What's more, even those young people whose jobs aren't slashed when the minimum wage is increased still get higher prices. If you have more money in your wallet, you have still been robbed of its buying power because of price inflation.

But who needs rational economic thinking when you can instead feel all warm and fuzzy and special inside by conning Zombies into voting for you even though, in fact, you know you are killing jobs and inflating prices?

SO NOW WE move on to the second economic lie the liberal machine uses to hypnotize future Obama Zombies—the evil, nefarious "wage gap" between men and women. Have you heard that women make seventy-seven cents to every dollar a man makes? It's been the liberal line for a while now. During the election, B.H.O. ran a TV ad in battleground states specifically targeting women, hyping up the inequity in pay between the sexes. The ad starts off by saying how many women work to support their families but are paid only seventy-seven cents to the dollar of their male counterparts. In the background we see women in professional attire and women in hard hats. The ad then accuses John McCain of not understanding our economy since he opposed a law that guaranteed equal pay for equal work.

While on the stump in New Mexico, B.H.O. said this:

> The choice could not be clearer. It starts with equal pay. Sixty-two percent of working women in America earn half or more of their family's income. But women still earn 77 cents for every dollar earned by men in 2008. You'd think that Washington would be united in its determination to fight for equal pay.[10]

So, are women really paid less than men?

Yes, it is true that men tend to earn more than women, but don't assume it's gender discrimination. Let's walk through a scenario: If a business could really get the same quality of work from women for the same job at such a discounted rate, why wouldn't employers hire all women? It would be bad business to keep all men on hand. The smart employers would drop their men and swoop up all the women for a discounted price. There's no way other businesses could compete. So perhaps there are other differences that account for the pay gap between men and women.

Cait Murphy, an editor at *Fortune*, blew the phony wage gap myth out of the water, noting that men and women get paid differently because they're engaging in different lifestyle choices that affect pay scales. Murphy, who is a woman, cited peer-reviewed research done by another woman, June O'Neill, an economist who served as director of the Congressional Budget Office under Bill Clinton.

As Murphy writes, "What [O'Neill] found was that women are much more likely over the course of their lives to cut back their hours or quit work altogether than men, for issues involving the family."[11] Women's lifestyle choices matter when it comes to full-time employment because "you go part-time or take years out of the labor force, that has an effect on earnings down the line, due to loss of seniority or missed promotions."

It has nothing to do with sexism. Murphy argues that "of women aged 25–44 with young children, more than a third were out of the labor force; of those women who did have jobs, 30% worked part-time." Again, this has considerable effects when one is moving in and out of the labor force, as many wages take into account seniority of service. Moreover, getting promotions is often a function of years served and experience gained.

"All told," says Murphy, "women are more than twice as likely to work part-time as men and over the course of their lifetimes, work outside the home for 40% fewer years than men. That accounts for a significant chunk of the pay gap."

But that's not all. There's also something, um, a bit more

understated, but very important in determining wage factors. Murphy continues:

> Despite the many advances the women's movement has brought the U.S., what it hasn't done, thank heavens, is make men and women the same. The simple fact is—and there is nothing nasty or conspiratorial about it—the sexes continue to choose different avenues of study and different types of jobs.
>
> Here's an illustrative example. The college majors with the top starting salaries, according to the National Association of Colleges and Employers, are: chemical engineering (almost $60,000), computer engineering, electrical engineering, industrial engineering, mechanical engineering. Men make up about 80% of engineering majors. Women predominate among liberal arts majors—whose salaries start at a little more than $30,000. Putting it all together . . . these differences—in choice of work, years in the workforce, and hours of work—could account for as much as 97.5% of the differences in pay between men and women.

Other differences? Men are more likely to work more hours than women; men are more likely to take hazardous jobs than women are, which is why more men are truck drivers, firefighters, police officers, construction workers, flight engineers, and coal miners than are women. And guess what? Dangerous jobs equal higher pay than, say, secretarial jobs. Again, it's all about choices.

Here's what the liberal machine will never tell its dronelike youth Zombies: The "pay gap" for women shrinks to ninety-eight cents for every dollar earned by men, after factoring in work experience, education, and occupation.[12] And women in their twenties in big cities, including New York and Dallas, are making nearly 20 percent more than men in their twenties.[13] You go, girls! In some categories, one researcher found, the starting salaries for women as investment bankers and dietitians, for instance, were considerably higher than men's.[14]

Is there actual discrimination in some cases? I'm sure that occurs. But the beauty of the free market is that the company that discriminates for the sake of discrimination will be bad-mouthed and the wronged employee can also go to a competitor. Moreover, the employee can sue.

But here's the grandest irony of all this leftist silliness. Did you know that while B.H.O. was a United States senator he paid his female staffers *less* than his male ones? Obama's female employees made on average seventy-eight cents for every dollar a man earned. In real numbers, women brought home an average salary of $44,953.21, which was $12,472 less than the $57,425 average salary that the then-senator paid men. It gets better. McCain's female staffers not only earned 24 percent *more* on average than Obama's gals, but they also earned more than McCain's male employees.[15]

Were the women less qualified in Obama's office than the men? I have no clue. Whatever the reason, McCain closed the "gender gap" without the force of government.

Oh, and here's another inconvenient truth: women's wages grew more during *conservative* administrations than liberal ones. In fact, the administrations of Reagan, George H. W. Bush, and George W. Bush had higher "labor market progress for women" compared to the administrations of Clinton and Carter. For instance, women's "annual wage growth relative to men's" for the Reagan administration was 1.6 percent, compared to 0.21 percent for Clinton.[16]

Moral of the story? Liberals' economic lies have lobotomized my generation.

OUT OF ALL the mindless buzzwords liberals use, none is more annoying than *green jobs*, which is the third major economic lie liberals tell. Obama promised to create 5 million green jobs. So far, he's allotted nearly $100 billion for green schemes.[17]

So what is a "green" job? Good question. Nobody really knows. I get these images of Captain Planet scurrying about tall buildings with a windmill on his back, but in reality, green jobs are a big fat myth—one that Obama Zombies wholeheartedly embrace.

You remember Zombie Jessy Tolkan, right? She's part of the faux youth organization the Energy Action Coalition, which pretends to represent forty different youth organizations on addressing "climate change." Back in 2007, Jessy and her cohorts initiated a conference called Power Shift, where they flew in around six thousand young people to Washington, D.C. In addition to reduction in CO_2 emissions, the group's legislative demands included government "investment" in "green jobs."

While in the nation's capital, Jessy went on television with the granddaddy of all Zombies, Chris Matthews, to discuss the youth vote and climate change. On air, Tolkan continued with the usual lies about how our sea levels are rising, glaciers are melting, the wildfires and droughts are all the result of global warming, that Sarah Palin loves clubbing baby seals . . . you know, the normal liberal talking points.

Tolkan then declared: "It's an essential problem. It is my future. Millions of people's lives are at risk. This is not a matter of if. It's a matter of having to do it right now, without a doubt. I have to say, it's going to be good for the American economy. We have the opportunity to create millions of new green jobs."[18]

Marcie Smith, a college Zombie participating in 2009's Power Shift conference in Washington, D.C., argued that green jobs were needed to address "climate justice." She even had the stones to compare her global-warming comrades to the leaders of the civil rights movement! Marcie told CNN:

> I've been working on a lot of climate adjustment issues from the local level, the state level, the national level, as well as at the international levels. And I think that that's one of the really, really cool features of this movement, in particular, is that this is a movement of profound and historic solidarity and reconciliation . . . you have the daughters and the sons of the civil rights movement, of the suffrage movement, of the labor movement. You know, and all of these sort of veins of equality movements are coming together under the banner of climate justice which is really, really important and profoundly historic.[19]

But we still haven't learned about all those green jobs and how they will be created. For starters, governments cannot create private-sector jobs; they can only move resources around. A government redistributes money within the economy. It doesn't create wealth; it only confiscates wealth. But if green energy is such a good idea, venture capitalists will produce it using their own money.

Green jobs are all bark but no bite. But don't take my word for it. Let's see how it's been instituted by our friends overseas.

Obama himself tells us that we should look to countries such as Spain that have "harnessed their people's hard work and inge-nuity with bold investments" in green energy. So how's it working out for Spain? Thus far, they've spent almost $30 billion on their "green energy economy," which tallies to an average of $855,000 for each green job. Guess who foots the bill for these "green jobs"? You got it. The taxpayers.

That's some "investment," eh? Despite the fact that the Spanish government spends $8 billion a year to create a flurry of "green" jobs, their economy is actually hemorrhaging jobs.[20] According to Gabriel Calzada of Universidad Rey Juan Carlos in Spain, his country's "experience reveals with high confidence, by two different methods, that the U.S. should expect a loss of at least 2.2 jobs on average, or about 9 jobs lost for every 4 created."[21]

Let me be clear. I'm not against alternative energy. I welcome new developments. Freedom and innovation rock! It's just that politicians and the lobbyists who fund them shouldn't be using our money to pick winners and losers in the alternative energy market. That's a surefire way to crush jobs.

The sad truth is that U.S. unemployment is at its highest level in twenty-six years and climbing. Obama rushed through the largest spending bill in American history, commonly known as the "stimulus" package. But the stimulus package did nothing to spur job growth and investment. Nada. Zip. Nothing.

Look, if government spending were a magic bullet, the Soviet Union would never have fallen; it would have been an economic juggernaut, a model for our success. Moreover, Cuba, Venezuela, and every other socialist tyranny around the world would be economic nirvanas.

The green jobs movement isn't about stimulating the economy. It's anti-growth. Offshore, we have an estimated 86 billion barrels of oil.[22] In oil shale alone, within the Rocky Mountains, we have an estimated 800 billion barrels.[23] Alaska and the Dakotas also hold billions of barrels of oil. That means we currently sit atop more than three times all the oil in Saudi Arabia, enough to meet our energy needs for the next four hundred years. But the anti-growth green people have made it illegal to drill.

For liberals, despite what they think about themselves, it's always about more control. They want to regulate and ration every part of the economy because they know deep down they are so much smarter than everyone else.

LEFTIST LIE NUMBER four revolves around one of the most treasured phrases in the Obama Zombie lexicon: *economic and social justice.*

Let's see how Obama lies about "economic fairness" and economic justice. During a primary debate, Charlie Gibson questioned Obama on the soundness of raising taxes on capital gains (stock values), noting that such an increase would likely lead to a decrease in government revenue. Gibson noted that in each instance when the capital gains tax was lowered, the government took in more money. In essence, lower taxes was generating wealth, not stripping it. Gibson then smartly asked Obama why he would raise capital gains, given that obviously there are no positive financial outcomes.

Obama's answer was stunning. He didn't deny the negative economic impact but said that he'd consider tax hikes anyway in the name of "fairness."

Now, we'll get into who actually pays taxes in a moment, but think about that for a second. Obama's worldview stresses that the profit system as we know it is unfair. In Obama's world, governments are economically responsible for their people; it's not individuals being responsible for themselves.

In his acceptance speech at the 2008 convention, Obama said

that John McCain "subscribed to that old, discredited Republican philosophy—give more and more to those with the most and hope that prosperity trickles down to everyone else. In Washington, they call this the Ownership Society, but what it really means is— you're on your own. Out of work? Tough luck. No health care? The market will fix it. Born into poverty? Pull yourself up by your own bootstraps—even if you don't have boots. You're on your own." To Obama, the "promise of America" is "the fundamental belief that I am my brother's keeper; I am my sister's keeper."

Um, when did you ever sign up to be your sister's keeper, B.H.O.? Isn't your illegal immigrant aunt living in squalor in America? Why aren't you helping her, Messiah?

But I digress.

So where does all this Marxist economic bilge come from? Well, B.H.O. freely tells us that in college he hung around Marxists; for twenty years he attended a Marxist-rooted church, and he even titled his bestselling book after a Marxist and racist-inspired sermon. He's also influenced by Michelle "Never Been Proud of My Country Before" Obama. Here's our patriotic first lady holding forth on the virtues of stealing a person's hard-earned money: "The truth is, in order to get things like universal health care and a revamped education system, then someone is going to have to give up a piece of their pie so that someone else can have more."[24]

Here is where liberals don't understand economics. At all. When wealth is created, it's not a zero-sum game. Everyone benefits. "Rich" people invest, start businesses, and create jobs.

But liberals think somehow this all leads to greediness. "People before profits," lefties like to say. Yet it is exactly because of profits that people are better off! That is capitalism; it's the most successful economic system in the world, albeit one that is ruthlessly under assault by Obama and his bevy of czars.

Economic fallacies have hit Zombies like wrecking balls. A recent poll found that more than a third of younger Americans preferred socialism to capitalism. Another 30 percent were undecided on what was the better economic model. In all, only 37 percent of younger adults said that capitalism is a better system than socialism.[25]

Madness!

But it fits with the narrative that is foisted on the Zombie, that capitalism is mean and that government is compassionate. Far from it! The freest economies in the world have the highest standard of living per person. In those countries that limit government intrusion and overreach, keep taxes marginally low, and respect free trade worldwide, the people are the most prosperous. Socialist governments are the ones that must ration everything, from food to health care. Moreover, free economies, which any socialist enterprise is not, enshrine property rights and reward hard work. Ever notice how our "poor" people are fat and plump . . . with cable TV, no less?

Last year, Young America's Foundation intern Alyssa Cordova had a great idea to bring the inequity of "redistribution of wealth" down to a level her peers could understand. Armed with a video camera, she set out to interview students at George Mason University about what they thought about redistribution . . . of grades. In fact, she had a petition for people to sign that would allow the administration at her school to redistribute grade point averages. She brilliantly used all the Zombie rhetoric. She said that there are people who currently aren't meeting the GPA requirements to graduate, and there are people at the very top that don't need the extra points, so, in the name of fairness and equality, let's allocate those points down the GPA ladder. Alyssa continued by saying that it's not the fault of people at the bottom who may be struggling and working just to get by.

The responses to Alyssa's petition were priceless. *Why would you take points away from people who earned it*, said one student sternly. *People who worked for their grades should be allowed to keep them*, exclaimed another. Alyssa set the trap. You work for your grade. You study your tail off to get that A. It's yours. You deserve it. Then Alyssa showed her true intent. She asked the same people who just finished saying that grade redistribution was wrong what they thought of redistribution of income. Would these same folks support raising taxes on the top 5 percent of earners? *Yeah*, the Zombie replied even before Alyssa was done with the question. Another guy said the top 5 percent are "freaking millionaires" and aren't going "to miss those little bit of dollars" versus a person who doesn't make as much money. It's all different, proclaimed the Zombies. Alyssa, smelling blood, followed up by asking, "So you think it's okay to take from people who earn their money but not from people who earn their grades?" *Exactly*, proclaimed the Zombie. In the end, the Zombies kept saying there is no parallel, it's not the same thing, while in the same breath saying it's fine to soak the "rich." The YouTube video ("Petition to Redistribute GPAs") is a great tool to bring the immorality of government redistribution down to a level people can relate to.[26]

What Obama Zombies need to understand is that *social justice* is merely a euphemism for *socialism;* respecting property and freedom is the real justice, not what some little college kid or Washington bureaucrat thinks is unfair. What's interesting is that liberals are all for "spreading the wealth around" except when it's their own.

WELL, BOYS AND girls, the moment has finally arrived. It's time to bust a gaping hole in the fattest liberal lie of all—that the rich don't pay their fair share in taxes.

Tax cuts for the rich! Tax cuts for the rich! Bush just cared about the rich (and Halliburton)!

There is no limit to how far liberals will go to stoke the flames of class warfare. The liberal mantra is that the lower class pays all the taxes while the rich folks tool around in their yachts clinking champagne glasses while paying zilch. But, as usual, the greatest enemy of the Obama Zombie is the facts.

In 2007, the top 1 percent of earners paid no less than 40 percent of all federal income taxes while the bottom 95 percent paid around 39.4 percent. In other words, 1.4 million people shouldered a larger tax load than a combined 134 million people. The nonpartisan Tax Foundation underscored such inequity this way: "The share of the tax burden borne by the top 1 percent now exceeds the share paid by the bottom 95 percent of taxpayers."[27]

Looking at the top 10 percent, that group paid more than 70 percent of the taxes required by the government! It's looking like "tax cuts for the rich" really means tax cuts for those who . . . pay taxes! In reality, the bottom 50 percent of income earners pay only about 2 percent of all federal income taxes.

Zombies, how much more do you want to slash the taxes of half of all wage earners? They barely pay anything already.

It gets better. Every time a major tax break was passed, whether it was under Ronald Reagan or George W. Bush, the left howled that it was a tax cut for the rich. Yet each time, the percentage of income taxes paid by the rich went *up*, and the percentage of taxes paid by the bottom decreased dramatically. In fact, since Ronald Reagan's historic tax cut in 1981, the share of taxes for the bottom 50 percent went from 7 percent down to 2 percent, and the share paid by the top 1 percent went from 17 to 40 percent![28]

Crying "tax cuts for the rich" is a scam. The rich are shouldering the tax burden. The fact that the bottom pays practically nothing is no cause for celebration, but for concern. We have more and more people dependent on government largesse and yet the number of people paying for it is declining. We're becoming a nation of moochers and leeches.

And how about George W. Bush? He showered the "rich" with tax breaks galore, no? In reality, the Bush tax cuts initiated in 2001 and 2003, among other things, lowered the 15 percent rate to 10 percent, the 27 percent rate to 25 percent, the 30 percent rate to 28 percent, the 35 percent rate to 33 percent, and the top marginal tax rate from 39.6 percent to 35 percent.[29] What is the largest-percentage cut? The one that went from 15 to 10 percent on the lowest income tax quintile! That rate cut was even higher than the one at the very top, which was just under 4 percent. The whole "tax cuts for the rich" was pure bunk, a lie that liberals shamelessly popularized.

These are tax cuts that Obama plans on letting expire, which means that every rate in every bracket would increase.

But rather than bludgeon "rich" folks over the head with a pipe, liberals should celebrate their job creation. Please point me to the poor person who provided you with a job. You know it's those evil rich people who have the money, acumen, risk temperament, and strategy to create jobs and employment for the rest of us. Bottom line: If you tax something, you get less of it. Slash taxes and reduce burdens of government, and prosperity will follow. Liberals endlessly excoriate the idea of "trickle-down" economics, blasting it as some scheme that just gets the very top wealthy while no one else prospers. The left's idea is trickle-down, too, though. It just uses the brute force of government to command where the trickling down is going to occur. There's no such thing as bottom up. If you think there is, go to the very bottom of the bottom—your local panhandler—and see how many jobs he can provide you and your family.

We've already tried the liberal solution to economic growth. It's been an abject failure. Since 1964, when Lyndon Johnson's "War on Poverty" began, can you guess how much we've spent fighting it? Just a guess? That would be none other than $16 trillion.[30]

To put that in perspective, the total cost of all military wars in our nation's history was $6.4 trillion. That means the War on Poverty has cost nearly *three times* the amount of every war the U.S. has fought, *combined*.

Talk about a quagmire!

In fact, Obama is poised to spend more on welfare in 2010 alone than Bush spent on the entire Iraq War. If the amount the government spends on "welfare" to the poor were just converted to cash and given directly to them, the lot would be nearly four times the amount needed to catapult each poor family out of poverty.[31] But nah, that's too, um, logical. Building more and more inefficient bureaucracies is better because it creates human mouse-traps to keep poor people poor and thus dependent on liberal politicians to keep the money train rolling. That's how cynical the liberal machine is.

Actually, the numbers are even more odious. In 2007, for instance, the gap between poor people who needed welfare and the monetary number that would raise that household past the federal poverty level was $148 billion. That means that for all households in poverty in America, it would take $148 billion to get them all out of poverty. Eliminate poverty entirely. Guess how much was actually spent: $550 billion.[32] What was done with the extra billions? Good question. No one knows for sure.

The truth is that welfare spending has grown the fastest in

the past decade, at a rate of nearly 300 percent. By contrast, defense grew only 126 percent.[33] Candidate Obama told us that the "war in Iraq is costing each household about $100 per month." Guess how much social services across the nation cost you? About $638 a month for all of 2010!

It's time the Zombies realize that the War on Poverty has been a complete failure. Today nearly half the population doesn't pay any taxes and receives government benefits. We have a generation of welfare-addicted people who are dependent on the government. Strike that—dependent on those rich folks who pay their taxes.

Truth be told, even though George Bush increased welfare programs by 68 percent, with 2008 welfare spending topping $700 billion,[34] Obama still had the chutzpah to say that "George Bush spent the last six years slashing programs to combat poverty." Change? What change?

If liberals really did care for the poor and needy, they would champion policies that actually increased the standard of living. The formula is in plain sight. After Ronald Reagan slashed high tax rates and minimized onerous business regulations, America experienced the greatest sprout of upward mobility ever known to man. The United States generated more wealth from 1980 to 2007 than in every previous year combined. In other words, the economy was twice as large in 2007 ($57 trillion) as it was in 1980 ($25 trillion), prior to the Gipper's free-market initiatives.[35] But liberals would rather create entitled brats who are hooked on government, not hooked on phonics. Liberals know government programs create more dependence, which is exactly why they promote them.

Thanks to the Obama Zombies, we are now trillions more in debt. They swallowed hook, line, and sinker five of the biggest economic lies in the liberal machine's playbook.

Our children thank them.

Our children's children thank them.

Our children's children's children thank them.

Our children's children's children's children thank them.

Our children's children's children's children's children thank them.

After all, they're the ones who just got stuck with the bill.

8 I Want My MTV

Why MTV Is Catnip for Obama Zombies

Before the 2008 presidential election, ABC's John Stossel posed the following question: With all these "youth" organizations registering college students at rock concerts, rap concerts, or through other gimmicks, are we building quality voters or just quantity?

Stossel's results were astonishing. He asked young would-be voters how many states are in the United States. Apparently, like Obama, there were concertgoers who believed there are "fifty-seven states." One person Stossel asked replied, "Fifty-two?"[1]

What about U.S. senators? How many are there?

"I have no idea," said one genius. "Sixty-four, I think. Something like that."

"Fifty per state?" said another girl. "Five per state? Seven?"

Another first-time voter chimed in, "Oh no. I wanna say twelve. Am I so wrong?"

Yes, you are "so wrong." My reply: Hey, you—out of the gene pool!

How about landmark events in our nation's history? In the same *20/20* interview, Stossel asked first-time voters if they knew what "Roe v. Wade" signified.

"Segregation, maybe?" said one dude.

"Is Roe versus Wade where we declared bankruptcy?" asked another guy.

"Roe versus Wayne?"

Stossel's findings reflect a broader problem. A Zogby poll found that while 77 percent of Americans could identify two of Snow White's Seven Dwarfs, only 24 percent could name two Supreme Court justices.[2] The same poll also revealed that 60 percent of Americans were able to identify Homer as Bart Simpson's father, but that Americans failed miserably in naming one of Homer's legendary Greek poems (21 percent could). How about basic civics? Well, well. Seventy-three percent of those polled were able to name all three of the Three Stooges, but, sadly, only 42 percent could name the three branches of government.[3]

Am I saying that there should be restrictions on voting? Should there be tests? No, of course not. One main reason for the army of ignoramuses out there is our leftist-dominated education establishment. Western civilization and American civics are no longer staples of education. Multiculturalism has replaced George Washington. Schools offer classes like "Lesbian Novels Since World Word II" (Swarthmore College) and "The Phallus" (Occidental College).

Or how about the University of Pennsylvania's "Adultery Novel" class, which studies a series of nineteenth- and twentieth-century works about adultery and watches "several adultery films" to place adultery "into its *aesthetic*, social and cultural context" (emphasis added). Penn even finds room for Marx in a course on marital infidelity, viewing trysts through "sociological descriptions of modernity, Marxist examinations of family," and "feminist work on the construction of gender."

This is what the left means when they talk about "diversity" and "multiculturalism": heavy on nonsense and short on American education. But this kind of erasure of American identity and history goes a long way toward explaining the MTV-driven crap that preys on students' abysmal understanding of the workings of the most powerful and affluent country on the planet.

One of MTV's electoral battering rams is their—ahem— "nonpartisan" Rock the Vote program, which boasts that it doesn't hold allegiances to any particular party and makes sure that papers always include the nonpartisan moniker next to its name. But Rock the Vote (or "Crock the Vote" as I prefer to call it) is little more than a solidly hard-left vote machine used to crank out Zombies in warp-speed fashion.

Y'all remember Sheryl Crow, right? She's the same toolbag that "joked" about having a law that regulated the amount of toilet paper we use. "I propose a limitation be put on how many squares of toilet paper can be used in any one sitting." All to save the earth! Yeah, that Sheryl Crow. The same Sheryl Crow who performed the kickoff concert at the 2008 Democratic convention and while onstage told the crowd, "What I'm hearing from Senator Obama is a lot of like we heard from Robert Kennedy. No matter what campaign ad we see or how it's spun, hope is important."[4] Clearly, she's precisely the type of "nonpartisan" celebrity one should use to encourage young people to vote, right?

Rock the Vote thought so. The group tapped Crow, among other musicians, for public service announcements (PSAs) and concert tours in key battleground states, including Ohio and Virginia.

"There are such critical issues facing our country, from high gas prices to climate change that we need to do more than just register to vote, we need to get our friends registered too," the rocker said.[5] Crow offered free tracks from her *Detours* album to the first fifty thousand people who got three friends to register to vote and also provided a "free download" of her song "Gasoline" to anyone who signed up for Rock the Vote's mailing list.[6] In all, Rock the Vote's college tour targeted more than thirty key cities. At the Rock the Vote tour stop at a park near Virginia Commonwealth University, Crow started off by asking the students, "Do you believe in hope?"[7]

Actually, she used the word *change,* too. "A change will do you good," Crow belched from stage, adding, "I have to believe that the days of being motivated by fear and deception are behind us."

And what's a celebrity concert without a little antimilitary, antiwar drivel?

"And I have to believe that war never solved anything. And I have to believe that change, change, change, change is on its way."

Actually, Crow is right. War has never solved anything— except for ending slavery, fascism, Nazism, and communism. War is soooo overrated, people!

Remember that Rock the Vote has the pretext of nonpartisanship, so they can't endorse a candidate, since the organization is a registered 501(c)(3). Regardless, Crow made sure the thousand-plus crowd knew whom she endorsed, that is, of course, if they didn't see her endorse Obama from the freaking Democratic National Convention!

"So I guess you get the point, right?" she asked at the end. Yes, Sheryl, we get the point. You're a toolbag.

More humorously, Robert DeNiro also did a PSA announcement for Rock the Vote, declaring, "I don't care who you vote for, I just want you to vote." [8] Fair enough, right? Just one problem. DeNiro was saying these very words while there was a *huge* Obama sign in plain view directly behind him. Subtle, guys. Very, very subtle.

And if you're wondering if any McCain supporter or campaign material also appeared in Rock the Vote PSAs or concerts, what the hell are you snorting? The same stuff Obama snorted in college?

On *Larry King Live,* another Rock the Vote groupie, Christina Aguilera, couldn't contain her excitement over Obama:

> It's an exciting [election]. I mean, wow, what ground-breaking—what a groundbreaking time in history. I mean, we had a woman running for president, which was pretty much unheard of. An African-American running for president. So it's just exciting, the change that has come to our country and just to get involved and—I think, also, that's another reason why young people might be more motivated now to vote, just because they can see, you know, what might have even been unheard of or unthinkable even last election, it's right here and right now and very present and this is the moment. This is the moment. [9]

What do race and gender have to do with whether one can lead the free world? Lady Margaret Thatcher was an incredible head of state. Was it because she sits down when going to the bathroom instead of standing up? No. It's because she was a fierce and brilliant leader with vision, tenacity, grit, guts, and rock-solid values. Ideas matter, not gender or skin color.

But Rock the Vote knows what it's doing. Heather Smith acknowledges that "voting is a habit, that's why we've got them involved at a young age. They'll keep voting and I think in November you're going to see the largest increase of young voters at the polls in our nation's history."[10] Translation: Brainwash the kiddies at a young age to help form long-lasting voting patterns.

That's why Rock the Vote targets them when they're young. Prime pickings! Smith knows this, just as clearly as she knows that she's a Democrat. Yep, the executive director of Rock the Vote has donated fifteen hundred dollars to Young Voter Pac, a blatantly liberal get-out-the-vote organization run by Jane Fleming Kleeb, whose husband ran for the U.S. Senate in Nebraska as a Democrat.

"As young people stand at the forefront of this historic election we want to ensure that young voters are educated on the issues and motivated to take action on Election Day," Smith noted in a press statement. "Our Get Out the Vote efforts will inspire young voters to take their future into their hands and forever change the perception of the youth vote."[11]

And by "educated," Heather Smith means indoctrinated. The group uses not a single conservative spokesperson, nor do they espouse any conservative positions on issues. Rock the Vote doesn't represent youth voters, it represents liberal voters. For example, on health care, Rock the Vote signed on to a plan put together by a shell group called "Health Care for America Now," which is a coalition of left-wing groups including MoveOn.org, the Center for American Progress, and the National Council of La Raza. In fact, Health Care for America Now cooked up a blueprint for its followers on "How to Fight Back Against the Right."[12]

Fight back, eh? Remember that every time Heather Smith or some other toolbag from Rock the Vote is introduced as a "nonpartisan" voter-mobilization organization. In terms of "solutions" to health care, Rock the Vote adopts the left-wing position. Openly. Its "The Solution" page reads "One way to make sure you can get covered is with a 'public option.'" It goes on to quote Obama himself to buttress its selling points.[13] You can't get more entrenched in ObamaMania than that, folks!

During the election. Rock the Vote's PSA with the rapper Murs parroted the liberal line about "universal health care." "What is it hurting to get off your ass and take ten minutes to go do something that could affect the lives of your children," said Murs in the YouTube video.[14] "You have a voice as an American." (Oh, for real, yo? I got a voice. Naw, homey?! No shizzle!) "If you don't register, you won't have a voice," Murs ends by saying. But the PSA continues with flashing statistics of why the youth should vote. And here's where the party affiliation comes in:

13.3 Million

18–29 Year Olds

DO NOT HAVE

Health Insurance

1,049,398

Young Americans

Under The Age Of 29

Have Served In Iraq

And Afghanistan

Hmmm. Whom do you think Murs and his Rock the Vote gang were going to vote for?

In all, there is not one conservative position Rock the Vote advocates. Of course, the group is free to lobby on whatever positions it wants; conservatives love freedom, so feel free to yap your trap all you darn please, dear socialists. But can we please drop the laughable line in the mainstream media that this is an organization that represents the interests of young people? If by "young people" you mean Maxine Waters and Nancy Pelosi and B.H.O., then, yes. But by any fair assessment these groups are nothing short of a surrogate for the Democratic National Committee.

MTV also threw its hat into presidential election coverage. MTV held dialogues with presidential contenders before the Iowa primary and had a follow-up with many of them before Super Tuesday. MTV also hired fifty-one youth "reporters" to cover the election for a youth perspective in each state and the District of Columbia. And by "cover" the election I mean carry water for Democrats. A fair reading of MTV means assessing whom the network uses as its main political moderator. And what do you know. It's none other than the effete Gideon Yago, the mother of all metrosexuals. The uberwoman of all men has given more than a thousand dollars to left-wing causes,[15] including General Wesley Clark's presidential run in 2004 and Vote Vets, a group representing a small number of disgruntled antiwar veterans who also take up the cause of "clean energy." Yago hosted every presidential forum. But even if we dropped tight-pants Gideon from the equation, what if we looked at how MTV covered both conventions? Bias, anyone?

Let's start off with the Democrat convention. MTV's Sway Calloway covered Obama's infamous stadium acceptance speech and discussed how "thousands of young people have descended" on Denver. On the screen, we see Obama Zombie after Obama Zombie give his or her name and state, and without fail, people are sobbing uncontrollably. That hard-hitting MTV "journalist" Sway interviews a Zombie who says that Obama makes "people feel good about getting up in the morning." The same dude states, "we live in the best country in the world and now I feel it."[16]

Being the top-notch investigative journalist he is, Sway manages to locate one girl who is weeping wildly. "God, I'm just so happy to be here," she says. "I can't even find the words to express how happy and how proud I am at this moment, to know that there are other people [Obama] who have struggled and who have lived the same way I have. We have a candidate as president who has gone through the same struggles that I have in life."[17]

One young man, Joshua Lopez, says of Obama's big acceptance speech, "The dream is now a reality . . . when MLK talked about having a dream about people being judged by the contents of their character and not the color of their skin, you know, we get to this point right now, we can see a man who happens to be an African American gives this enormous speech and run for president of the United States, the dream is definitely realized."

Refusing to leave any journalistic stone unturned, our dear Sway finds yet another Obama Zombie, Brian Lee: "I really do think they [McCain and Obama] have different understandings of the economy. First and foremost because one person understands the economy and one person has no idea about the economy. That's a fundamental difference when you know your ABCs and . . . (stuttering) and the other person has no idea how to spell cat."[18]

Did you follow that "logic"? *Obama understands the economy because he understands the economy and McCain has no idea how to spell* cat. Oh, I get it now. Clear as mud.

Paul Rieckhoff, an antiwar veteran, praises Obama's speech as a big step "to remake the face of the party" so that it's not perceived as unpatriotic. He says that he has never seen so many American flags in one place.

The ever-skeptical Sway then plays a clip of Obama's acceptance speech: "Patriotism has no party. I love this country and so do you . . . the men and women who serve in our battlefields may be Democrats and Republicans and independents, but they have fought together and bled together and some died together under the same proud flag. They have not served a red America or a blue America. They have served the United States of America."

Tom Tarantino, another liberal veteran, commented for MTV that this line by Obama was "the absolute key . . . the military is one of the most single diverse minorities in the country . . . all types of people in this country choose to stand up for this country."

Actually, Tom, the military is one of the least ideologically diverse places around, where liberals make up a paltry 8 percent of the armed forces. Pathetic, homeboy. Get your friends to sign up!

"Obama didn't disappoint," said the hard-hitting and always fair-and-balanced Sway.

A Zombie reaction to Obama's education plan outlined that night, where you would get money for "serving your community": Bonner Springs of Kansas told MTV, "I can't really see any way of going about being someone who is in lower class and trying to go through and get a college education. There really needs to be a level playing field for people who want to work and want to try."

MTV's Jake: "80,000 Americans are now finally proud of their country again after 8 years of what we've had. It's just great seeing everyone; seeing the excitement; and seeing how proud everyone is. It's just phenomenal."

And that's how MTV covered Obama's convention speech, folks! There was not *one* critical piece of information. Not one! No tough questions. No analysis. Just fawning fluff piece after fawning fluff piece, all reinforcing the image of Obama as Rock Star of the Universe.

John McCain got similar coverage at his convention acceptance speech, right? Ha! And Michelle Obama doesn't believe America is a "downright mean" country?

Remember how the journalistic icon Sway and the MTV gang

couldn't find or feature one—not a *single*—young person who was critical of Obama at the convention? Well now, miraculously, in the opening segment of MTV's coverage of McCain's speech, Sway Calloway finds an Obama supporter at the RNC Convention![19] After interviewing two young McCain supporters, Sway goes to Bill. After acknowledging that Bill is liberal, Sway asks him what McCain has to do to convince him to vote for him. Bill says that McCain must explain how Obama's plan to tax the "wealthiest Americans is bad for the middle class as well as poor America." To be clear, in the *opening segment* of MTV's "nonpartisan" coverage of McCain's convention speech, good ol' MTV finds (or plants) a guy to parrot Obama's talking points!

If that weren't bad enough, Sway highlights the leftist protesters who descended on Minneapolis and finds a girl among them to say Sarah Palin shouldn't be running for vice president, because of her daughter's looming pregnancy. How progressive and feminist of her!

To put this in perspective, Sarah Palin rocked the GOP house with her convention speech. It was more talked about than McCain's was. There were thousands of adoring fans—thousands— at the Xcel Energy Center who fell in love with Palin as the VP candidate, and this nitwit Sway finds some schmuck on the street to trash her? Fair and balanced at its best, no?

After McCain's actual acceptance speech, the unstoppable Sway managed to find a disgruntled veteran to sound off on McCain as someone who doesn't care about soldiers' post-traumatic injuries.[20]

But MTV's bias was even more insidious. Somehow the network found another convention "attendee" to trash McCain on the war. Bill Halter: "I would've liked to hear John McCain address how he plans to bring the Iraq conflict to a conclusion."[21] Most

Republicans are strictly against an arbitrary timetable set by politicians and prefer drawdown or pullout dates to be set according to the commanders on the ground. It's remarkable that out of a crowd of tens of thousands of people with that understanding of Iraq, MTV found "Bill Halter" to talk negatively about Iraq.

So, to recap. MTV features Obama Zombie after Obama Zombie, wetting their pants over the Anointed One. No criticism. No tough questions. But at the Republican convention, well, you can't let conservatives get in the way! MTV features leftists to strike a discord in the hearts of young voters on McCain's military commitment. . . . even McCain's military record.

MTV develops its programming through the goggles of liberalism. Its programming team either is unaware or dismisses opposing views. There are no conservative correspondents, reporters, or even questions that tackle a conservative perspective. And that's just the coverage of the two convention speeches. MTV sponsored presidential forums with Democrat and Republican candidates. God knows an entire chapter could be written just on those performances. But I'll give you a few gems.

In MTV's "Countdown to the 'Super Dialogue,'" our crack reporter Sway says he asked young voters what issues they consider most important and, what do you know, he found students to say: "nationwide healthcare," "gay rights," "the war in Iraq," "college affordability," "Darfur," "withdraw some troops," "the environment and the energy crisis in our country are horrendous." Obama Zombie after Obama Zombie, liberal line after liberal line.

On December 3, 2007, at Southern New Hampshire University, John McCain participated in the dialogue, which was moderated by the girly boy Gideon Yago and the clueless Sway. In the forum, Yago shows McCain a video submitted from students at the University of Southern California. It went like this: "We believe that global warming is the greatest threat to our future. Every day we feel how real global warming is, with drought conditions fueling recent wild fires and rising sea levels eroding our coastlines; it's clear these threats are here now, not years away. Our next president needs to be a global leader on this issue; as young people who will inherit this problem we need a clear plan now."[22] As it turns out, these were no ordinary students. They were part of the group CalPIRG, a leftist activist student group started by Ralph Nader decades ago! PIRG falsely stands for Student Public Interest Research Groups. These are the biased of the biased. And MTV picked their video.

Actually, the PIRGs are another one of these allegedly "nonpartisan" youth mobilization efforts we hear so much about. For the 2008 election, the group teamed up with the other "nonpartisan" groups Rock the Vote, Declare Yourself, and HeadCount to churn out the student vote. These groups described themselves as the "four largest non-partisan voter registration groups."[23] The four horsemen, folks. Recall that Declare Yourself is run by left-wing producer Norman Lear; HeadCount was started to elect John Kerry; and Rock the Vote, well, you know about Rock the Vote.

With this type of "nonpartisanship," I wonder if MSNBC will have me on the program and allow me to identify myself as an Obama supporter. I will then go on to give Obama advice on how he is wrecking our economy with irresponsible spending. I'm as much of an Obama supporter as these groups are nonpartisan. Combined, these organizations boast that they have registered millions of young voters through voter drives on campuses, at concerts, and online. And with the star power these groups are packing, and with help from MTV, I tend to believe their numbers.

When the PIRGs at the University of California finished asking McCain the loaded global-warming question, MTV's cohost said,

"There you go, USC has spoken, Senator."[24] Actually, it was a gaggle of students who spoke, but that doesn't fit into MTV's left-wing narrative.

Manufactured questions like this were normal. When John "I ain't yo' baby daddy" Edwards spoke at his presidential dialogue, a student from the ONE campaign to end poverty asked, "Do you believe that AIDS and poverty are national security issues for the U.S.?" Right on cue, Edwards ran his fingers through his Breck Girl hair and said, "Yes."

Ron Paul was asked about the federal government's subsidizing birth control and human papillomavirus shots on campus. To his credit, Paul said that such funding is not the responsibility of taxpayers, but it goes to show the complete left-wing tilt of every question. There was not one conservative activist identified or given the microphone to ask a question. Keep in mind that there were more than four presidential forums, featuring more than five candidates.

Keeping with MTV's leftist activism, in 2007 the network partnered with the Clinton Global Initiative and the Campaign to Make Poverty History. The event was called "Giving—Live at the Apollo," and by "giving" the organizers meant redistribution of wealth in developed countries passed down to third-world spots in Africa. The forum was organized to "engage college students" on the world's most "pressing problems."

"Today's generation of young people hold more power than any generation before them to make a positive impact on the world," President Clinton said about the MTV forum.[25]

"College students are a potent force for positive social change, and we're thrilled to join with the Clinton Global Initiative to stimulate even greater civic participation on campus and worldwide," said Christina Norman, president of MTV.

So, what are these "pressing problems" youth care about? To elaborate at the Apollo event, Sway "finds" a recent graduate in the audience to interview live. It's Erica Williams, that employee for Campus Progress, which is the "youth" arm of the left-wing Center for American Progress. Thousands of people there and Sway just "happens" to stumble across a leftist activist. What are the odds? To Erica's credit, she embraces her employer, saying how Campus Progress "empowers young people" to get involved in the issues that they care about, "like about global warming, and Iraq, and academic affordability."²⁶ You see how this cycle works, don't you? Young people are bombarded with leftist propaganda from an array of celebrities, organized agitators in Washington, D.C., college professors, and networks including MTV, and then all these groups have the audacity to say that the liberal line is what young people care about. Funny how that works. Plant the propaganda seeds, water them constantly, weed out opposing views.

The always impartial Sway finishes with Erica by saying, "you're motivating me." Nowhere is Erica identified with a partisan, left-wing group. Only if you knew what Campus Progress does would you be able to identify the bias. But MTV gives her a platform as though she's a mainstream voice looking out for young people.

Norman, the former president of MTV, probably has no problem with such blatant bias. After all, she did contribute $4,600 to Obama's presidential run and $28,000 to the Democratic National Committee Service Corporation in 2007 and 2008 alone.²⁷

Norman is neck deep in liberalism, so duh, she's going to use her stature at perhaps the most important network dedicated to young people to shovel Obama's talking points on us all. The "potent force for positive social change" is nothing more than what the Democratic National Committee is planting in her ear. (Notice how the social change and the elimination of poverty are *always* via the hand of government bureaucrats, never through the power of the tried-and-true force of capitalism.)

So when MTV decided to highlight veterans of the Iraq and Afghanistan wars, it's no surprise it found those who suffered injuries. In July 2008, MTV put together a reality TV documentary called *Homecoming,* an hour-long special about veterans, hosted by Kanye West and Sway Calloway. Now, to other "nonpartisan" organizations, allowing Kanye "George Bush hates black people" West to be the center of attention may not jibe well with the nonpartisan moniker. But such rancorous partisan fools are exactly the type of persons MTV partners with.

As the *New York Times* reported, the premise of the show was Kanye and Sway's surprising a veteran named Lorenzo Zarate, who had returned from his deployment in Iraq. The MTV hosts come bearing gifts, giving Zarate six months' rent and setting him up with an internship at a local radio station. That's honorable of MTV. But that's not the documentary's angle. "Once the surprise subsides and the two men settle down in the living room, the talk turns to 'before I went' and 'when I got back.' " You see, Zarate suffers from severe post-traumatic stress disorder. And there's the angle. As the *Times* notes, *Homecoming* was part of MTV's 2008 election coverage to spotlight a "few of the roughly 1.6 million Americans who have served in Afghanistan and Iraq." In the documentary, Zarate tells Sway and Kanye of his battles with adjusting back to life in Austin, Texas.

"The Army could teach you to kill, kill, kill, but they can't teach you to come back home and be a civilian," he recounts. Zarate even tried to attain a college degree but was relegated to the back of the class because he "had to be fully aware of his surroundings."

"I couldn't have anyone behind me. I was always alert." Zarate's level of trauma was acute enough that his doctor advised him not to work, a problematic diagnosis since his wife was pregnant and they were behind on mortgage payments.[28]

Tirann Laws of Oklahoma City is also featured in *Homecoming*. His symptoms also prevented him from holding down a steady job. The third veteran interviewed, Shameeka Gray of Charlotte, North Carolina, was in the same boat as the other two individuals.

Dave Sirulnick, an executive vice president at MTV, told the *Times* that *Homecoming* doesn't exaggerate the difficulties facing GIs. "These stories are emblematic of a lot of veterans, certainly not all veterans, but a lot."

Sirulnick observed that "over the last three years we [MTV] have found—this is not scientific—but we have found that well over 70 percent of the veterans we speak to have had some sort of" post-traumatic stress disorder. In reality, the number isn't nearly as high, and most servicemen returning home do not have those symptoms. Would it have killed MTV to highlight veterans who are proud of their time in Iraq? Explaining the valuable leadership skills they gained? How about the heroism? Yes, war is hell. And that must never be diminished or overlooked; lives are, tragically, lost and disrupted. But to focus on just the negative is the ultimate antiwar propaganda machine. It discourages rather than cultivates interest in joining the United States military. Moreover, such documentaries foster antiwar sentiments.

Is it any surprise, then, that the Iraq War was the second most important issue for voters 18–29 surveyed on Election Day?[29] Young people are thinking nearly 70 percent of veterans are coming home maimed and psychologically scrambled.

But it wasn't just biased forums and documentaries that MTV was promoting. As part of MTV's "Choose or Lose" election coverage, the "Street Team '08" covered the 2008 election supposedly from a "youth perspective." An MTV press release even boasted that some of the reporters were children of "once-illegal immigrants." Just an FYI, execs at MTV: most people don't boast about such things. According to the *Boston Globe*, MTV's Street Team '08 went through an "intensive three-day orientation" where they received "lessons on ethics and journalism" and "maintaining objectivity."[30]

So get this: To maintain objectivity and fulfill ethics in journalism, one of MTV's "reporters" was Jane Fleming Kleeb, who, as I noted earlier, is an outward lib. But don't take my word for it. Jane describes herself as "the Executive Director of the Young Voter PAC which helps Democratic candidates and State Parties win with the 18–35 year-old vote through endorsements, on-the-ground support, training, strategy and money."[31] As I also pointed out, Jane's husband, Scott, was the Democrat Senate nominee.

Jaime McLeod, the Vermont "reporter," is a gay rights activist who, in her MTV profile, gives props to Kobutsu Malone, a rabidly anticapitalist, anti–death penalty, and antiwar Buddhist priest.

Minnesota "reporter" Carissa Jackson covered the Republican convention by highlighting leftist protest groups. Because that's objective and all. This is how Carissa titles her article: "Students Saying No to War, Yes to Schools."[32] Yep. As balanced as a teeter-totter with Michael Moore on one side. Carissa profiles a bunch of nitwits on the steps of the Minnesota State Capitol who were part of the group Youth Against War and Racism. Participants apparently staged a "theatrical arrest of 'Dick Cheney' and 'Big Oil Bob,' whom the group considers to be" war criminals.

Other reports featured the "Rise of the Christian Left."[33] The Philadelphia correspondent, Cassidy Hartmann, profiled women to dismiss the selection of Sarah Palin as nothing more than "pandering" to women and evangelicals. One Zombie called her a "token," while others on the video report decried the pick as "demeaning" and insulting.[34]

MTV IS SERIOUS about bringing young people to the polls.

"Now is the time to have your voice heard," Gideon Yago told the presidential forum audience. "Let's put to rest the notion that young people don't show up to the polls."

Granted, MTV's forums aren't as bad as Cameron Diaz saying "If you think rape should be legal, then don't vote," or Diddy's "Vote or Die Campaign." (Hyperbole, anyone?) Still, MTV may be more lethal, because it cloaks itself in the appearance of objectivity. MTV's decidedly pro-left-wing stance on every political issue acts as a constant electoral battering ram against young people.

9

The Dynamic Duo: Jon Stewart and Stephen Colbert

Why Mediated Morons Matter

Jon Stewart

It was a special homecoming weekend for Northeastern University. More than five thousand students packed the Matthews Arena on the Boston campus to hear the feature speaker in what one school official labeled the "single best event" in his time on campus. From a Zombie perspective, he was right. The event featured the left's best spokesman, and it was on the eve of the November election, on October 17, 2008. A perfect forum to juice up support for the One. The speaker wasn't Obama, Bill Clinton, or Oprah. No, it was Jon Leibowitz, more commonly known by his stage name, Jon Stewart, of Comedy Central's *The Daily Show*.

Stewart stormed the Northeastern stage to a rock-star welcome as thousands of Zombies cheered liberalism's patron saint.

Then the conservative bash-fest began. Sarah Palin? "She said that small towns she really likes going to because that's the pro-America part of the country. You know, I just want to say to her, just very quickly: Fuck you."[1]

Actually, what Palin had said on the campaign trail was "We believe that the best of America is not all in Washington, D.C. We believe . . . that the best of America is in these small towns that we get to visit, and in these wonderful little pockets of what I call the real America, being here with all of you hardworking very patriotic, very pro-America areas of this great nation."

Stewart continued: "You know, NYC was good enough for fucking Osama bin Laden, it better be good enough for you. That's what I think."

"I can't take it anymore . . . after eight years of this divisiveness, we're back to this idea that only small-town America is the real America." Stewart groused that Palin was writing off "entire swaths of the country," saying that "cities are just a lot of towns piled on top of each other in one building." Meanwhile, Stewart took direct aim at the selection of Palin: "McCain made an interesting vice presidential choice. I like the woods . . . I just don't know if I would pull my vice president out of the woods randomly." Sounds a little like Stewart was doing his own version of "writing off a swath of the country."

The nearly hour-long "comedy" routine was little more than a liberal screed of talking points. Stewart "joked" about Palin's criticisms of Obama's cozy relationship with bomb-thrower Bill Ayers and even Obama's position on abortion. "I've never seen someone with a greater disparity between how cute they sound when they're saying something and how terrible what they're saying is," Stewart said while doing goofy impressions of the Alaska governor. "Don'tcha know, Obama, by golly, he just a terrorist? . . . Oh, you know, he just, gosh, kills babies, you know."

No one deemed Stewart's "cute" comment as sexist.

Speaking about McCain, Stewart said that he had "never seen a dude just wander off in the middle of the debate,"[2] looking for "Mr. Puddles," ascribing dementia to the Arizona senator. "I got sausages," the McCain impression went. Stewart, again in the faux comedy tone, painted McCain as irrational during the debates, flailing his arms around in disgust, pouting, throwing temper tantrums. "He looks like he's ready to fucking kill somebody," said Stewart. "Lasers are gonna come out of his eyes." But Obama? Well, he was calm, collected, and cool—going through his "plan," his "six-point plan," Stewart told the five-thousand-plus crowd.

And there you have the left's secret weapon, folks: a forty-something self-loathing New Yorker is liberalism's greatest spokesman today. Young people are drawn to Jon Stewart's nightly dose of zany facial expressions, liberal drivel, and F-bomb-laced commentary. Believe it or not, his program is where many young people get their daily news of what's going on in the real world. Sad? Yes. Surprising? Hardly. As we have seen throughout this book, Zombies don't think, they feel.

But it's all just comedy, right? We shouldn't take Jon "little man" Stewart seriously. I mean, he doesn't even take himself seriously. That's certainly the skirt he hides behind when his partisanship is called into question. This is hardly surprising given that Stewart's television program takes cues from the partisan, leftist smear group Media Matters.[3] But Stewart is often mean and downright nasty. Sarah Palin is not just politically flawed, in his estimation. Nope. According to Stewart, former governor Palin is comparable to the devastation in Germany that led to Hitler's rise to power. "Have you noticed how [Palin's] rallies have begun to take on the characteristics of the last days of the Weimar Republic?" he said to a crowd at the stuffy Waldorf-Astoria. " 'Who is Barack Obama?' Hey, lady, we just met you five fucking weeks ago."[4]

Or how about when the self-righteous "comedian" called the late conservative columnist Robert D. Novak a "115-year-old vampire demon," a "terrible person," and an "enemy of American democracy"?[5] During the Republican convention in Minnesota, Comedy Central paid for a billboard near the main airport that came from *The Daily Show*. It read, "Welcome, Rich White Oligarchs!"[6]

Stewart has compared Fox News to Al Jazeera[7] and relentlessly attacked the Bush administration, gloating that he looked forward to January 21, 2008, "as a comedian, as a person, as a citizen, as a mammal."[8] Serving up an inquisition for every conservative guest on his show (while giving liberals a free pass), Jon Stewart has thrust himself into the position of the Pied Piper of liberalism. And for that, he is crowned in glory by fellow nancy boys in the mainstream media.

In discussing Stewart as among *Time* magazine's hundred most influential people, Tom Brokaw may have engaged in the mother of all sycophantic, orgasmic fits of fawning, calling him America's "Athenian, a voice for democratic ideals and the noble place of citizenship, helped along by the sound of laughter."[9] Remember now, Stewart has a show . . . on Comedy Central, for Pete's sake. But in the mind of Brokaw, he's apparently our Greek god and protector of the planet.

Matt Lauer, an official Obama lapdog for NBC, referred to Stewart as "one of the most respected and listened to political voices in this country."

The *New York Times* absurdly called Stewart "the most trusted man in America." And in the profile on him, we know why he was graced with that title. As the *Times* reporter stated, "Mr. Stewart's comedic gifts—his high-frequency radar for hypocrisy, his talent for excavating narratives from mountains of information, his ability . . . 'to name things that don't seem to have a name'—proved to be perfect tools for explicating and parsing the foibles of an administration known for its secrecy, ideological certainty and impatience with dissenting viewpoints."[10] And even though the *Times* was admitting that Stewart got off on flaming the Bush administration night after night, it somehow had the audacity to claim that *The Daily Show* "is animated not by partisanship but by a deep mistrust of all ideology." So long as that ideology is conservatism.

Newsweek called *The Daily Show* "the coolest pit stop on television." The *Daily Variety* called it "almost impossible not to appreciate how sharply it tears down falsehoods permeating the political world," even while the paper accurately called the program "anti-Republican."[11] David Remnick, the editor of the *New Yorker* magazine, called Stewart America's "most astute—and obviously, most hilarious—press watchdog and overall political bullshit monitor. His most effective move is to cull through the tapes of all the countless banalities, hypocritical contradictions and attempted snow-jobs executed in boundless profusion on our airwaves and on political podiums. He just puts them on the air and you watch with slack-jawed amazement."[12] Stewart has also been labeled the "voice of reason in an insane world" and the "epicenter of real news."[13] In an online poll, *Time* called him America's most trusted news anchor, dwarfing Brian Williams by 15 percentage points.[14]

You read that correctly. A leftist comic delivering fake news is "the most trusted news anchor."

So just how much in the tank is Stewart for liberals? The Pew Research Center's Project for Excellence in Journalism analyzed content from *The Daily Show* for the entire 2007 year in a report titled "Journalism, Satire or Just Laughs? 'The Daily Show with

Jon Stewart,' Examined," and, surprise, surprise, found blatant bias: Republicans "were more often the targets of Stewart's humor. In the mix of on-air guests, Democrats and Republicans appeared in near equal numbers. But a more qualitative impression suggests that those Republican guests are far more likely to be challenged by the host."[15]

An example was the interview with John Bolton, former ambassador to the United Nations. It quickly became heated as Stewart attacked the Bush administration over the brouhaha involving Joe Wilson and his wife, former CIA agent Valerie Plame.

"Why the games? Why, when you go after and you out a C.I.A. agent [Valerie Plame Wilson], why not just come out and say, 'she was the person who sent Joe Wilson. He was wrong and all I did was tell newspaper reporters that fact.' Why then pretend, 'no, we didn't say that. We had nothing to do with it.' Man up and come out and say these people have to be sympathetic to the President. Why lie about it?"[16]

Another Pew example involves Stephen Hayes, who had written a favorable biography of Dick Cheney. When Hayes acknowledged that the Bush White House mishandled Iraq, Stewart responded thus:

"Then stop making the rest of us feel like idiots when we question their strategy on the war on terror and stop making—and I don't mean you, I mean them—I think that they've gone, they've seemingly gone out of their way to belittle people and he's [Cheney] actually literally come out and said if you don't elect us, we might get hit again. That to me is—I can't jibe the portrait you paint of the steadfast leader with the fearmongering, not bright guy that I've seen."[17]

You see what I mean about carrying water for the left, right? Pew even juxtaposes his interviews with conservatives to his interviews with leftists. One such interview was with Michael Moore, who had just released *Sicko*, a documentary that praised Cuba's health-care system.

Stewart encouraged Moore to talk more about the film but never challenged Moore's theories. As Moore turned to his getting bumped off Larry King Live because of news about Paris Hilton, the sense of camaraderie continued. "But then I thought about it and I figured," Moore reasoned sarcastically, "you know . . . you know, the priorities are in order. Paris Hilton, healthcare for all . . . you know . . ." Stewart sympathetically replied, "I think if she's ok, aren't we all ok." Moore agreed, playing on the same joke. "She is our proxy . . ." Stewart continued, "In many respects, she is the canary in our coal mine."[18]

This is Pew, no partisan outfit, mind you. After all the group's research, this conclusion is reached:

What explains these differences? Why do Republicans find themselves more a topic of ridicule than Democrats? We cannot answer that definitively here, but can suggest some possibilities. One explanation is that the show's writers and producers and Stewart himself are simply liberal, and in the course of offering their comedy are also offering their own political views. Another possibility is that the agenda is fundamentally more anti-establishment than anti-Republican.[19]

Hmmm, I'm gonna go with (a), Stewart is just a partisan hack. When he starts off his show with a monologue, it's used as his leftist bully pulpit. As Pew noted, *"The Daily Show* aims at more than comedy. In its choice of topics, its use of news footage to deconstruct the manipulations by public figures and its tendency toward pointed satire over playing just for laughs, *The Daily Show* performs a function that is close to journalistic in nature—getting people to think critically about the public square."[20] And by "think critically," they meant to say serve as a battering ram for the left. Whatever it takes is a small price to pay to churn out converted Zombies.

Granted, Stewart hasn't completely slobbered over Obama during his first year in office. Every fish makes its way out of water occasionally. Stewart has taken him to task on his failed pledges to close Gitmo and rescind "Don't Ask, Don't Tell." Those rhetorical bombs from Stewart, however, are still launched from a leftist perspective.

WISELY, STEWART DEFLECTS his leftist credentials through self-deprecation. Any time he's asked about his impact on the elections or the role he fosters in the newsrooms, there's always a self-effacing joke, or as Stewart has remarked, "When the focus of the country turns to matters you've been dealing with, for a moment you could almost believe what you do matters. Then you go back and remember, 'Oh, yea, we don't.'"[21]

This is, of course, bunk. One of the most lethal rhetorical

weapons is comedy. It's a win-win. You score points while claiming that your disgruntled opponent can't take a joke. Double points.

One of the clearest (and most memorable) examples of Stewart hiding behind "comedy" was his infamous encounter on CNN's debate show, *Crossfire*. Stewart, on tour promoting his book *America (The Book)*, sat down in the CNN studios on October 15, 2004, just before the election between George W. Bush and John Kerry. Stewart immediately jumped all over hosts Paul Begala and Tucker Carlson for "hurting America" with the style of debate their program employed. "Stop, stop, stop, stop hurting America." And they were hurting America because, in Stewart's words, they were "partisan, what do you call it, hacks." Stewart lectured the guys on what honest debate looks like, and how they needed to stop "spinning" for their candidates of choice. Stewart asked childishly absurd questions such as "why do we have to fight?" and "why do you argue?" Begala, a fellow liberal, explained to Stewart that in a country with liberals and conservatives, their show would of course feature debate and disagreement, but Stewart would have none of it.

"I'm here to confront you; we need help from the media, and they're hurting us." Carlson compared and contrasted the questions he and Begala would ask to the questions Stewart asked Kerry. "How are you holding up? Is it hard not to take the attacks personally?" And here's where Stewart hides behind his façade of comedy while lecturing the rest of us on our moral inferiority: "I didn't realize that . . . the news organizations look to Comedy Central for their cues on integrity."

When Stewart is confronted with an alternative opinion and his credentials come into question, he reverts back to "Oh, I'm just a comedian. Hardy-har-har." "The show that leads into me is puppets making prank phone calls," he told Carlson.

In a similar vein, at the Democratic National Convention in 2008, Stewart told *USA Today*, "The whole idea that we're the beacon of integrity is ridiculous. We get far more attention from you guys [media] than we should." [22] He's also minimized his role by saying his job amounts to just "throwing spitballs." [23] In one instance, when Matt Lauer asked Stewart if the increased number of young people turning out in the presidential election was partially attributable to *The Daily Show*'s success, the pissant shrugged it off while finding room to cast more stones at John McCain. "I don't doubt that humor can bring people into a system. I also think it helps to have some candidates, you know, who are not necessarily Matlockian," alluding to a television character who was well liked by older folks. [24]

But in reality, Stewart and his bevy of Ivy League writers do view their job as to entertain—at the expense of conservatives. And Stewart himself becomes wildly unfunny, as he did on the set of *Crossfire*, when he either is confronted with tough questions (he becomes defensive) or lectures the media on their journalistic role. At the end of his *Crossfire* appearance, Carlson was rightfully fed up with a moralizing speech from a guy who, in Tucker's words, sniffs the throne of liberals. "I do think you're more fun on your show. Just my opinion," said Carlson. The little funny man's response? "You know what's interesting, though? You're as big a dick on your show as you are on any show," replied Stewart.

And thus the veil is lifted. The partisan hackery belongs to Stewart. But even as he writes himself off as not having influence or being beneath political influence, it's really a ploy to gain even more adulation and influence with the media elites and adoring leftist audiences who will cheer and applaud like circus animals, laughing slavishly at whatever comes out of Stewart's self-loathing mouth.

At the Democrat convention in Denver in 2008, Stewart hosted a breakfast with political writers from the *New York Times, Wall Street Journal*, Associated Press, and other news outlets. He blasted Fox News's "fair and balanced" slogan as an insult "to people with brains," claiming that if it weren't for *Fox News Sunday* host Chris Wallace, the network would even find a way to frame news that Obama cured cancer as an "economic disaster."[25]

"I'm stunned to see Karl Rove on a news network as an analyst." Well, Jon, what about the hundreds of other "analysts" who are clearly Democrats but grace CNN, MSNBC, and yes, even Fox News? Or better yet, James Carville, who was instrumental in Bill Clinton's election victories? Nope, not the same, says Jon. "I don't think [Carville's] being passed off as a sage,"[26] reported the *Washington Post*'s Howard Kurtz. Stewart scolded the gaggle of reporters to "earn your authority back"[27] and discontinue the off-the-record dinners with politicians. "That colors your vision of them so clearly and so profoundly." When challenged on this point with the argument that getting to know candidates is important, even if in a background setting, Jon responded, "I don't say access is useless. But the more you get sucked into it, the more you become part of that machinery."[28]

For all the talk that Stewart is just a funnyman, he gets pretty darn serious about Fox News and other intricacies of media coverage. It's a typical Zombie multiplier, as is the case every time you attack Fox News: it's street cred among the liberal cognoscenti, even as his Zombie-packed audience is too stupid to realize the schizophrenia of his positions.

Is he funny? Sure, I'll give him that. Even though conservatives bear the brunt of his jokes, I do find Stewart smart and sometimes entertaining. Conservatives are generally slow on what's in with pop culture, and that has to do with the fact that we're more interested in ideas than iconography. Britney Spears and Paris Hilton ain't exactly our "peeps." Plus, personal responsibility isn't exactly chic these days. But Stewart's tiresome years of unrequited cheap shots tailored to the under-thirty crowd are paying off. He is a pop cultural icon, much like this president. It is cool to support him; that's the fad. But make no mistake about it: Stewart is a dedicated liberal foot soldier (that is, if liberals actually became "soldiers").

On the decidedly left-wing website Daily Kos, one writer, under the headline "The debt we owe Jon Stewart," credited Stewart with Obama's lead in the polls.

> There are a lot of reasons why Obama is ahead in the polls, and why we can be cautiously optimistic about the outcome of this election. One of these reasons is the work of Jon Stewart and his *Daily Show* for the past nine years. Despite the fact that the *Daily Show* is on cable, and thus doesn't have the ratings of more mainstream political shows, it has had a fundamental impact on how many voters, particularly young voters who have come of age during its lifetime, view politics and political discourse.[29]

The piece proclaimed, "Jon Stewart has been the best weapon our country has had against the last eight years of fearmongering, wedge issues, and cultural wars. If the Democrats take the White House this year, we all owe a debt of gratitude to him for his unflinching search for truth."[30]

You can't get any more left-wing than Daily Kos. And it doesn't get any more revealing, either. Liberals see Stewart as their antidote to Fox News, as their counterpart to Sean Hannity, Glenn Beck, Bill O'Reilly, and the king of talk radio, Rush Limbaugh.

• • •

TUCKER CARLSON CALLED Stewart a "butt boy" for his soft interviews with John Kerry. His interviews with Obama show Stewart essentially giving Obama a thorough colonoscopy and enjoying it, to boot.

Just before the 2008 election, on October 29, Obama was a guest on the show via satellite in Florida. The cheers and applauses for Obama were so obvious that even Stewart acknowledged to Obama that "clearly our show is not a swing show, if you will." The questions were anything but tough, anything but inquisitive, anything resembling thought-provoking, and remember, this is the same Stewart who likes lecturing the media on integrity and Fox News for being a lapdog for the Republican Party.

The first question from Stewart: "How are you holding up? How are things going?"[31]

Whoa! Take that, Barack!

This happened to be the same night Obama ran his infamous thirty-minute infomercial, which had Stewart asking another powerhouse question, Greek-god style, this time about the infomercial. "Will it annoy us, or will we like it?" "Or will we feel comforted?"

Awww. "Will it comfort us?"

Still, Stewart managed to muster the tough questions: "So much of this [election] has been about fear of you: an elitist; a celebrity; a Muslim, terrorist sympathizer; a socialist; a Marxist; a witch . . . the whole socialism and Marxism thing, if you do win, is that a mandate for socialism in this country? . . . Has any of this fear stuff . . . do you think it has stuck with the electorate? Are you finding that on the trail?"

Stewart was there to offer Obama a venue and to assist him in batting down what they consider falsehoods. Obama's response:

I think there's a certain segment of certain hard-core Sean Hannity fans that probably wouldn't want to go have a beer with me [audience laughter]. But for the average voter, they're saying to themselves, "What's all this stuff about? I'm trying to figure out whether I can hang on to my house or who's gonna help me get a job. What about my health care? My premiums have doubled over the last couple of years." So I don't think they are paying too much attention to this stuff. And the whole socialism argument, that doesn't fly too well. The evidence of this seems pretty thin. I said today, they found proof that when I was in kindergarten that I shared some toys with my friends and that was clearly a sign of subversive activity. Now, Jon, I will say that being on your program is further evidence of these tendencies.

Stewart laughed on cue.

Stewart closed the segment with this cringe-worthy question, knowing full well that Obama was going to take it and turn it to a campaign stump speech: "Is there a sense that you have, you know, two years ago when you began this journey the country was not necessarily in the shape it's in now. Is there a sense that you don't want this?"

Obama:

I actually think this is the time you want to be president. If you went into public service thinking that you can have an impact now is the time you can have an impact. We tend to be a pretty conservative country. I don't mean conservative politically per se, but conservative in the sense, you know, that things are kind of going along pretty well and we don't want to mess with it too much. And then every once in a while you have these big challenges and big problems and it gives an opportunity for us to really move in a new direction. I think this is one of those moments, on things like energy and health care and the economy and education. I think people recognize that what we've been doing isn't working and that means people are going to be more open to change.[32]

Nice coordination, guys!

Prior interviews with Barack offered the same bro-mance ambience, including this probing one back in 2007: "There's a certain inspirational quality to you. Is that really something America is gonna go for?"[33] Or this affirmation: "Here's to staying above the fray, and not having the red-blue divide anymore." Ha! How's that working out for you now, Jon? Obama has been the most politically divisive president in recent memory, but that matters not. It's feeling over fact, faith over hope for the Zombie. Really, entire chapters could be dedicated to Stewart's bro-mantic relationship to Obama during interviews.

Compare and contrast those man-crush sessions to any one of the interviews Stewart conducted with McCain. It was a grilling. It wasn't a lovefest. Stewart was playing liberal inquisitor, especially over the Iraq War.[34] While duking it out with McCain over Iraq, Stewart defended Senator Harry Reid's proclamation that the war was lost (just before the famous and successful surge kicked into high gear).

"In fairness to Senator Reid," said Stewart, ". . . I think what he was saying . . . that militarily . . . you can't win it militarily. I think he said it clumsily but what he said was, it is a political solution not a military solution."

McCain gave his normal line about winning, and not surrendering to the enemy. But what's striking is how Stewart was feeding liberal line after liberal line back to McCain's stance on Iraq.

"Shouldn't we get away from the language of win or lose in Iraq and get more to a descriptive success; metrics; deadlines if you will; timetables [laughter, applause, from the circus animals]."

McCain said sure, if you want to set a timetable for surrender. Stewart called that assertion "unfair" and added: "Isn't the president saying I don't want to set timetables, but our patience is not unlimited, so what he's saying is we're not going to pull our troops out between now and the end of time." How can you say we need a deadline, "but I don't want to pin it down because that's surrender?" Stewart concluded.

Think to yourself, what's funny about this exchange? Stewart likes to pawn off his program as just comedy and throwing spitballs, but where's the punch line? If this brother is not on the DNC's payroll, he's getting gypped!

Stewart to McCain: "Supporting the troops: They say that asking for a timetable or criticizing the president is not supporting the troops. Explain to me why that is supporting the troops less than extending their tours of duty from twelve months to fifteen months, putting them in stop-loss, and not having Walter Reed be up to snuff. How can the president justify that? How can he have the balls to justify that?" [35]

McCain is booed by Stewart's audience after he says the men and women in Iraq are fighting for a worthwhile cause; they're fighting for freedom, and they're proud to be there.

Stewart: "The majority of [military] guys I talk to say that the political scene is not my scene. I'm a soldier." (As though McCain doesn't know what soldiers think, and recall the deafening silence from the left at the time when Obama's plan to escalate troop levels in Afghanistan was identical to the rhetoric of President Bush.)

Stewart adds this gem: "You cannot look a soldier in the eye and say questioning the president is less supportive to you than extending your tour for three months; you should be coming home with your family. And that's not fair to put on people that criticize.

"This is not about questioning the troops and their ability to fight and their ability to be supported. That is what the administration does, and that is almost criminal."[36]

And this is just part of one interview with John McCain, as Stewart has gone toe-to-toe in plenty of others. He goes after conservatives, and did so constantly during the 2008 election. After the election, the *New York Times* asked J. R. Havlan, a writer for *The Daily Show*, if Obama's victory was a "mixed blessing," to which Havlan said, "It's probably no secret where our politics lie."[37] Clearly it's not a secret, J.R., and that's the point. Little people of the world, unite!

Stephen Colbert

In 2006, the Republicans in Congress took a beating. They lost both the Senate and the House. The result didn't seem that surprising, given an unpopular war waged by an unpopular president, and with a Republican majority that acted like Democrats and spent tax dollars as though they were Monopoly bucks. But was there more to this drubbing? And by more, did Jon Stewart's partner in crime, Stephen Colbert, have anything to do with the Republican implosion at the polls? Why am I even mentioning Stephen Colbert in a discussion about the election and defeat of candidates? We'll call it the "truthiness" factor, the famous term coined by Colbert to reflect making up facts and relying on feeling to reach conclusions . . . rather than reaching conclusions based on facts and analysis. But Stephen Colbert actually may have influenced the election, and liberals praise him for it. After the 2006 election, the liberal *New York Times* columnist Frank Rich wrote about his "favorite moment from the fabulous midterms of 2006,"[38] and that was Colbert's now-infamous gig at the White House Correspondents Dinner. Colbert began:

Wow! Wow, what an honor! The White House Correspondents Dinner. To actually—to sit here at the same table with my hero, George W. Bush, to be this close to the man. I feel like I'm dreaming. Somebody pinch me. You know what? I'm a pretty sound sleeper; that may not be enough. Somebody shoot me in the face. Is he really not here tonight? Damn it! The one guy who could have helped.

Colbert, in his buffoonish way, playing an idiot, continued:

. . . it is my privilege to celebrate this president, 'cause we're not so different, he and I. We both get it. Guys like us, we're not some brainiacs on the nerd patrol. We're not members of the factinista. We go straight from the gut. Right, sir? [to President Bush] That's where the truth lies, right down here in the gut. Do you know you have more nerve endings in your gut than you have in your head? You can look it up. Now, I know some of you are going to say, "I did look it up, and that's not true." That's 'cause you looked it up in a book. Next time, look it up in your gut. I did. My gut tells me that's how our nervous system works.

Every night on my show, *The Colbert Report*, I speak

straight from the gut, okay? I give people the truth, un-filtered by rational argument. I call it the "No Fact Zone." Fox News, I hold a copyright on that term.[39]

Is he funny? Yes. I think he's more funny than Stewart. But the two are cut from the same leftist cloth. His faux reality is one jab at conservatives after another. It has made Colbert heroic to the left. His "comedy" to liberals is a takedown of conservatives. There weren't too many laughs at the White House Correspondents Dinner. Many of the attendees thought the jokes were too over-the-top and highly disrespectful. But with the speech live on C-SPAN, it quickly went viral and became a rallying cry for liberals nationwide. Liberal bloggers dubbed the routine as the "turning point in revealing that the emperors of the media often wear no clothes." Or as *Vanity Fair* put it, "the speech turned Colbert into a kind of folk hero for the left."[40]

And you know what? It's true. Colbert's salvos wrapped up in "comedy" included "I believe the government that governs best is the government that governs least. And by these standards, we have set up a fabulous government in Iraq." On President Bush's low approval rating, Colbert said, "Guys like us, we don't pay attention to the polls. We know that polls are just a collection of statistics that reflect what people are thinking in 'reality.' And reality has a well-known liberal bias."

President Bush was obviously uncomfortable. And liberals were beside themselves. How couldn't they be with lines like this: "I stand by this man. I stand by this man, because he stands for things. Not only for things, he stands on things, things like aircraft carriers and rubble and recently flooded city squares. And that sends a strong message, that no matter what happens to America, she will always rebound with the most powerfully staged photo-ops in the world."

In 2005, Colbert spun off from *The Daily Show*. He played virtually the same character, but served mostly as one of Stewart's fake correspondents. Colbert's role is the "blindly egomaniacal, Bill O'Reilly–esque talk-show host," as *Vanity Fair* described it.[41] His role was to embody what he called conservatives who "know with their heart," but don't "think with their head"—the oh-so-famous "truthiness." Liberal writer Steven Daly of the *Sunday Telegraph* in London praised Colbert as the "titular host [who] offers a fun-house-mirror reflection of the bellicose Right-wing opinionizers of Rupert Murdoch's Fox News" who dominate political discourse with "lengthy and obnoxious opinion-slots that are somehow passed off as 'news.'"[42]

Colbert's lines may be funny, but the message is calculated to eviscerate conservatives. At the correspondents' dinner, he continued his shtick, painting conservatives as a bunch of baboons:

I'm sorry, I've never been a fan of books. I don't trust them. They're all fact, no heart. I mean, they're elitist, telling us what is or isn't true or what did or didn't happen. Who's *Britannica* to tell me the Panama Canal was built in 1914? If I want to say it was built in 1941, that's my right as an American! I'm with the president. Let history decide what did or did not happen.

And there's the Fox-bashing, of course. He is a fake Fox correspondent, after all! "Fox News gives you both sides of every story: the president's side, and the vice president's side." But it's not contempt for Washington per se that drives Colbert, it's contempt for conservatives. His whole persona is to mock conservatives. It's to make conservatism so unpalatable that no one from his audience, TV or rival, would back a Republican. The left realizes this. In an article for the *Huffington Post* called "Obama owes presidency to . . . Stephen Colbert," Greg Mitchell, editor of *Editor & Publisher*, opined on how the "faux rightwing blowhard" has "filtered into our political/media consciousness."[43]

Colbert rarely gets out of character. In fact, he spends nearly his entire day in it, by his own admission, and he looks forward to driving home and listening to his playlist, so that he can be normal again (conservatism to him is abnormal) when he gets to his wife and kids.[44] Colbert is a sitcom taken seriously. But there are rare glimpses into what motivates Colbert.

Most revealing was an interview he had with Daly of the *Sunday Telegraph* in May 2008.[45] The interview occurred in Colbert's Manhattan office, and since Daly is a fellow lib, Colbert let his hair down. Daly, like most on the left, affirmed the character of Colbert as the pretend "Fox News Bill O'Reilly" who "takes great pride in shouting down unpatriotic," or as Daly wrote, "dissenting" guests and "occasionally having their microphones switched off midsentence."[46]

Explaining the inspiration, Colbert noted: "At the heart of this is America as the chosen country of God. It's conflation of the Statue of Liberty and the crucifix: American religiosity and American destiny are one and the same. That's why George Bush was chosen by God to lead the world. Manifest destiny is an old idea, but now it's just expressed in different ways."

Continuing his rare expression out of character, Colbert said,

> The odd thing about the triumphalism of the character is that it works best in an atmosphere of victimhood. These characters [aka conservatives] say people have personal responsibility and they attack people for playing victims. But an ongoing theme with the Christian Right in the

U.S. is the "War Against Christmas." That somehow there are sinister forces—read Jews, Muslims, lesbians—that wish to destroy Christmas. It ignores the fact that Christianity is more dominant with our culture than in any other Western society. In a way, they're very much in line with language an Islamic fascist might use, talking about the decadence of the West.

Not so funny, eh? Colbert is earning his leftist street cred with statements like that. It's a peek into the worldview that drives the character that is Stephen Colbert. Like Stewart, Colbert offers an apologia for liberalism. He attempts to bat down conservative arguments. Colbert is giving us a line that we hear from liberal outlets such as the Daily Kos and MoveOn.org.

Daly noted that the day the interview took place was also the day when Susan Jacoby, author of *The Age of American Unreason*, was booked on the show. Jacoby, a liberal, offers a blistering critique of "the same pathology that Colbert embodies," wrote Daly. That pathology the liberal author defined as "bullet-headed, patriotic incuriosity."

"Knowing things that other people don't know is the definition of elitist," Colbert said in character while interviewing Jacoby. Before the cameras were rolling, Colbert told Daly that his "conservative" persona has more trust in "the invisible hand of the free market" than in "knowledge" and "facts." "The market will take care of poverty. I call it dribble-down economics," he said mockingly. "The rich eat everything—and don't get me wrong, I'm rich—and some of it crusts on their beard, and the poor are allowed to feed on their beard. You can't say they're not being provided for—that's class warfare."

Much of his material is funny. Conservatives aren't humorless, as the false cliché goes. But we understand, and we've seen the effects, of the man who will address a Hollywood audience as "godless sodomites." We understand his worldview. And, more importantly, so does Colbert. Speaking of his "mentor" Bill O'Reilly, Colbert says, "I have a genuine admiration for O'Reilly's ability to do his show. I'd love to be able to put a chain of words together the way he does without much thought as to what it might mean, compared to what you said about the same subject the night before."[47] By turning conservative ideas into satire and jokes, he and his merry band of eighty-six staffers[48] have helped lobotomize a generation of Zombies who have written off the successful ideas of limited government and free markets. Colbert even warns his guests that "he's willfully ignorant of everything we're going to talk about."[49]

YOUNG PEOPLE ARE increasingly getting their news from Colbert and Stewart.[50] A poll released by Rasmussen Reports found that 30 percent of those ages 18–29 say that both *The Daily Show* and *The Colbert Report* are replacing more traditional news outlets;[51] 35 percent disagree and another 35 percent are undecided.[52] Amazing! Nearly a third view the dynamic throne sniffers as legitimate news outlets, and another third are not sure what to think? America, your future is not looking good.

Many young people even boast of their fondness for news delivery via liberal comedians. Jen Jablow, an anthropology major at the University of Pennsylvania, said during the campaign that "I think of watching network newscasts as something my parents do. I can't imagine my friends sitting down to watch an actual network newscast at 6:30 because we're doing other things at that time. It's a lot quicker to go online. I customize my news." Like many her age, Jablow is hooked on Comedy Central's fake news shows.[53]

I'm certainly not saying they should go back to the Brian Williamses and Katie Courics. No! Lord, have mercy! Quite the opposite. The cultural shift is obvious, a shift that Obama picked up on. But replacing any type of traditional news source with acerbic comedians is crazy. Young people would rather laugh than think, feel than analyze. Humor is a feeling, so it plays right into the left's best weapon: emotion. It's the liberal disease: Give me free goods and services! Have those damned "rich" people pay for them! I'm entitled! Me, my, me, my! The left has gone from trusting Dan Rather and Brian Williams to following the likes of Jon Stewart and Stephen Colbert. Ideologues masquerading as "fake journalists." Of course, a generation raised on *The Simpsons* and *South Park* has a tendency to abandon a network evening format that hasn't changed in decades.

Stewart is cool! Colbert is cool! Obama is cool! See the narrative? Heck, back in 2006 *Rolling Stone*'s cover story declared Stewart and Colbert "America's Anchors!" Matthew Kolasa, a University of Pennsylvania student, admitted that he learned a lot by watching *The Daily Show*. It's not just for laughs. "Within his political satire, Stewart makes really interesting points. He can make an argument with such smartness and wit. I think the U.S. senators could take a lesson from him."[54]

Taking on the image of an egomaniacal character comes easily to Colbert. His dark personal life, with the tragic deaths of his father and two brothers when he was a child, left him emotionally scarred, toying with his identity, even the identity of his last name. It was always pronounced Colbert, not Col*bear*. As a kid, he immersed himself in a fantasy world of role-playing games, science fiction novels, and Dungeons & Dragons. Colbert was a wandering actor, a wannabe poet, and a standup comic. He's devoted his life to playing someone else.[55] It's an exercise in self-hatred. Hopefully Colbert finds *his* voice, not somebody else's.

There you have it—two men angry at life, masking their anger and sorrows in comedy; they are unpaid volunteers for liberalism, and cronies for Barack Obama.

Conclusion

A Six-Point Battle Plan for Awakening Obama Zombies from
Their Brainless Slumber

Okay, so we've identified the chicanery of Barack Obama and his Zombie-inducing surrogates. We've blown past the rhetoric versus the reality. We've demonstrated that Obama is not the second coming of Jesus Christ. We've seen a president who distrusts his country, genuflects to dictators around the world, and takes massive dumps on the idea of American exceptionalism. Meanwhile, as we've also seen, the journalists covering him are more interested in being on the Messiah's good side and helping him govern than in holding him accountable.

So now I'm going to give you a few quick tools for deprogramming Obama Zombies and waking them from their slumber. Engagement is the key. John "Grandpa" McCain was an awful candidate with an even more awful youth outreach program. The GOP is in big trouble if they don't have steadfast engagement. The numbers aren't looking good. The GOP is getting older,[1] and younger voters are aligning with liberal candidates. Republicans are increasing in age, Democrats decreasing.

Now granted, much of the mania has to do with the Cult of Obama and the fact that today young people become liberal through osmosis—they just don't hear conservative ideas argued in academia, Hollywood, and most of the media.

Yep, so there's a problem.

Yet there are glimmers of hope. With all the heavy doses of liberal nonsense they are exposed to on a daily basis, young people still break only as 31 percent liberal, 30 percent conservative.[2] Heck, I'll take 30 percent right now. We can easily build on it. ObamaMania is showing signs of cracking. As the reliably liberal Associated Press even noted, since the election the Obama "fervor has died down—noticeably." "While young people remain the president's most loyal supporters in opinion polls, a lot of people are wondering why that age group isn't doing more to build upon their newfound reputation as political influencers."[3]

The "dorm storming" people for Obama on campus have stopped; the dancing in the streets is over; the bouncing Obama girls on YouTube have faded. The sizzle has fizzled. And that's why conservatives need to wake up and take action.

The youth vote is vital. "Millennials," or whatever we are called this week by political scientists, could possibly make up the single largest voting bloc in the future, so conservatives need to get with the program; we need to shake, rattle, and roll Obama Zombies and get them to do what their liberal lobotomies have prevented them from doing—*thinking*!

Here's a six-part battle plan for how we can do it:

1. Back to the Basics

It can't be stressed enough: John McCain was an atrocious presidential candidate. Gramps was uninspiring, inarticulate, and uncharismatic, and he looked like death. To some ignoramuses in Washington and New York, however, McCain's loss is a sign to give up conservative ideas, to buck conservative principles, and to appeal to so-called moderates.

That's the wrong direction. We need an unapologetic espousal of the core principles of conservatism: limited government, a strong military, traditional values, and personal responsibility. John McCain banked his presidential aspirations on "reaching across the aisle" and his supposed appeal to "independents." The problem is twofold: First, it doesn't work, or else we'd be addressing President McCain right now. And second, voters respond favorably to those candidates who passionately and persuasively present their ideas. That's why the so-called moderate bloc swings back and forth like a pendulum. It's not static.

On too many issues, McCain was never anchored in a core set of beliefs. He attained the status of "maverick" by giving his conservative base the middle finger on everything from tax cuts to "climate change" to Guantanamo Bay to campaign financing. In short, he sought liberal approbation from the media and his colleagues at the expense of conservative principles. "Bipartisanship" was his highest goal. To be clear, folks, I'm all for compromise, but I'd rather see liberals concede to our values than vice versa.

Our message is one that will resonate with younger voters. Since young people never hear conservative ideas, those ideas by definition sound fresh, rebellious, and provocative: all things that interest young and hungry minds. So let's get back to the basics. It's about time our leaders start juxtaposing the philosophies of liberalism and conservatism. They are two markedly different worldviews, one that embraces government and one that embraces liberty.

While liberals like to tout themselves as progressives, the dirty little secret is that they are far from progressive in any modern sense of the word. Their allegiance to top-down, bureaucratic management is right out of a thirteenth-century feudal system where "kings" and "lords" gave orders for how all the "peasants" would live in society. Today, just replace *king* or *lord* with *liberal,* for it is they who through legislative fiat empower Washington bureaucrats over us.

But for us, the conservatives, protecting the inalienable rights of individuals is the only reason that government exists. We are not sheep led by a governmental shepherd; rather, we are the shepherds and the government is around to ensure that some thief doesn't mess with our flock. In other words, government is there to enforce laws in order to maintain a civil and free society, not to tell us how to live our lives.

Our America is one that doesn't bail out the irresponsible, doesn't engage in the politics of greed and envy, doesn't try to socially engineer outcomes, but does respect America's role as a superpower that persistently pursues victory against her country's enemies. Our leaders must espouse policies that embody this philosophy. If not, we will continue to get more Zombies, not less. The largest ideological bloc in America is made up of those who consider themselves conservative.[4] Let's start acting like it.

Our candidates need to arouse passion and excitement. All of Obama's slogans and all of Obama's gimmicks would have been meaningless if he hadn't inspired his supporters. We need bold action, not Liberalism Lite.

2. The Job Stimulus That Wasn't

Obama's disastrous economic policies are creating a great window for conservatives to reach out to young people. Jobs are scarce. Economic opportunity is lagging. Overall youth unemployment is the worst since World War II, way above 20 percent. We will not grow up with the same prosperity our parents did; we are a generation shackled by Obama-driven spending sprees. Obama's lack of experience during the campaign was actually seen as an asset to younger voters.

"I like that he's new," gushed Neil Stewart, a freshman at the University of Colorado in Boulder. "He's new and modern and breaking with the past," said Jose Villanueva, a senior at Claremont McKenna College in California.

To Zombette Jennifer Zamarripa, a University of Denver law school student, B.H.O.'s "inexperience meant he came in with a fresh look and isn't quite as jaded by the political system as most other people are." She added, "We need some freshness in our government right now."[5]

Well, congratulations, kiddos. You and the rest of our generation are now the grand prize winners of . . . a boatload of debt!

I know the Obama Zombies aren't too fond of those math-number thingies, but even they must wake up to the fact that Obama's collectivist schemes are a torpedo aimed at the interests of Generation Y voters. Obama didn't give us change, he gave us more of the same. While B.H.O. has framed his agenda as a break from the "failed policies of the Bush administration," all the Messiah is really doing is doubling down on all of Bush's reckless borrowing, spending, and bailouts. Zombies: You do realize that Obama is killing our chances to be in a better financial position than our parents, right? Take our federal deficit and debt as an example. The Obama administration expects a ten-year budget deficit of approximately $9 trillion, which means that Obama will spend around $1 trillion more than he takes in every year![6] The national debt now stands at $12 trillion as of 2009 and will likely double to $24 trillion by 2019![7] Put that number in perspective: Kobe Bryant is paid around $25 million a year by the Los Angeles Lakers. He would have to play 960,000 seasons in order to break even with our projected national debt!

This is absolute criminal financial insanity.

Obama is on pace to pile up more debt than any other president in our nation's history *combined*.

Here's what that means for you: You, me, and every Zombie who voted for Barack will be responsible for hundreds of thousands of dollars for the Obama spending binge. There's another name for it, too: it's called generational theft, forcing us and our children to pay for Obama's "let's live it now" programs.

We send executives like Bernie Madoff to prison for running these kinds of Ponzi schemes, yet federal bureaucrats can treat our money as though it's theirs. But since these schemes are the product of the Messiah, no jail time (yet, at least).

3. Piss Off a Liberal: Get a Job, Make Money, and Be Happy

In the immortal words of Obama supporter Diddy, "It's all about the Benjamins, baby."

Make money, work hard, spur capitalism, and enjoy your life. Nothing—and I mean *nothing*—will infuriate liberals more.

Creating wealth, and the opportunities for others that capitalism fuels, is the best gift you can give your fellow man, not some lame AmeriCorps "please pay me to pretend to work while I promote lefty causes" gambit. Put another way, what I'm saying is to totally and completely ignore Michelle "I've never been proud of my country" Obama. On the campaign trail in Ohio she urged young people to stay away from evil corporate America:

> We left corporate America, which is a lot of what we're asking young people to do. Don't go into corporate America. You know, become teachers. Work for the community. Be social workers. Be a nurse. Those are the careers that we need, and we're encouraging our young people to do that. But if you make that choice, as we did, to move out of the money-making industry into the helping industry, then your salaries respond.[8]

B.H.O., for his part, echoed the same anticorporate sentiments during his address to graduates at Arizona State University. The One encouraged them not to focus on "how much money you make and how big your corner office is, whether you have a fancy enough title or a nice enough car," which, Obama put it, would "compromise your values, principles and commitments" to the larger community. Instead, the Savior of Humanity said they needed to make a "commitment instead to doing what is meaningful to you, what helps others, what makes a difference in this world." That expensive business or engineering degree you worked hard to earn? Shoot, bro, you need to toss that and trade it in for a gig working at a nonprofit community outreach center:

> Did you study business? Why not help our struggling nonprofits find better, more effective ways to serve folks in need. Nursing? Understaffed clinics and hospitals across this country are desperate for your help. Education? Teach

in a high-need school; give a chance to kids we can't afford to give up on—prepare them to compete for any job anywhere in the world. Engineering? Help us lead a green revolution, developing new sources of clean energy that will power our economy and preserve our planet.[9]

Gang, the most charitable thing you can do, the most compassionate thing you can do, is make a boatload of money and directly assist those in need. As conservative satirist P. J. O'Rourke said, "There's nothing the matter with honest moneymaking. Wealth is not a pizza, where if I have too many slices you have to eat the Domino's box. In a free society, with the rule of law and property rights, no one loses when someone else gets rich."[10] As O'Rourke notes, you'll make more of a difference by the more money created. "Don't chain yourself to a redwood tree. Instead, be a corporate lawyer and make $500,000 a year. No matter how much you cheat the IRS, you'll still end up paying $100,000 in property, sales and excise taxes. That's $100,000 to schools, sewers, roads, firefighters and police. You'll be doing good for society. Does chaining yourself to a redwood tree do society $100,000 worth of good?"[11]

Only if you're Al Gore, I suppose.

I don't say this to burst idealistic bubbles and whatnot, but all the "we can change the world" mumbo jumbo we hear on commencement day is utopian and immature. Truly. We've got to grow up. Capitalism is the most effective and compassionate system to work people out of poverty and provide real, sustainable jobs. I'd rather see a community served by some profit-driven capitalist pig who invests money in a community to open up a business for financial gain, thereby employing large swaths of people, than some smug, self-important college graduate who heads to the inner city to help the "poor" through some AmeriCorps or Peace Corps job that is so unnecessary that it has to be propped up by taxpayer dollars. Paying people to volunteer? Doesn't that sort of defeat the spirit of philanthropy? Please, spare us.

We *need* rich folks, idiots! Who the hell do you think cuts your paycheck? Do you really want a poor boss? I don't. I'd rather my paycheck not bounce so I can feed myself and, Lord willing, someday my family. As Adam Smith noted, "By pursuing his own interest [an individual] frequently promotes that of the society more effectually than when he really intends to promote it. I have never known much good done by those who affected to trade for the public good." [12]

4. Learn to Frame the Message

Message framing is key in waking up the Obama Zombie. Yes, our generation is entitled—we think we have a right to everything. But we're also individualistic in the good sense, too. We value freedom, ideas, and innovation. So leverage it in the form of smart message framing.

Obama was able to harness the power of social and new media to unleash an army of Zombies onto the public, while using machinery that was built and empowered by free markets. You see, folks, we have a built-in base with young people: they crave choice and services that big government can never supply. McCain's message was about self-sacrifice, which was, eh, okay. Most of the time, Mac had just "John McCain" signs behind him at the podium and onstage, while Barack Obama always had "Hope" and "Change" and multiple variations of "Yes, we can."

We need a message, and it should be undergirded by this: the ability to live your life without Obama's massive and sprawling interference. Liberals love to blame capitalism for economic woes, but ours is an economy that is *over*regulated, not under.

The facts: In total, the Federal Register, which keeps a running count of all the regulations and provisions that govern our lives, has topped eighty thousand pages, with sixty federal departments, commissions, and agencies at a compliance cost of over a trillion dollars, and nearly $50 billion more for the government to enforce.[13] That's some unregulated, out-of-control capitalist economy we've got going! Riiiight.

Even more disgusting, and I do really mean disgusting, Americans pay more in taxes—federal, state, local, payroll, sales, property, corporate, etc.—than they spend on food, clothing, and housing combined! And if you're not a welfare queen, all those days you spend working, well, lop off 103 of them, which is the number needed at the office just to pay your federal, state, and local taxes.[14] Holy smokes, people! For those Zombies in the workforce, a third of your freaking life is spent working to pay for some government scheme.

It doesn't take long to see that the left basks in a "government knows best" mentality. The most prominent left-wing "think" tank, the Center for American Progress, proudly reported that nearly two-thirds of young people polled endorsed the idea that "government has a responsibility to pursue policies that benefit all of society and balance the rights of the individual with the needs of the entire society," as opposed to "the primary responsibility of government is to protect the rights of the individual." Alas, the poll reflects more the attitude of the left-wingers directing the question than it does those answering it.

What has separated America from every other country is the foundational principle that government protects the rights of individuals. But one of the most prominent left-wing organizations in

Washington, D.C., this one run by John Podesta, who was Obama's transition chief, praises the notion of a government that coercively takes what it does not earn and redistributes it to favored constituencies. As longtime columnist George Will observed, "The Left exists to enlarge the state's supervision of life, narrowing individual choices in the name of collective goods."[15] Our message must be freedom from such coercion; no longer can we pay lip service to small government. We must act and demonstrate how government ruins lives, how government is the least efficient and least compassionate entity.

Conservatives are at a natural rhetorical disadvantage, since liberals make utopian promises that never come true. Liberals can and do always promise heaven on earth. But reality always pimp-slaps them in the end. Remember LBJ's so-called War on Poverty, which was allegedly created to make people less dependent on the federal government? Well, guess what? The reverse happened. Not only did the massive social programs and welfare policies fail to eliminate poverty, but they fueled and fostered generational welfare dependency that has hobbled families and crippled communities. Way to go, liberals! How compassionate of you!

Remember: As government increases, freedom decreases. Whatever government gives you it can take from you.

5. Twitter This

And once we have our message locked and loaded, we need to use every available outlet to spread our ideas. I hope it's clear by now that young people are getting their information via YouTube, Facebook, Twitter, text messaging, and a host of other social networking venues. Besides college campuses, we must meet young people where they're at—on the Net. Web 2.0, baby! Our generation is getting its information virally, so we must flood those arenas with engaging content that is razor sharp in its analysis.

Let's not forget that Obama had a machine of ninety people working on his new media team—an operation that produced the largest phone bank in world history, captured 13 million email addresses and 1 million cell phone numbers, and even created applications for the iPhone. Sure, B.H.O.'s message was old-school liberalism, but nobody would deny his MyBO website was a powerhouse. Obama, Axelrod, and Plouffe devoted globs of resources to make their campaign site an unprecedented success. There's nothing wrong with learning from our opponents. B.H.O. gave us a formula for interacting and connecting with millions of youth across the country. It's time to put those tools to work. The next GOP nominee better *not* bring back Pork Invaders. Good grief!

6. Donate That Money

For you older whippersnappers out there, you can make a difference, too, in waking up the Obama Zombie. The conservative movement doesn't run on ethanol. Like all grassroots organizations, it runs on cash. Obama raised a record-smashing $750 million. It wasn't just the cultic personality but the huge cash loads that made blanketing his message possible. Irony of ironies, one of the most anticapitalist presidential candidates in American history was one of the most effective at poaching massive mother lodes of dirty capitalist dough. So what's the solution?

Get your wallets out and put your money where your future is. There are organizations that are specifically reaching out to the next generation, introducing them to the conservative ideas that aren't heard in the classroom. Trust me, there is nothing like seeing Michelle Malkin, Ann Coulter, Dinesh D'Souza, Walter Williams, or Peter Schweizer on a liberal campus totally wiping the floor with some smug professor or clueless student.

Let's not forget how Ronald Reagan got onto the political scene. His famous 1964 "Time for Choosing" speech to support Barry Goldwater's election bid was bankrolled by three wealthy businessmen. LBJ ended up crushing Goldwater, but that speech by Reagan—which was aired on NBC—raised millions of dollars, solidified a base of hundreds of thousands of supporters, and launched the political career of the greatest modern president.[16]

Moral of the story: Conservative wallets must open, because liberal ones like George Soros's already have and will continue to.

There are many conservative organizations that reach out to young people. I prefer Young America's Foundation (www.yaf.org), having worked there four years and seen firsthand how the organization introduces young people to alternative ideas that are seldom taught in American classrooms. Get involved and give generously. Do it now. As in right this second, before Michael Moore eats another young person for breakfast.

Admittedly, we have an uphill battle on our hands. But conservatives are realists; we don't live in the fantasy world of welfare unicorns and government sugar fairies like the left does. Being a liberal is easy. Promising every constituency under the sun "free" goodies (otherwise known as goodies paid for by *you!*) takes little effort, except for the ability to lie one's you-know-what off.

Smashing the Obama cult is going to take a united effort.

Can we awaken our generation of Obama Zombies?

"Yes, we can!"

Notes

Introduction

1. "Watch Online: BCN Highlights Student Reaction to Obama Win," Bowdoin campus news, November 6, 2008, http://www.bowdoin .edu/news/archives/1bowdoincampus/005623.shtml.
2. Jocelyn Vena, "Young voters across the country share their reactions— both positive and negative—to Barack Obama's election-night win," MTV News, November 5, 2008, http://think.mtv.com/044FDFFFF009 8989A0016009953B5/.
3. Jason Linkins, "After The Election: Impromptu Rally At White House Draws Massive Crowd," Huffington Post, November 5, 2008, http:// www.huffingtonpost.com/2008/11/05/after-the-election-improm_ n_141437.html.
4. Ibid.
5. "Video: Oh My God," MTV News, November 6, 2008, http://think .mtv.com/044FDFFFF0098989A00170099545E/.
6. Vena, "Young voters across the country share their reactions."

7. Andrew Romano, "He's One of Us Now," *Newsweek*, February 18, 2008.

8. Luke Russert, NBC News transcript, November 5, 2008.

9. Chris Harris, "Super Tuesday Youth Voter Turnout Triples, Quadruples In Some States," MTV News, February 6, 2008, http://www.mtv.com/news/articles/1581027/20080206/id_0.jhtml.

10. Albert R. Hunt, "Letter from Washington: Republicans worry as youth vote desert the party," *New York Times*, September 2, 2007.

11. Alex Beinstein, "Barack Obama Youth Director Hans Riemer," October 25, 2007, http://www.alexbeinstein.com/2007/10/barack-obama-youth-director-hans-riemer.html.

12. Natalie Morales, "Importance of the youth vote," NBC *Today*, February 4, 2008.

13. Paul Waldman, "The youth vote, the culture wars, and Barack Obama," *American Prospect*, November 21, 2007, http://www.prospect.org/cs/articles?article=the_youth_vote_the_culture_wars_and_barack_obama.

14. David Schaper, " 'Camp Obama' Trains Campaign Volunteers," National Public Radio, June 13, 2007, http://www.npr.org/templates/story/story.php?storyID=11012254.

15. Ryan Lizza, "Battle Plans; How Obama Won," *New Yorker*, November 17, 2008.

16. Olivia Ward, "Looking at how Obama brought youth to the polls," *Toronto Star*, November 10, 2008.

17. Ibid.

18. Andrew Chung, "Seeking out the MTV crowd," *Toronto Star*, February 4, 2008.

19. Ibid.

20. Michael Whack, "The "BAM" . . . The OBAMA Handshake!," Organizing for America Community Blogs, January 12, 2008, http://my.barackobama.com/page/community/post/michaelwhack/CVBJ.

21. Suzanne Goldenberg, "Generation gap: After a lifetime with Bush, only the hippest candidate will do," *Guardian* (London), February 2, 2008.

22. Romano, "He's One of Us Now."

23. "Our Fading Heritage: Americans Fail a Basic Test on Their History

and Institutions," American Civic Literacy Program, 2008, http://
www.americancivicliteracy.org/2008/summary_summary.html.

24. Sara Hebel, "Obama, helped by youth vote, wins presidency and
makes history," *Chronicle of Higher Education,* November 5, 2008.

25. Ibid.

26. Sara Lipka and Reeves Wiedeman, "Young voters overwhelmingly
favored Obama, swinging some battleground states," *Chronicle of
Higher Education*, November 14, 2008.

27. Ibid.

Chapter 1: The Media Muzzle and the Hope-a-Dope Mantra

1. "Obama in Jeans," CNN video, May 8, 2009, http://www.cnn.com/
video/#/video/politics/2008/05/08/obama.jeans.cnn.

2. Richard Leiby, "Obama Delivers the Zingers at Journalists' Dinner,"
Washington Post, May 10, 2009.

3. Ashley Parker, "For Washington journalists, one night to laugh," The
Caucus, *New York Times* blog, May 10, 2009, http://thecaucus.blogs
.nytimes.com/2009/05/10/white-house-correspondents-association
-dinner/.

4. Mike Allen and Michael Calderone, "Washington Post cancels lobbyist event amid uproar," Politico, July 3, 2009, http://www.politico
.com/news/stories/0709/24441.html.

5. Brent Baker, "Revolving Door from Journalism to Team Obama Now
Up to a Dozen," Media Research Center, July 29, 2009, http://www
.mrc.org/biasalert/2009/20090729104616.aspx.

6. Richard Wolffe and Daren Briscoe, "Across the Divide: How Barack
Obama is shaking up old assumptions about what it means to be
black and white in America," *Newsweek*, July 16, 2007.

7. Ibid.

8. Daniel Schorr, "A New, 'Post-Racial' Political Era in America," NPR
transcript, January 28, 2008, http://www.npr.org/templates/story/
story.php?storyId=18489466.

9. Lyndsi Thomas, "ChiTrib's Zuckman: Obama Success Story Just as
Impressive as McCain POW Story," Newsbusters.org, July 9, 2008,

http://newsbusters.org/blogs/lyndsi-thomas/2008/07/09/chitribs
-zuckman-obama-success-story-just-impressive-mccain-pow-story.

10. Jill Zuckman, "Fighting the 'Who?' factor: Candidates considered outside the top tier struggle to get even a once-over from voters," *Chicago Tribune*, June 28, 2007.

11. Jill Zuckman, "On the campaign trail, Palin has the folksy persona down," *Chicago Tribune*, September 16, 2008.

12. David Von Drehle, "Does Experience Matter in a President?" *Time*, March 10, 2008.

13. Ibid.

14. Richard Wolffe, "Our time for change has come," *Newsweek*, January 14, 2008.

15. "Obama Love Fest: NBC Reporter Admits Objectivity Difficult Amid Candidate Fervor," Breitbart TV, January 8, 2008, http://www.breit bart.tv/?p=26294.

16. Jacques Steinberg, "On the Press Bus, Some Questions over Favoritism," *New York Times*, March 1, 2008, http://www.nytimes.com/2008/03/01/us/politics/01press.html.

17. Joe Klein, "Why Barack Obama Could Be the Next President," *Time*, October 23, 2006.

18. Ibid.

19. "The Invisible Primary—Invisible No Longer," Pew Research Center's Project for Excellence in Journalism, October 29, 2007, http://www.journalism.org/node/8187.

20. "How the Press Reported the 2008 General Election," Pew Research Center's Project for Excellence in Journalism, October 22, 2008, http://www.journalism.org/node/13307.

21. Eli Saslow, "As Duties Weigh Obama Down, His Faith in Fitness Only Increases," *Washington Post*, December 25, 2008.

22. Media Bias Facts, Media Research Center, http://www.mediare search.org/biasbasics/biasbasics3.asp.

23. Bill Dedman, "Journalists dole out cash to politicians (quietly)," MSNBC, June 25, 2007, http://www.msnbc.msn.com/id/19113485/ns/politics/.

24. "Obama's Selma Speech," March 5, 2007, http://blogs.suntimes.com/sweet/2007/03/obamas_selma_speech_text_as_de.html.

25. "Obama, Clintons honor activists at Selma, Ala.," Associated Press, May 5, 2007, http://www.kcby.com/internal?st=print&id=6301042 &path=/news/national.

26. "Obama's Margin of Victory: The Media," Media Research Center, http://www.mrc.org/SpecialReports/2008/obama/obama.asp.

27. Ibid.

28. Felix Gillette, "Primary Scream," *New York Observer*, February 5, 2008, http://www.observer.com/2008/primary-scream.

29. Martin Snap, "Barack as a Jedi knight," *Contra Costa Times* (Calif.), April 14, 2008, http://my.barackobama.com/page/community/post/ martinsnapp/gGBJOg.

30. Lili Haydn, "Why Obama is like a desert lover," Huffington Post, February 29, 2008, http://www.huffingtonpost.com/lili-haydn/why -obama-is-like-a-deser_b_89285.html.

31. Jose Antonio Vargas, "Obama Fervor Is Breaking on the Web," *Washington Post*, February 23, 2008.

32. Sam Fulwood III, "For Obama, hipness is what it is," Politico, April 24, 2009, http://www.politico.com/news/stories/0409/21522 .html.

33. Ibid.

34. Ibid.

35. Alex Leo, "CNN Story On Obama's 'Swagga' The Most Embarrassing Ever?" Huffington Post, April 29, 2009, http://www.huffingtonpost .com/2009/04/29/the-most-embarrassing-cnn_n_193095.html.

36. Ibid.

37. John Kass, "Obama's mystical (national media) disconnect from sleazy Chicago politics," *Los Angeles Times,* May 11, 2008, http:// latimesblogs.latimes.com/washington/2008/05/mediasobamaluv .html.

38. "Obama's Political 'Godfather' In Illinois," Associated Press, March 31, 2008.

39. Ibid.

40. Todd Spivak, "Barack Obama and Me," *Houston Times*, February 28, 2008.

41. Katie Couric, *CBS Evening News,* August 24, 2009.

42. Noel Sheppard, "MSNBC Anchor: 'Socialist' Is Becoming the New

N-word," Newsbusters.org, August 10, 2009, http://newsbusters.org/blogs/noel-sheppard/2009/08/10/msnbc-anchor-socialist-becoming-new-n-word.

43. Noel Sheppard, "Obama Official: 'At the White House, We Love MSNBC,' " Newsbusters.org, May 5, 2009, http://newsbusters.org/blogs/noel-sheppard/2009/05/05/obama-official-white-house-we-love-msnbc.

44. Top 20 Contributors to Barack Obama during 2008 presidential campaign, Opensecrets.org, https://www.opensecrets.org/politicians/contrib.php?cid=N00009638&cycle=2008.

45. "Democratic National Cmte: Top Contributors," Opensecrets.org, https://www.opensecrets.org/parties/contrib.php?cmte=DNC&cycle=2008.

46. Suzy Jagger, "Google unveils 'trillion-dollar' clean energy program," TimesOnline, October 3, 2008, http://business.timesonline.co.uk/tol/business/industry_sectors/technology/article4870334.ece.

47. Thomas Claburn, "Google CEO Eric Schmidt Calls for Innovation Bailout," *InformationWeek,* November 18, 2008.

48. Rob Preston, "In Search Of An Economic Solution: Schmidt's Views," *InformationWeek*, December 1, 2008.

49. Ibid.

50. Owen Thomas, "Google Execs Pay $150,000 for Obama Bash," December 27, 2008, http://valleywag.gawker.com/5119039/google-execs-pay-150000-for-obama-bash.

51. "Apple, Google face FTC antitrust probe," *Deal,* May 5, 2009, http://www.thedeal.com/corporatedealmaker/2009/05/apple_google_face_ftc_antitrus.php.

52. "Apple, Silicon valley line up behind Obama," October 25, 2008, http://www.9to5mac.com/apple-obama.

53. *World News Tonight with Charlie Gibson*, ABC, January, 4, 2008.

Chapter 2: Will You Be My (Facebook) Friend?

1. will.i.am, "Why I Recorded *Yes We Can*," Huffington Post, February 3, 2008, http://www.huffingtonpost.com/william/why-i-recorded-yes-we-can_b_84655.html.

2. Matthew Fraser and Soumitra Dutta, "Barack Obama and the Face-book Election," *U.S. News & World Report,* November 19, 2008, http://www.usnews.com/articles/opinion/2008/11/19/barack-obama-and-the-facebook-election.html.

3. will.i.am, "Why I Recorded *Yes We Can*."

4. Andrew Rasiej and Micah L. Sifry, "The Web: 2008's Winning Ticket," Politico, November 12, 2008, http://www.politico.com/news/stories/1108/15520.html.

5. Amber Lee Ettinger, "I Got a Crush on Obama," YouTube, June 13, 2007, http://www.youtube.com/watch?v=wKsoXHYICqU&feature=PlayList&p=vY3x8oj4XFI.

6. "Hollywood Declares Themselves," YouTube, October 1, 2008, http://www.youtube.com/watch?v=olpCyDA4kYA.

7. Norman Lear, DiscoverTheNetworks.org, http://www.discoverthenetworks.org/individualProfile.asp?indid=1945.

8. Brooks Barnes, "Getting Out the Vote, Keeping Up with Youth," *New York Times,* August 1, 2008.

9. Rasiej and Sifry, "The Web: 2008's Winning Ticket."

10. Alexander Burns, "McCain camp lacked in high-tech," Politico, November 22, 2008, http://www.politico.com/news/stories/1108/15888.html.

11. David Talbot, "White House 2.0. A group of Boston geeks helped Barack Obama turn the Web into the ultimate political machine. Will he use it now to reinvent government," *Boston Globe,* January 11, 2009.

12. Ibid.

13. Ellen McGirt, "How Chris Hughes Helped Launch Facebook and the Barack Obama Campaign," FastCompany.com, March 17, 2009, http://www.fastcompany.com/magazine/134/boy-wonder.html.

14. Brian Stelter, "The Facebooker Who Friended Obama," *New York Times*, July 7, 2008.

15. Brian C. Mooney, "Technology aids Obama's outreach drive," *Boston Globe,* February 24, 2008.

16. McGirt, "How Chris Hughes Helped Launch Facebook and the Barack Obama Campaign."

17. Ibid.

18. Mooney, "Technology aids Obama's outreach drive."

19. Joe Garofoli, "Appetite for change finally draws young voters to the polls," *San Francisco Chronicle*, January 6, 2008.

20. Ibid.

21. Mark Hennessy, "Obama to continue exploiting potential of web as president," *Irish Times*, November 11, 2008.

22. Catherine Holahan, "Can Obama Turn Friends into Votes?" *Business-Week* Online, August 27, 2008, http://www.businessweek.com/technology/content/aug2008/tc20080825_808232.htm?campaign_id=rss_tech.

23. Ibid.

24. McGirt, "How Chris Hughes Helped Launch Facebook and the Barack Obama Campaign."

25. Ibid.

26. Ibid.

27. Ibid.

28. Jose Antonio Vargas, "Obama's Wide Web," *Washington Post*, August 20, 2008.

29. McGirt, "How Chris Hughes Helped Launch Facebook and the Barack Obama Campaign."

30. Jose Antonio Vargas, "Politics Is No Longer Local. It's Viral," *Washington Post*, December 28, 2008, http://www.washingtonpost.com/wp-dyn/content/article/2008/12/26/AR2008122601131.html.

31. Colin Delaney, "Obama Campaign's New Media Staff was NOT a Part of the Tech Team," Epolitics.com, January 28, 2009, http://www.epolitics.com/2009/01/28/obama-campaigns-new-media-staff-was-not-a-part-of-the-tech-team/.

32. McGirt, "How Chris Hughes Helped Launch Facebook and the Barack Obama Campaign."

33. Michael Cornfield, "New Technology and the 2008 Election," in Larry J. Sabato, ed., *The Year of Obama* (New York: Longman, 2008), p. 213.

34. Ibid., p. 214.

35. "David Plouffe's Strategy Update: October 14, 2008," YouTube, October 13, 2008, http://www.youtube.com/watch?v=R92Fg5sznLQ&feature=channel.

36. David Saltonstall, "Obama Push for 'Text Generation' To Get the Message," *Daily News* (New York), October 29, 2008.

37. Vargas, "Obama's Wide Web."

38. "Bronx students discuss Obama's race speech," YouTube, March 28, 2008, http://www.youtube.com/watch?v=r9IldaegABO.

39. Vargas, "Obama's Wide Web."

40. Ben Smith, "Largest phone bank ever," *Politico,* December 9, 2007, http://www.politico.com/blogs/bensmith/1207/Largest_phone_bank_ever.html.

41. Ibid.

42. Vargas, "Obama's Wide Web."

43. Jim Kuhnhenn, "Obama uses speech for high-tech outreach," *Boston Globe,* August 28, 2008, http://www.boston.com/news/politics/2008/articles/2008/08/28/obama_uses_speech_for_high_tech_outreach/?page=1.

44. Ibid.

45. Saltonstall, "Obama Push for 'Text Generation' To Get the Message."

46. Obama '08: The Official iPhone Application, http://my.barackobama.com/page/content/iphone.

47. Cornfield, "New Technology and the 2008 Election," p. 224.

48. David Carr, "How Obama Tapped Into Social Networks' Power," *New York Times*, November 9, 2008, http://www.nytimes.com/2008/11/10/business/media/10carr.html?_r=1.

49. Jose Antonio Vargas, "Obama Raised Half a Billion Online," *Washington Post,* November 20, 2008, http://voices.washingtonpost.com/44/2008/11/20/obama_raised_half_a_billion_on.html.

50. "Young Voters in the 2008 Election," Pew Research Center for the People & the Press, November 12, 2008, http://pewresearch.org/pubs/1031/young-voters-in-the-2008-election.

Chapter 3: The Dave Matthews Electoral Magnet— And Other Ways to Manufacture a Crowd

1. "Celebrity-packed pledge for Obama," Huffington Post, January 19, 2009, http://www.huffingtonpost.com/2009/01/19/celebrity-packed-pledge-f_n_159046.html.

2. Tina Daunt, "On the stump for Barack Obama until the final curtain," *Los Angeles Times*, October 31, 2008, http://articles.latimes.com/2008/oct/31/entertainment/et-cause31.

3. Jay Newton-Small, "Obama's Celebrity Army," *Time*, February 4, 2008.

4. "Celebrities React to Obama Win: Oprah, Pitt, Lohan, Alba, Clooney, Madonna, More," Huffington Post, November 5, 2008, http://www.huffingtonpost.com/2008/11/05/celebrities-react-to-obam_n_141305.html.

5. Ibid.

6. "Sherri Shepherd Sobs Over Obama Win," Huffington Post, November 5, 2008, http://www.huffingtonpost.com/2008/11/05/sherri-shepherd-sobs-over_n_141398.html.

7. "Madonna, Oprah, others react to Obama win," MSNBC, November 5, 2008, http://www.msnbc.msp.com/id/27557276/ns/entertainment-celebrities/.

8. Ibid.

9. Eric Bates, "Dave Matthews speaks out for Barack Obama," *Rolling Stone*, April 17, 2008, http://www.rollingstone.com/news/story/20093048/dave_matthews_speaks_out_for_barack_obama.

10. Ibid.

11. Ibid.

12. http://gawker.com/5005030/obamas-dirty-trick-involved-dave-matthews.

13. Martha Irvine, "Tough Political Realities Have Quieted Youth 'Obamamania,'" Huffington Post, September 22, 2009, http://www.huffingtonpost.com/huff-wires/20090922/us-obama-youth-hangover.

14. http://www.reuters.com/article/pressRelease/idUS152365+03-Mar-2009+PRN20090303.

15. Lindsay Lohan, "Uh Oh," MySpace, September 14, 2008, http://blogs.myspace.com/index.cfm?fuseaction=blog.view&friendID=29730276&blogID=432883808.

16. Ibid.

17. Ibid.

18. "Matt Damon On Palin: 'Like A Really Bad Disney Movie . . . Totally Absurd,' Palin Responds (VIDEO)," Huffington Post, September 10, 2008, http://www.huffingtonpost.com/2008/09/10/matt-damon-on-palin-like_n_125334.html.

19. Lohan, "Uh Oh."

20. Natalie Finn, "Who Knew? Sarah Palin 'Terrifies' Pink," E!Online, September 12, 2008, http://www.eonline.com/uberblog/b28783_who_knew_sarah_palin_terrifies_pink.html.

21. "T.I. & Russell Simmons Get Political At MTV VMA Awards," Access Hollywood, September 8, 2008, http://www.accesshollywood.com/mtv-video-music-awards/ti-and-russell-simmons-get-political-at-mtv-vma-awards_article_11146/.

22. "Diddy Goes Off On John McCain For Picking Sarah Palin (VIDEO)," Huffington Post, September 1, 2008, http://www.huffingtonpost.com/2008/09/01/diddy-goes-off-on-john-mc_n_123081.html.

23. Maryclaire Dale, "Springsteen Rocks Obama Rally in Philly," Associated Press, October 4, 2008, http://abclocal.go.com/wpvi/story?selection=news/politics&id=6432174.

24. "The Boss mourns for the USA," Daily Telegraph (Australia), October 7, 2008.

25. George Rush and Bill Hutchinson, "Bruce Springsteen, Billy Joel headline Barack Obama midtown cash bash," Daily News (New York), October 17, 2008.

26. "Jay-Z, LeBron James get out vote for Obama," Associated Press, October 30, 2008, http://www.msnbc.msn.com/id/27455428/.

27. Vidya Rao, "Oprah effect: Can celebs sway voters?" MSNBC, October 25, 2008, http://www.msnbc.msn.com/id/27227264//.

28. Ibid.

29. Ibid.

30. Cindy Clark, "Stars want YOU to register to vote," USA Today, November 25, 2008.

31. "Jam the vote," Relix, November 2008, http://www.headcount.org/docs/headcount-relix-10-08-pdf.

32. Shannon Bond and Lea Radick, "Rock stars motivate new generation of voters," Medill News Service, August 25, 2008, http://news.medill.northwestern.edu/washington/news.aspx?id=97959.

33. Erica Lamar, "T.I. to the people: 'Respect my vote!'" Vibe, July 30, 2008, http://www.vibe.com/news/news_headlines/2008/07/ti_respect_my_vote/.

34. Alex Macpherson, "Film & Music: Rock & pop: Inside man: Hip-hop star TI is on unbeatable form, full of reflection, revelation and 'jam-

min'-ass kicks.' All he has to do now is get out of prison," *Guardian* (London), March 6, 2009.

35. Kathleen Brady Shea, "Hip-hopping for the vote; A nonpartisan 'summit' in Phila. used music celebrities as an incentive," *Philadelphia Inquirer*, April 21, 2008.

Chapter 4: The Peacenik Phantom

1. "The 15th Biannual Youth Survey on Politics and Public Service," Harvard University Institute of Politics, Fall 2008, p. 10.

2. Ibid., p. 12.

3. Ibid., p. 13.

4. Ibid., p. 12.

5. http://www.supportbillayers.org.

6. "Bill Ayers," Discoverthenetworks.org, http://www.discoverthenet works.org/individualProfile.asp?indid=2169.

7. Ibid.

8. Dinitia Smith, "No Regrets for a Love of Explosives; In a Memoir of Sorts, a War Protester Talks of Life With the Weathermen," *New York Times*, September 11, 2001.

9. Jack Stripling, "In Defense of Ayers," *Inside Higher Ed,* October 14, 2008, http://www.insidehighered.com/news/2008/10/14/ayers.

10. Barack Obama, *Dreams from My Father* electronic edition (New York: Three Rivers, 2004), p. 100.

11. William J. Broad and David E. Sanger, "Obama's Youth Shaped His Nuclear-Free Vision," *New York Times*, July 4, 2009.

12. "Sen. Barack Obama Delivers Remarks at The MTV/MySpace Presidential Forum," CQ Transcriptions, October 29, 2007.

13. Ibid.

14. Broad and Sanger, "Obama's Youth Shaped His Nuclear-Free Vision."

15. Michael D. Shear and Howard Schneider, "Obama's Worldwide Star Power Finds Limits," *Washington Post*, September 20, 2009.

16. "Envisioning A World Without America," *Investor's Business Daily*, September 18, 2009, http://www.ibdeditorials.com/IBDArticles.aspx?id =338166890369546.

17. Ryan Lizza, "Making It," *New Yorker,* July 21, 2008.

18. "Sen. Barack Obama Delivers Remarks at the MTV/MySpace Presidential Forum."

19. Mark Steyn, "Come west, young man," *National Review Online*'s The Corner, March 27, 2008, http://corner.nationalreview.com/post/?q=YzU4YjIwMTBjNDdjZmRiNzkwMGUwNGEyMzMxMzE5OWU=.

20. Jim Michaels, "Thousands of Enemy Fighters Reported Killed," *USA Today*, September 26, 2007.

21. Nile Gardiner, "Barack Obama's Top 10 Apologies: How the President Has Humiliated a Superpower," Heritage Foundation Web Memo 2466, June 2, 2009, http://www.heritage.org/research/europe/wm2466.cfm.

22. "Remarks by President Obama at Strasbourg Town Hall," White House Office of the Press Secretary, April 3, 2009, http://www.whitehouse.gov/the_press_office/Remarks-by-President-Obama-at-Strasbourg-Town-Hall/.

23. "Obama's interview with Al Arabiya television," January 27, 2009, http://www.alarabiya.net/articles/2009/01/27/65096.html.

24. "Remarks by President Obama to the Turkish Parliament," White House Office of the Press Secretary, April 6, 2009, http://www.whitehouse.gov/the_press_office/Remarks-By-President-Obama-To-The-Turkish-Parliament/.

25. Alex Alexiev, "Obama's Fantasy Islam," *National Review Online*, June 11, 2009, http://article.nationalreview.com/?q=YWUwODZjNjhkNDJhNjE5YzllOTZkZjZiZjdlZjZkZjl=&w=MA==.

26. Steve Benen, "American exceptionalism . . . ," *Washington Monthly*'s Political Animal, April 5, 2009. http://www.washingtonmonthly.com/archives/individual/2009_04/017614.php.

27. "Obama Calls Chavez Gift a 'Nice Gesture,' " Fox News, April 19, 2009, http://www.foxnews.com/politics/first100days/2009/04/19/obama-calls-americas-summit-productive-demands-follow/.

28. Jake Tapper, "President Obama Jokes About Ortega Rant," ABC News, April 17, 2009, http://blogs.abcnews.com/politicalpunch/2009/04/president-ob-20.html.

29. "Deepak Chopra," "Can We Stop Being a Super Power, Please," Huffington Post, July 20, 2009, http://www.huffingtonpost.com/deepak-chopra/can-we-stop-being-a-super_b_241254.html.

30. Ibid.

31. "Americans Are Most Likely to Base Truth on Feelings," Barna Group, February 12, 2002, http://www.barna.org/barna-update/article/ 5-barna-update/67-americans-are-most-likely-to-base-truth-on -feelings.

32. Joel Achenbach, "BYU Democrats and More Utah Pics," *Washington Post's* Achenblog, January 31, 2008, http://voices.washingtonpost .com/achenblog/2008/01/byu_democrats_and_more_utah_pi.html.

33. Keith Olbermann, "Republicans have hijacked 9/11," MSNBC, September 10, 2008, http://www.msnbc.msn.com/id/26645619/.

34. "Generation 9/11: Education professor conducts landmark survey of college students' responses to September 11, 2001," University of Texas at Austin Feature Story, http://www.utexas.edu/features/ 2005/generation/index.html.

35. Sharon Jayson, "Will 9/11 define a generation?" *USA Today*, September 11, 2006.

36. Melissa Dahl, "Youth vote may have been key in Obama's win," MSNBC, http://www.msnbc.msn.com/id/27525497.

37. Matthew Kalman, "On Gaza TV, Hamas' bunny brainwashes kids, declaring 'I will eat the Jews!' " *Daily News* (New York), February 12, 2008.

38. David Horowitz, *The Professors: The 101 Most Dangerous Academics in America* (Washington, D.C.: Regnery, 2006), pp. 40–41.

39. Ibid., p. 45.

40. Ibid., p. 46.

41. "Clark: Getting 'shot down in plane' doesn't make McCain qualified," CNN, June 29, 2008, http://www.cnn.com/2008/POLITICS/06/29/ clark.mccain/index.html.

42. Jim Geraghty, *National Review Online's* The Campaign Spot, April 8, 2008, http://campaignspot.nationalreview.com/post/?q=NjFlOWO0 ODUlYmVmMjJmZjg4YWVmNDhjYjVkZmJjMzk=.

43. "Harkin Suggests Military Background Makes McCain Unfit to be Commander-in-Chief," Fox News, May 22, 2008, http://www.fox news.com/politics/elections/2008/05/22/harkin-suggests-military -background-makes-mccain-unfit-to-be-commander-in-chief/.

44. Matthew Balan, "Schultz Defends His 'McCain is a Warmonger' Com-

ment on CNN," Newsbuster.org, April 7, 2008, http://newsbusters
.org/blogs/matthew-balan/2008/04/07/schultz-defends-his-mccain-
warmonger-comment-cnn.

45. Fred Hiatt, "The Belligerent vs. the Naif?" *Washington Post,* May 26,
2008.

46. "Politics, Civilian and Policy," *Military Times* Poll, December 31,
2007, http://www.militarycity.com/polls/2007activepoll_politics
.php.

47. "Politics, Civilian and Policy," *Military Times* poll, December 31,
2007, http://militarycity.com/polls/2007guardreservepoll_politics
.php.

48. Asheesh Siddique, "Infighting: Do We Root for the Home Team?"
Campusprogress.org, June 27–30, 2006, http://www.campusprog
ress.org/features/972/infighting-do-we-root-for-the-home-team.

49. "The 15th Biannual Youth Survey on Politics and Public Service,"
Harvard University Institute of Politics, Fall 2008, p. 18.

Chapter 5: Global-Warming Ghouls

1. David de Rothschild, *The Live Earth Global Warming Survival Handbook: 77 Essential Skills to Stop Climate Change—or Live Through It*
(New York: Rodale, 2007), p. 143.

2. Tombari Bonkoo, "Obama the Only Presidential Candidate to Promote Live Earth Concert," Associated Content, July 7, 2007, http://
www.associatedcontent.com/article/304735/obama_the_only_pres
idential_candidate.html?cat=47.

3. Ibid.

4. De Rothschild, *The Live Earth Global Warming Survival Handbook,*
p. 142.

5. Ibid., p. 134.

6. Ibid., p. 58.

7. Ibid., p. 50.

8. Ibid., p. 94.

9. Ibid., p. 90.

10. Ibid., p. 38.

11. Ibid., p. 92.

12. "Media Hype on 'Melting' Antarctic Ignores Record Ice Growth," The Inhofe EPW Press Blog, March 27, 2008, http://epw.senate.gov/public/index.cfm?FuseAction=Minority.Blogs&ContentRecord_id=F1F2F75F-802A-23AD-4701-A92B4EBBCCBF.

13. Henry Payne, "Polar Bears: More Journalistic Malpractice," U.S. Senate Report Debunks Polar Bear Extinction Fears," *National Review Online*'s Planet Gore, May 15, 2008, http://planetgore.nationalreview.com/post/?q=NjI5YmIzNzgxMjE3NDJkZTkyMDMyOGY0OGZiZTM5ZTk=.

14. Greg Keller, "Environmental alarms raised over consumer electronics," *Seattle Times*, May 13, 2009, http://seattletimes.nwsource.com/html/nationworld/2009214989_apeugreenergadgets.html.

15. George Monbiot, "Drastic action on climate change is needed now—and here's the plan," *Guardian* (London), October 31, 2006, http://www.guardian.co.uk/commentisfree/2006/oct/31/economy.politics.

16. Andrew C. Revkin, "Whose Climate Is it, Anyway?" *New York Times*, November 2, 2007, http://dotearth.blogs.nytimes.com/2007/11/02/whose-climate-is-it-anyway/.

17. Alex Williams, "Jolly and Green, with an Agenda," *New York Times*, November 25, 2007.

18. Lawrence Solomon, "Limited role for CO2," *National Post* (Canada), February 2, 2007, http://www.canada.com/nationalpost/story.html?id=069cb5b2-7d8l-4a8e-825d-56e0f112aeb5&k=0.

19. Phil Chapman, "Sorry to ruin the fun, but an ice age cometh," *Australian*, April 23, 2008, http://www.theaustralian.news.com.au/story/0.25197.23583376-7583.00.html.

20. Piper Fogg, "Saving the Planet, by Degrees," *Chronicle of Higher Education*, October 20, 2006.

21. Jennifer Weeks, "Planet Earth 101: Why more and more campuses are seeing green in going green," *Boston Globe Magazine*, October 5, 2008.

22. "What Is a Sustainable University," *Chronicle of Higher Education*, October 20, 2006.

23. Lisa W. Foderaro, "Without Cafeteria Trays, Colleges Find Savings," *New York Times*, April 29, 2009.

24. Ibid.

25. Richard Monastersky, "Colleges Strain to Reach Climate-Friendly Future," *Chronicle of Higher Education*, December 14, 2007.

26. Will Potter, "The First Certified 'Green' Dormitory," *Chronicle of Higher Education*, March 26, 2004.

27. Monastersky, "Colleges Strain to Reach Climate-Friendly Future."

28. Richard Monastersky, "Truth in Advertising: Middlebury College's Biomass Plant," *Chronicle of Higher Education*, October 20, 2006.

29. Ibid.

30. Ibid.

31. Monastersky, "Colleges Strain to Reach Climate-Friendly Future."

32. Scott Carlson, "In Search of the Sustainable Campus: With eyes on the future, universities try to clean up their acts," *Chronicle of Higher Education*, October 20, 2006.

33. Ibid.

34. Ibid.

35. Monastersky, "Colleges Strain to Reach Climate-Friendly Future."

36. Ibid.

37. Ibid.

38. Editorial, "Wind ($23.37) v. Gas (25 Cents)," *Wall Street Journal*, May 12, 2008.

39. Ibid.

40. Ibid.

41. Monastersky, "Colleges Strain to Reach Climate-Friendly Future."

42. Marc Morano, "Celebs Ignore Death, Poverty on MTV Enviro Series," CNSNews.com, April 25, 2005, http://ff.org/centers/csspp/library/co2weekly/2005-04-28/celebs.htm.

43. Ned Martel, "Eco-Lessons Taught in a Surfer-Girl Patois," *New York Times,* March 28, 2005.

44. Morano, "Celebs Ignore Death, Poverty on MTV Enviro Series."

45. Alessandra Stanley, "Sounding the Global-Warming Alarm Without Upsetting the Fans," *New York Times*, July 9, 2007.

46. Ibid.

47. "Live Earth is promoting green to save the planet—what planet are they on?" *Daily Mail* (London), July 7, 2007, http://www.dailymail.co.uk/femail/article-466775/Live-Earth-promoting-green-save-planet--planet-on.html.

48. "Cameron Diaz's Potty Mouth," *Radar Online*, May 9, 2009, http://www.radarmagazine.com/exclusives/2009/05/cameron-diazs-potty-mouth.

49. "More Than 700 (Previously 650) International Scientists Dissent Over Man-Made Global Warming Claims," U.S. Senate Minority Report, December 11, 2008, http://epw.senate.gov/public/index.cfm?FuseAction=Minority.PressReleases&ContentRecord_id=d6d95751-802a-23ad-4496-7ec7e1641f2f.

50. Erika Lovely, "Scientists urge caution on global warming," Politico, November 25, 2008, http://dyn.politico.com/printstory.cfm?uuid=D0C4924D-18FE-70B2-A808D77A9C1FFFD3.

51. Comment on Grist.org by Andy Revkin, March 8, 2008, http://www.grist.org/member/view-all/comments/2231.

52. Andrew C. Revkin, "In Debate on Climate Change, Exaggeration Is a Common Pitfall," *New York Times*, February 25, 2009.

53. Steven Milloy, "The *Real* Inconvenient Truth: Some facts about greenhouse and global warming," Junk Science, August 2007, http://www.junkscience.com/Greenhouse/.

54. Dudley J. Hughes, "Carbon Dioxide Levels Are a Blessing, Not a Problem," *Environment & Climate News*, Heartland Institute, May 1, 2007, http://www.heartland.org/policybot/results/20952/Carbon_Dioxide_Levels_Are_a_Blessing_Not_a_Problem.html.

55. Michael Asher, "Temperature Monitors Report Widescale Global Cooling," Daily Tech, February 26, 2008, http://www.dailytech.com/Temperature+Monitors+Report+Worldwide+Global+Cooling/article10866.htm.

56. Michael Asher, "Blogger Finds Y2K Bug in NASA Climate Data," *Daily Tech,* August 9, 2007, http://www.dailytech.com/article.aspx?newsid=8383.

57. "Green fuels produce twice as much carbon as fossil fuels," Tele graph.Co.Uk, April, 14, 2009, http://www.telegraph.co.uk/earth/greenertransport/5153781/Green-fuels-produce-twice-as-much-carbon-as-fossil-fuels.html.

58. "Think twice about 'green' transport, say scientists," Breitbart.com, June 7, 2009, http://www.breitbart.com/article.php?id=CNG.243153c6a091a3b942a75077729e8c92.c51&show_article=1.

59. Ian Murray, "Time to recycle recycling," Competitive Enterprise Institute, June 6, 2008, http://cei.org/articles/time-recycle-recycling.

Chapter 6: Health-Care Hypnosis

1. "Income, Poverty, and Health Insurance Coverage in the United States: 2008," Congressional Budget Office, September 2009, http://www.census.gov/Press-Release/www/releases/archives/news_con ferences/014226.html.

2. Michael D. Tanner, "Who are the uninsured?" *Philadelphia Inquirer*, August 20, 2009.

3. "Income, Poverty, and Health Insurance Coverage in the United States: 2008."

4. "Obama's mother of all political lies and the town hall mayhem it caused," *Naked Emperor News*, August 10, 2009, http://www.breit bart.tv/naked-emperor-news-obamas-mother-of-all-political-lies -and-the-town-hall-mayhem-it-caused/.

5. "White House releases list of health executive visitors," Associated Press, July 23, 2009, http://www.latimes.com/news/nationworld/ nation/la-na-healthcare-talks23-2009jul23.0.220833.story.

6. David Espo, "Drug firms cut secret deal with Obama, Congress," Capitol Hill Blue, June 21, 2009, http://www.capitolhillblue.com/ node/18223.

7. "The truth about health insurance," *Wall Street Journal*, August 12, 2009.

8. Hilton Friedman, "How to Cure Health Care," Hoover Digest, 2001, http://www.hoover.org/publications/digest/3459466.html.

9. Devon Herrick and Ariel House, "Competition, Deregulation Can Make Health Insurance Affordable," Heartland Institute, http:// www.heartland.org/publications/health%20care/article/24019/Com petition_Deregulation_Can_Make_Health_Insurance_Affordable.html.

10. Ann Coulter, "Liberal Lies About National Health Care: First In a Series," *Human Events* Online, August 19, 2009, http://www.hu manevents.com/article.php?id=33213.

11. Natalie Morales, "Importance of youth vote," NBC *Today* show, February 4, 2008.

12. Barack Obama, Northwestern University Commencement Address, June 16, 2006, http://www.obamaspeeches.com/079-Northwestern -University-Commencement-Address-Obama-Speech.htm.

13. Lois Romano, "Generation Y: Ready to rock the 2008 election," *Washington Post*, January 10, 2008.

14. Michael Pollan, "Big food vs. big insurance," *New York Times*, September 9, 2009.

15. Jim Geraghty, "A Long and Contradictory Laundry List of Promises," *National Review Online*'s The Campaign Spot, http://campaignspot .nationalreview.com/post/?q=Y2UzZWO2YTAxNmRmMDk2ZDE4ZDB1 ZTEyMTA1ZDFmNDI=.

16. Ed Morrissey, "A brief lesson on markets and rationing," HotAir.com, July 21, 2009, http://hotair.com/archives/2009/07/21/a-brief-les son-on-markets-and-rationing/.

17. Erica Williams, "For Young Americans, Health Care Reform Is Our Fight," Huffington Post, August 6, 2009, http://www.huffington post.com/erica-williams/for-young-americans-healt_b_252858.html, accessed October 27, 2009.

18. David Walker, "Long-Term Fiscal Outlook: Action Is Needed to Avoid the Possibility of a Serious Economic Disruption in the Future," testimony before the Senate Budge Committee, General Accounting Office, January 29, 2008, http://gao.gov/new.items/d08411t.pdf.

19. Ibid.

20. Shawn Tully, "5 freedoms you'd lose in health care reform," CNNMoney.com, July 24, 2009, http://money.cnn.com/2009/07/24/ news/economy/health_care_reform_obama.fortune/.

21. Robert Book, "Who Will Make Your Health Care 'Choices'?" Heritage Foundation's Foundry blog, July 29, 2009, http://blog.heritage .org/2009/07/29/who-will-make-your-health-care-choices/.

22. "Young people the biggest losers in health care reform?" Rock the Vote press release, July 28, 2009, http://www.rockthevote.com/ about/press-room/press-releases/wall-street-journal.html.

23. Karyn Schwartz and Tanya Schwartz, "Uninsured young adults: A profile and overview of coverage options," Kaiser Family Foundation, June 2008.

Chapter 7: The Economic Igor

1. Paul R. La Monica, "Behind the minimum wage debate," CNNMoney .com, September 5, 2008, http://money.cnn.com/2008/09/05/ markets/thebuzz/index.htm.

2. Ben Adler, "Democrats try to get hip to young voters," Politico, September 26, 2007, http://www.politico.com/news/stories/0907/6015.html.

3. Barack Obama speech at the AFL-CIO Labor Day Picnic in Cincinnati, Ohio, September 7, 2009, http://www.whitehouse.gov/blog/Labor -Day-Reform-and-the-Fight-for-Whats-Right/.

4. James Sherk, "Raising the minimum wage will not reduce poverty," Heritage Foundation, January 8, 2007, http://www.heritage.org/ Research/Labor/bg1994.cfm.

5. Scott Mayerowitz, "Relief for Workers at Bottom: Minimum Wage Goes Up," ABC News, July 24, 2009, http://a.abcnews.com/Business/ Story?id=8159485&page=1.

6. David Neumark, "Delay the Minimum-Wage Hike," *Wall Street Journal*, June 12, 2009.

7. Tim Kane, "Minimizing Economic Opportunity by Raising the Minimum Wage," Heritage Foundation, March 4, 2005, http://www.heri tage.org/research/economy/wm676.cfm.

8. "The Young and the Jobless," *Wall Street Journal*, October 3, 2009.

9. Diane Stafford, "Unemployment rate hits record low for young people in July," *Kansas City Star*, August 27, 2009, http://www.kansas city.com/business/story/1409954.html.

10. Fred Lucas, "Obama's for Equal Pay, Yet Pays Female Staffers Less Than Males," CNSNews.com, June 30, 2008, http://www.cnsnews .com/Public/Content/Article.aspx?rsrcid=32005.

11. Cait Murphy, "Obama Flunks Econ 101," CNNMoney.com, June 6, 2007, http://money.cnn.com/2007/06/04/magazines/fortune/muphy_pay act.fortune/index.htm.

12. James Sherk, "Paycheck Fairness Act Unfairly Burdens Employees and Employers," Heritage Foundation, July 30, 2008.

13. Rachel Breitman, "Young women earn more than men in big U.S. cities," Reuters, August 3, 2007, http://www.reuters.com/article/ domesticNews/idUSN0334472920070803.

14. Wendy McElroy, "Why Men Earn More," Fox News, February 24, 2005, http://www.foxnews.com/story/0.2933.148407.00.html.

15. Fred Lucas, "Obama Pays Women Only 78 Percent of What He Pays Men," CNSNews.com September 18, 2008, http://www.cnsnews .com/public/Content/Article.aspx?rsrcid=35972.

16. Casey B. Mulligan, "Vote Republican if You Want Equal Pay," *Wall Street Journal*, September 12, 2008.

17. Kate Sheppard, "Obama's Green Achievements At 100 Days," Grist .org, April 29, 2009, http://www.grist.org/article/2009-04-29 -obamas-green-achievements-at/.

18. *Hardball with Chris Matthews*, MSNBC, November 5, 2007.

19. CNN *Newsroom*, transcript, March 2, 2009.

20. Nick Loris, "Spanish & Solar: A Model to Follow or a Cautionary Tale?" Heritage Foundation's The Foundry blog, September 25, 2009, http://blog.heritage.org/2009/09/25/spanish-solar-a-model-to -follow-or-a-cautionary-tale/#more-15726.

21. Tony Blankley, "The Myth of 5 Million Green Jobs," Real Clear Politics, May 27, 2009, http://www.realclearpolitics.com/articles/2009/ 05/27/economic_reality_of_5_million_green_jobs_96680.html.

22. Report to Congress: Comprehensive Inventory of U.S. OCS Oil and Natural Gas Resources, Energy Policy Act of 2005—Section 357, U.S. Department of Interior, February 2006.

23. "Oil Shale Development in the United States, Prospects and Policy Issues," prepared for the National Energy Technology Laboratory of the U.S. Department of Energy by the RAND Corporation, 2005, http://www.rand.org/pubs/monographs/2005/RAND_MG414.pdf.

24. Michael Goldfarb, "Michelle Will Steal Your Pie," April 9, 2008, http://www.weeklystandard.com/weblogs/TWSFP/2008/04/michelle _will_steal_your_pie.asp.

25. "Just 53% Say Capitalism Better Than Socialism," April 9, 2009, Rasmussen Reports, http://www.rasmussenreports.com/public_con tent/politics/general_politics/april_2009/just_53_say_capitalism_ better_than_socialism.

26. "Petition to Redistribute GPA's," YouTube, April 17, 2009, http:// www.youtube.com/watch?v=_p8DFUnYtPo.

27. Scott Hodge, "Tax burden of top 1% now exceeds that of bottom

95%," Tax Foundation, July 29, 2009 http://www.taxfoundation.org/blog/show/24944.html.

28. Gerald Prante, "Summary of Latest Federal Individual Income Tax Data," Tax Foundation, http://www.taxfoundation.org/taxdata/show/250.html.

29. Chris Edwards, "Tax Policy Under President Bush," Cato Institute, August 14, 2006, http://www.cato.org/pub_display.php?pub_id=6621.

30. Robert Rector, Katherine Bradley, and Rachel Sheffield, "Obama to Spend $10.3 Trillion on Welfare," Heritage Foundation, September 16, 2009.

31. Ibid.

32. Ibid.

33. Ibid.

34. Ibid.

35. Arthur B. Laffer, Stephen Moore, and Peter J. Tanous, *The End of Prosperity* (New York: Simon & Schuster, 2008), p. 89.

Chapter 8: I Want My MTV

1. John Stossel and Elizabeth Vargas, "Rock the Vote; Maybe you shouldn't," ABC *20/20,* October 10, 2008.

2. "New National Poll Finds: More Americans Know Snow White's Dwarfs Than Supreme Court Judges, Homer Simpson Than Homer's *Odyssey,* and Harry Potter Than Tony Blair," Zogby International, August 15, 2006, http://www.zogby.com/Soundbites/readclips.cfm?ID=13498.

3. Ibid.

4. "Stevie Wonder, Sheryl Crow, Will.I.Am play at Barack Obama's Democratic convention," *New Musical Express,* August 29, 2008.

5. "Sheryl Crow Offers Free Albums to Voters," *New Musical Express,* August 21, 2008.

6. "Sheryl Crow Exchanges Free Album Download For New Voters," *Rolling Stone,* August 21, 2008, http://www.rollingstone.com/rockdaily/index.php/2008/08/21/sheryl-crow-exchanges-free-album-download-for-new-voters/.

7. "Sheryl Crow @ Rock The Vote Tour Richmond VA 2008," YouTube, October 28, 2008, http://www.youtube.com/watch?v=OT35wtkLnjY.

8. "Robert DeNiro—Election Protection," YouTube, October 28, 2008, http://www.youtube.com/watch?v=_IzN11De9cY.

9. Larry King, "Predicting the Youth Vote in 2008; Christina Aguilera Rocks the Vote; Luke Russert remembers his dad," CNN *Larry King Live,* June 25, 2008.

10. Ibid.

11. "Rock the Vote Launches 'Get out the Vote' Campaign," Rockthevote .com, October 14, 2008, http://www.rockthevote.com/about/press -room/press-releases/rock-the-vote-launches-get.html.

12. Jason Rosenbaum, "How to Fight Back Against the Right," Health Care for America, August 5, 2009, http://blog.healthcareforameri canow.org/2009/08/05/how-to-fight-back-against-the-right.

13. "Get smart like that on health care; you will care when you need it and can't get it," Rockthevote.com, http://www.rockthevote.com/ issues/health-care.html.

14. "Murs Rocks the Vote PSA," YouTube, September 19, 2008, http:// www.youtube.com/watch?v=ptXubszjdaE.

15. "Gideon Yago," News Meat, http://www.newsmeat.com/fec/bystate_ detail.php?st=NY&last=Yago&first=Gideon.

16. "Choose or Lose presents: Obama decoded," MTV, September 3, 2008, http://think.mtv.com/044FDFFFF0002D79C000800992F08/ User/Blog/BlogPostDetail.aspx.

17. Ibid.

18. Ibid.

19. "It's the Senator's turn to tell his story," MTV, September 5, 2008, http://think.mtv.com/044FDFFFF0098989A001700992FE8/.

20. "It Felt Like a History Lesson," MTV, September 5, 2008, http:// think.mtv.com/044FDFFFF0098989A001700992FE6/.

21. Ibid.

22. "The MTV/MySpace Presidential Dialogue," December 3, 2007, http://www.mtv.com/videos/news/193255/12-of-23-the-grand-can yons-best-friend.jhtml#id=1575664.

23. "Nation's Leading Voter Registration Groups Join Forces with MySpace for 'Ultimate College Bowl' to Register College Students to

Vote," Student PIRGs, September 9, 2008, http://www.studentpirgs
.org/release/news-releases/nations-leading-voter-registration-groups
-join-forces-with-myspace-for-ultimate-college-bowl-to-register-col
lege-students-to-vote.

24. "The MTV/MySpace Presidential Dialogue."

25. "Clinton Global Initiative teams up with MTV to engage college students in global action," October 12, 2008, MTV, http://mtvpress
.com/activism/release/clinton_global_initiative_teams_up_with_
mtv_to_engage_college_students_in_g/.

26. "CP's Erica on MTV w/Bono, Alicia Keys, Shakira, Clinton," YouTube,
October 29, 2007, http://www.youtube.com/watch?v=HaKoN6w5eZ
Q&feature=channel.

27. "Christina Norman," Opensecrets.org.

28. Brian Stelter, "Back from the war and on MTV's radar," *New York
Times*, July 28, 2008.

29. Scott Keeter, Juliana Horowitz, and Alec Tyson, "Young Voters in
the 2008 Election," Pew Research Center Publications, November 12,
2008, http://pewresearch.org/pubs/1031/young-voters-in-the-2008
-election.

30. Jenn Abelson, "MTV wants digital army to bring back the buzz,"
Boston Globe, January 12, 2008.

31. Jane Fleming Kleeb, "What happened to the NH Youth Vote?" NDN,
January 1, 2008, http://ndn.org/node/1751.

32. Carissa Jackson, "Students Saying No to War, Yes to Schools," MTV,
September 17, 2008, http://think.mtv.com/044FDFFFF0098A14000
08009934F2/User/Blog/BlogPostDetail.aspx.

33. Brian Rich, "Rise of the Christian Left," MTV, November 3, 2008,
http://think.mtv.com/044FDFFFF0098A06900170099518D/.

34. Cassidy Hartman, "Philly women on Palin," MTV, September 12,
2008, http://think.mtv.com/044FDFFFF0098A0C60017009932F1/.

Chapter 9: The Dynamic Duo: Jon Stewart and Stephen Colbert

1. Mary Katherine Ham, "Jon Stewart to Sarah Palin: '[Expletive] You,"
Weekly Standard's The Blog, October 19, 2008, http://www.week

lystandard.com/weblogs/TWSFP/2008/10/jon_stewart_to_sarah_pa
lin_exp.asp.

2. Jessica Torrez-Riley, "Jon Stewart at NU," Beantown University blog,
October 17, 2008, http://beantownuniversity.blogspot.com/2008/10/
jon-stewart-at-nu.html.

3. Jacques Steinberg, "An All-Out Attack on 'Conservative Misinforma-
tion,' " *New York Times*, November 1, 2008.

4. George Rush and Joanna Rush Molloy, "Palin Unappealin' to Jon,"
Daily News (New York), October 9, 2008.

5. Tim Graham, "Jon Stewart Trashes Novak as Heartless 'Vampire
Demon,' Enemy of Democracy," Newsbusters.org, September 19,
2006, http://newsbusters.org/node/7747.

6. Joel Topcick, " 'The Daily Show' Welcomes GOP to the Twin Cities,"
Broadcasting & Cable, August 24, 2008, http://www.broadcasting
cable.com/blog/BC_Beat/10210-_The_Daily_Show_Welcomes_GOP_
to_the_Twin_Cities.php.

7. Bill Moyers, transcript, PBS, July 11, 2003.

8. Michiko Kakutani, "Is Jon Stewart the most trusted man in America?" *New York Times*, August 15, 2008.

9. Tom Brokaw, "Jon Stewart: The 2005 Time 100," *Time*, April 18,
2005.

10. Kakutani, "Is Jon Stewart the most trusted man in America?"

11. Jon Weisman, "The Groundbreakers: Television: Jon Stewart," *Daily
Variety*, October 31, 2008.

12. David Smith, "How a satirist became America's most influential TV
personality," *Observer* (London), September 14, 2008.

13. Leonard Doyle, "You can't be serious: How a comedian became the
most influential voice in American politics," *Independent* (London),
August 19, 2008.

14. "Now that Walter Cronkite has passed on, who is America's most
trusted newscaster?" *Time,* http://www.timepolls.com/hppolls/ar
chive/poll_results_417.html.

15. "Journalism, Satire or Just Laughs? 'The Daily Show with Jon Stewart,' Examined: Attacking Politicians: Who Gets Ridiculed," Pew Research Center's Project for Excellence in Journalism, May 8, 2008,
http://www.journalism.org/node/10956.

16. Ibid.

17. Ibid.

18. Ibid.

19. Ibid.

20. Ibid.

21. Tom Leonard, "Palin is a dream to satirists," *Daily Telegraph* (London), October 14, 2008.

22. Gary Levin, "Behind the convention's 'Daily' grind; Jon Stewart on the road in Denver," *USA Today*, August 28, 2008.

23. Kakutani, "Is Jon Stewart the most trusted man in America?"

24. Scott Whitlock, "Matt Lauer Lauds Liberal Jon Stewart: 'Respected and Listened To,'" Newsbusters.org, August 28, 2008, http://news busters.org/blogs/scott-whitlock/2008/08/28/matt-lauer-lauds-lib eral-jon-stewart-respected-listened.

25. Howard Kurtz, "No joke: Jon Stewart takes aim at 24-hour cable news 'beast,'" *Washington Post*, August 26, 2008.

26. Ibid.

27. Levin, "Behind the convention's 'Daily' grind."

28. Kurtz, "No joke."

29. DParker, "The debt we owe Jon Stewart," Daily Kos, October 4, 2008, http://www.dailykos.com/storyonly/2008/10/4/135834/621.

30. Ibid.

31. "Obama's *Daily Show* Interview," Huffington Post, October 29, 2008, http://www.huffingtonpost.com/2008/10/29/obamas-daily-show -intervi_n_139123.html.

32. Ibid.

33. Mo Rocca, AOL news blog, August 24, 2007, http://news.aol.com/ newsbloggers/2007/08/24/jon-stewart-interviews-barack-obama/.

34. "*Daily Show* interview with John McCain," April 24, 2007, http:// www.thedailyshow.com/watch/tue-april-24-2007/sen—john-mccain -pt—1.

35. Ibid.

36. Ibid.

37. Dave Itzkoff, "Can We Laugh? Yes, We Can," *New York Times*, November 7, 2008.

38. Frank Rich, "Throw the Truthiness Bums Out," *New York Times*, November 5, 2006.

39. "Colbert Roasts President Bush—2006 White House Correspondents'

Association Dinner," Google videos, http://video.google.com/video play?docid=869183917758574879#.

40. Seth Mnookin, "The Man in the Irony Mask," *Vanity Fair*, October 2007.

41. Ibid.

42. Steven Daly, "Stephen Colbert: the second most powerful idiot in America," *Sunday Telegraph* (London), May 18, 2008.

43. Greg Mitchell, "Obama Owes Presidency To . . . Stephen Colbert?" Huffington Post, February 21, 2009, http://www.huffingtonpost.com/ greg-mitchell/obama-owes-presidency-tos_b_159664.html.

44. Mnookin, "The Man in the Irony Mask."

45. Daly, "Stephen Colbert: the second most powerful idiot in America."

46. Ibid.

47. Maureen Dowd, "America's Anchors," *Rolling Stone*, October 31, 2006.

48. Mnookin, "The Man in the Irony Mask."

49. Daly, "Stephen Colbert: the second most powerful idiot in America."

50. "Key News Audiences Now Blend Online and Traditional Sources," Pew Research Center for the People & the Press, August 17, 2008, http://people-press.org/report/?pageid=1353.

51. "Nearly One-Third of Younger Americans See Colbert, Stewart As Alternatives to Traditional News Outlets," Rasmussen Reports, March 25, 2009, http://www.rasmussenreports.com/public_content/life style/entertainment/march_2009/nearly_one_third_of_younger_ americans_see_colbert_stewart_as_alternatives_to_traditional_news_ outlets.

52. Ibid.

53. Gail Shister, "Young adults eschew traditional night news for 'The Daily Show,'" Philly.com, May 13, 2007, http://www.philly.com/ inquirer/columnists/gail_shister/20070513_Young_adults_eschew_ traditional_nightly_news_for_quot_The_Daily_Show_quot_html? page=2.

54. Ibid.

55. Mnookin, "The Man in the Irony Mask."

Conclusion

1. "Independents Take Center Stage in Obama Era," Pew Research Center for the People & the Press, May 21, 2009, http://people-press .org/report/?pageid=1516.

2. Lydia Saad, " 'Conservatives' Are Single-Largest Ideological Group," June 15, 2009, http://www.gallup.com/poll/120857/Conservatives -Single-Largest-Ideological-Group.aspx.

3. Martha Irvine, "Tough political realities quiet youth 'Obamamania,' " Huffington Post, September 22, 2009, http://www.huffingtonpost .com/huff-wires/20090922/us_obama_youth_hangover.

4. Saad, " 'Conservatives' Are Single-Largest Ideological Group."

5. David Von Drehle, "The Year of the Youth Vote," Time, January 31, 2008.

6. Jeff Mason, "Obama to raise 10-year deficit to $9 trillion," Reuters, August 21, 2009, http://www.reuters.com/article/newsOne/idUS TRE57K4XE20090821.

7. Mark Knoller, "National debt now tops $12 trillion," CBS News Political Hotsheet, November 17, 2009, http://www.cbsnews .com/blogs/2009/11/17/politics/politicalhotsheet/entry5686644 .shtml.

8. Byron York, "Michelle's Struggle," National Review Online, February 29, 2008, http://article.nationalreview.com/?q=MmEyN2RkNzcwYz gyZDY2MDBiY2U5MjJ1ZGMwNDM2ODg=.

9. "Obama ASU speech: Full text," Huffington Post, May 13, 2009, http://www.huffingtonpost.com/2009/05/13/obama_asu_speech_ tex_n_203287.html.

10. P.J. O'Rourke, "Fairness, Idealism and Other Atrocities," Los Angeles Times, May 4, 2008.

11. Ibid.

12. University of North Carolina Economics Department, http://www.unc .edu/depts/econ/byrns_web/Economicae/HET/Pioneers/Smith.htm.

13. Wayne Crews and Ryan Young, "America's Hidden Trillion-Dollar Tax," Investor's Business Daily, May 27, 2009, http://www.ibdedito rials.com/IBDArticles.aspx?secid=1502&status=article&id=32831840 0128627&secure=1&show=1&rss=1.

14. "America Celebrates Tax Freedom Day," Tax Foundation, March 31, 2009, http://www.taxfoundation.org/taxfreedomday/.

15. George Will, "March of the Polar Bears," *Washington Post*, May 22, 2008, http://www.washingtonpost.com/wp-dyn/content/article/2008/05/21/AR2008052102428.html.

16. Nicole Hoplin, "Obama Takes a Page from Reagan's Playbook," *Human Events*, October 29, 2008, http://www.humanevents.com/article.php?id=29237.

Acknowledgments

I've always imagined that writing a book would be quite the undertaking. And boy, oh boy, was I right. For six months, my life was focused on one thing, and one thing only: *Obama Zombies*. The bad news was that my social life was shelved. *Sigh*. The really bad news was that my social life was shelved because of Obama. *Double sigh*. The good news is that my social life is no longer shelved. *Hurrah!*

In all seriousness, there are many people that helped make this book a reality. Wynton Hall of Wynton Hall & Co. fame: you've emerged as a trusted mentor, confidant, and friend. You are the best at what you do, the supreme communications counselor and strategist. You answered every literary question I had, even if I called you at 1:00 a.m., with more of a vent than an actual question. And you read and gave counsel on the hundreds of pages I wrote. My sincerest thanks, brother.

My deep gratitude to the team at Threshold: the Executive Vice President and Publisher, Louise Burke; as well as Mary Matalin; and Mitchell Ivers, my trusty editor, who offered indispensible guidance and masterful edits. A special thanks to Anthony Ziccardi, who believed in this project from the very beginning. Thank you for your visionary leadership.

Glenn Hartley and Lynn Chu, I couldn't have asked for better agents. Thank you for being in my corner.

To my colleagues at Young America's Foundation, America's campuses are better off today because of your steadfast commitment to introduce young people to real diversity—*intellectual* diversity. Ron Robinson, you are a strategic genius and a tireless advocate for the conservative cause. I've been blessed to call you boss. Patrick X. Coyle and Roger Custer, you guys run the best student conferences and campus lecture programs in the country. I've been blessed to call you colleagues.

I'm usually asked how a kid who grew up in Brooklyn, New York, and went to college in Rhode Island found his way to Washington, D.C. . . . and as a conservative, no less! Liberals, for that, you have my awesomely awesome parents to thank. Their financial sacrifice allowed me to dodge that institution that normally ruins adolescents and fries brain cells: public school. To my dad, Joseph, you've been the ideal father. You've been the most supportive person in my life, always there for me when I needed direction and advice. I will always remember when you ignited my intellectual curiosity on those road trips to basketball camp. To my mom, Joyce, your work ethic and passion have always been a source of inspiration. Thank you.

To the Meeks household, you'll always be family. It was Cindy who assured that my nightly dinners didn't consist of just Cheerios and pancakes. My stomach thanks you! And it was Daris who offered me blunt feedback on everything in life and a constant stream of unforgettable jokes.

Alyssa Cordova, yes, you were a great intern (non-Clintonesque, people!), but you've turned out to be an even better friend. A. J. Rice, you're one of the most creative and talented individuals I know. Thanks for your insights and support.

Jedediah Jones, it's been many years since our days at Roger Williams University. I will never forget your constant encouragement and mentorship. To June Speakman, one of the few "tolerant" professors on campus. Thanks for sticking by this troublemaker!

As a young professional, I've been humbled to have the support of political heavyweights. Michelle Malkin, thank you for allowing me to contribute to your inestimable crew over at HotAir .com. It's been an honor to work with you. To Ann Coulter, thank you for your early backing of *Obama Zombies,* and for your always making yourself available for my questions. To Andrew Breitbart, thank you for your wise counsel and friendship.

I also want to thank all the great radio hosts who, over the years, have been kind enough to invite me on their shows to blabber about my views or who have featured my work, including: El Rushbo, Sean Hannity, Mark "the Great One" Levin, Glenn Beck, Laura Ingraham, Jerry Doyle, Mike Gallagher, Roger Hedgecock, Rick Roberts, and Monica Crowley. Your courage and unapologetic defense of liberty and freedom has been contagious. I'd also like to thank Thomas Sowell, whose books have contributed enormously to the development of my worldview. Thank you, sir, for your intellectual leadership.

To God, the giver of life and the savior of mankind: I have not earned Your grace, but You've bestowed it upon me nonetheless.

Lastly, I must thank all you Zombies out there who allowed

this project to become a reality. If it weren't for your multiple and public O-gasms, your undue trust in Washington bureaucrats, and your inability to think critically, I would've never landed my first book deal. For this, I do hope His Holiness Barack Hussein Obama visits you in a dream, and gives you the mother of all O-gasms.

Peace and love,
Jason Mattera

Index